TIM DiLENA

WHAT DOES GOD HAVE TO SAY?

A BIBLICAL WORLDVIEW *from* A *to* Z

bookVillages

To my friend Carter Conlon—

You inspire me and you have inspired this book's genesis.

Thank you for listening to the Holy Spirit's voice while doing your cardio one cold November morning. Your out-of-breath phone call will forever be remembered: "Tim, I think I have an idea from the Holy Spirit . . ." Those words not only changed my life but will change thousands of lives.

Thank you for believing with me for a billion souls.

And thank you for caring enough for those billion souls that you knew we needed to give them a biblical worldview.

Let's finish well together.

CONTENTS

FOREWORD

The storm was beyond anything they had imagined. Ignoring the words that God had given them (see Acts 27:9–11), they sailed off, believing that their own reasoning was sufficient to get them to their desired end.

Looking back, we shake our heads at how foolish they actually were. I suppose the real question now is whether our generation has learned anything from their obvious folly. As the saying goes, "Here we go again." Right before our eyes, evil is becoming increasingly purported to be good, and good, evil. The Word of God warns that this course of continual disregard of truth will lead our society to the same end as they experienced. Before long, their idyllic journey took a turn into the crisis which had been clearly foretold.

Without any doubt, we find ourselves today exactly where they were back then. As they did, we are doing our best to undergird this faltering generation, even to the point of throwing overboard things that were formerly accepted, trusted, and proven. Our professed wisdom has turned out to be as foolish as direction without God has always been. We are now in a storm of epic proportions. The kingdoms of this world are rapidly sinking. Before you follow them into their downward spiral, remember that there is still hope. In a desperate moment, someone called for the man of God who claimed to have words from God.

I'm hoping today that this is the reason you now hold this book in your hands. There is still Truth. God's Truth. Words from God that are able to give you hope and a future. Paul the apostle told the people to "take some meat," for up to that point they had eaten little for many days. Because of this, they were faint in the face of their predicament. In the same way, this present church age needs to return to biblical thinking. To come back to solid truth, proven truth, and directional truth. We need not be afraid of the weightier truths because Jesus told us that His truth would set us free. The book in your hands is about this kind of truth.

Pastor Tim Dilena is a trusted friend and a sincere seeker of God's word for your sake. The contents of this book will help you to find safety and finish your journey to Victory. The ship was going to break apart. The land was going to be strange and unfamiliar. Yet God's words through Paul would prove faithful and bring everyone who trusted in them to safety. Hanging on to pieces of wood, everyone was able to make it to shore.

In the same way, the victory of the cross and the truth that comes with it will help you and get you to the place of safety, which comes with both the warnings and promises of God. Today, despite what anyone says, your future is in the embracing of *what God has to say*.

—*Carter Conlon*

INTRODUCTION

Building According
to Code

*"The best proof of God's existence is
what follows when we deny it."*
WILLIAM SULLIVAN[1]

In 1992, Hurricane Andrew ravaged southern Florida, destroying thousands of homes in its path. However, in an area where the wreckage resembled a war zone, one house remained standing, still firmly anchored to its foundation. When a reporter asked the homeowner why his house had not been blown away, he replied, "I built this house myself. I also built it according to the Florida state building code. When the code called for 2" x 6" roof trusses, I used 2"x 6" roof trusses. I was told that a house built according to code could withstand a hurricane, and it did."

Just as the Florida state code offers clear instructions on how to build in preparation for storms, God has given us His stormproof building code. Jesus Himself spoke about the importance of building our lives according to that code, referring to those who do so as *wise*. Consider His words in the finale to the greatest sermon ever preached on earth, the Sermon on the Mount:

> Therefore, everyone who hears these words of Mine, and acts on them, will be like a wise man who built his house on the rock. And the rain fell and the floods came, and the winds blew and slammed against that house; and yet it did not fall, for it had been founded on the rock. And everyone who hears these words of Mine, and

does not act on them, will be like a foolish man who built his house on the sand. And the rain fell and the floods came, and the winds blew and slammed against that house; and it fell—and its collapse was great. (Matthew 7:24–27)

There are some important conclusions we can draw from Jesus' parable. First, we are all involved in building. Second, the materials for storm proofing are found in obedience to the Word. Going to church and reading the Bible are good things, but *obeying* God is the key! And lastly, the real test comes when the storms hit.

With one glance at today's society, it is evident that a storm is already upon us. This storm is the majority calling evil "good" and good "evil" (see Isaiah 5:20)—and a battle ensues when the Church calls evil "evil" and good "good." All the while, a tsunami of filth is slamming against God's house and our own homes. If these two houses are not built according to code, they will fall—and, as the parable says, great will be their fall.

The prophet Jeremiah also warned about a great fall that would result from refusing to obey God—a fall that would be experienced both nationally and individually.

"Were they ashamed because of the abomination they had done?
They were not ashamed at all,
Nor did they know even how to be ashamed.
Therefore they will fall among those who fall;
At the time that I punish them,
They will collapse," says the Lord.

This is what the Lord says:
"Stand by the ways and see and ask for the ancient paths,
Where the good way is, and walk in it;
Then you will find a resting place for your souls.
But they said, 'We will not walk in it.'
And I set watchmen over you, saying,
'Listen to the sound of the trumpet!'
But they said, 'We will not listen.'

Therefore hear, you nations . . .

Behold, I am bringing disaster on this people,

The fruit of their plans,

Because they have not listened to My words,

And as for My Law, they have rejected it also."

(Jeremiah 6:15–19)

Clearly there is a great cost to warnings unheeded. It is therefore imperative that you and I take the time to ensure that we are building according to code. We are living in a critical hour when the Church must be equipped to stand and speak—and to speak with one voice! Over these next twenty-six chapters, we will be exploring a biblical worldview from A to Z, or in other words, God's building code!

Now the first question we must address is: What is a worldview? A worldview is the lens through which one *sees* and *defines* life. It is our tool for interpreting life. There are some foundational topics that every worldview should address, such as man's origin and purpose, death, and the afterlife. I believe every worldview must also be able to reckon with the worst moments in human history. For example, what does your worldview have to say about the Holocaust or about a massive earthquake that leaves tens of thousands dead?

Everyone has a worldview, but not every worldview has God in it. People tend to build their worldview on six different grounds. Relativism: The majority decides. Subjectivism: How do I feel? Pragmatism: Does it work? Rationalism: I think. Postmodernism: I only care about right now. Biblical: The Bible says!

Some key elements of a biblical worldview, to be discussed further in the coming chapters, include: Absolute and objective truth exists. Truth is defined in the Bible. Jesus Christ was God in the flesh. God is Creator of the universe. The Holy Spirit indwells every Christian. Jesus' death, burial, and resurrection are the source of our freedom. Salvation is a gift from God and cannot be earned. Satan is a real enemy. There is a heaven and a hell. Christians must be public about their faith.

These are statements not often easily grasped or readily embraced. In fact, a recent survey revealed that only slightly more than one-third of American Christian pastors possess a biblical worldview[2]. Others claim to hold a biblical worldview yet deviate from it when they cannot reconcile certain aspects of God's Word with their own lifestyle or opinions. However, to paraphrase Augustine, "If you believe what you like in the Gospel and reject what you don't like, it is not the Bible you believe but yourself."[3] What happens when God is left out of your worldview, or if compromise makes you the god of your worldview? You are essentially cheating on building code materials. Palatable perhaps, yet great will be its fall.

One of the darkest books in the Bible, the book of Judges, gives us a picture of what I believe lies at the heart of the problem. Judges spans more than 300 years, and it is known as "the dark years" of Hebrew history. It was a time that very much resembles our day. Notice the reoccurring phrase:

> In those days there was no king in Israel; everyone did what was right in his own eyes. (Judges 17:6)

> In those days there was no king of Israel. (Judges 18:1)

> Now it came about in those days, when there was no king in Israel. (Judges 19:1)

> In those days there was no king in Israel; everyone did what was right in his own eyes. (Judges 21:25)

Four times the Scriptures tell us the problem: There was no king in Israel. That is exactly what has happened in our world today. We have removed the King of Kings from schools, public places, and the courts. We even want to take the King out of Christmas. The result? When you remove the King, man becomes king. When man becomes king, truth becomes personal. When truth becomes personal, you get to choose how to define "your truth."

I was recently in a hotel room eating dinner and decided to turn on the TV. I ended up watching an episode of *Everybody Loves Raymond* where Amy, who had been a virgin, and her boyfriend, Robert, had a physical relationship. Amy's religious parents then show up at her apartment. Of course, any moral and religious people in sitcoms are usually portrayed as condemning stiffs who preach rules, not Jesus.

Here is what scared me about the episode, revealing the spirit of this age: Amy looked at her parents, who had by then figured out what had happened, and said, "Mom, Dad, I have decided it's not a sin for Robert to spend the night." How dangerous is that talk! It is postmodernism in its purest form. Suddenly truth becomes the preference of the individual. Amy became her own decision-maker on moral issues, choosing what is sin and what is not.

If that is true and correct, we are left with three options: (1) We all need to ask Amy for her list so that we will know what she considers sin for all of us. (2) We each decide for ourselves what is sin and what is not. Or (3) we trust a loving, righteous God—who cannot lie—to tell us what is sin.

The Bible says, "There is a generation that is pure in its own eyes, yet is not washed from its filthiness" (Proverbs 30:12 NKJV). Pure in its own eyes. What a picture of our generation—a generation that loves to look good without being good. Houses not built to code can certainly look good, but it will be a different story once the storm hits.

Solomon, the wisest man in history, made the same statement twice in the book of Proverbs. When God speaks twice, the matter is certain and definite (see Genesis 41:32). I think we ought to pay close attention to Solomon's words found in both chapters 14 and 16:

> There is a way that seems right to a man, but its end is the way of death. (Proverbs 14:12 ; 16:25 NKJV)

Think about some of the things man believes that "seems right" today: *There are many ways to God. We must honor all religions. Everything is acceptable as long as you are sincere. We must be tolerant of everyone's lifestyles and definitions.*

Man can do something that seems right, yet the end is destruction. What does this mean? Quite simply, we cannot trust ourselves or the conclusions we draw. As the Bible says, "For the mouth speaks what the heart is full of" (Matthew 12:34 NIV), and "the human heart is the most deceitful of all things, and desperately wicked" (Jeremiah 17:9 NLT). Truth *must* come from outside of ourselves, not from within. We must discover what God says is right. Unfortunately, the bandwagon seems to be replacing the Bible. Matters are decided based on popularity rather than principle, horizontal pressure over vertical authority. Though we may have facts, what we need is truth.

In John 18:38, Pilate asked Jesus, "'What is truth?' And when he had said this, he went out again" (NKJV). Pilate asked the question of the centuries, yet he would not sit long enough to listen to the answer. Let us not make the same mistake. It is a question worthy of our due diligence in seeking the answer—so that what we construct might endure.

I will issue a warning to those who choose to live by a biblical worldview today: Some people will conclude that you are insane. Look at what Paul spoke to the political leaders of his time and their response:

> "So, having obtained help from God, I stand to this day testifying both to small and great, stating nothing but what the Prophets and Moses said was going to take place, as to whether the Christ was to suffer, and whether, as first from the resurrection of the dead, He would proclaim light both to the Jewish people and to the Gentiles."
>
> While Paul was stating these things in his defense, Festus said in a loud voice, "Paul, you are out of your mind! Your great learning is driving you insane." (Acts 26:22–24)

I love Paul's response: "I am not insane, Most Excellent Festus. What I am saying is the sober truth" (Acts 26:25 NLT). Though the world may conclude we are out of our minds, in reality, living by the Bible is embracing sober truth.

Different worldviews will constantly be vying for your attention. The warnings have been issued. The storm is already upon us. We have lived long enough by "what seems right." It is time to get right—to believe right and to do what is right. I invite you on this journey of examining a biblical worldview. God has graciously given us His stormproof code. Let's build accordingly.

THE ATONEMENT

It's Time to Declare Bankruptcy

*"The whole world is bankrupt, it's just that
not everyone has declared bankruptcy yet."*
C. S. Lewis[1]

How does the story of a man getting a speeding ticket in a little Texas city outside of Dallas go viral on YouTube? None of my tickets ever went viral. It was the story of a young man, Hayden Carlo, who drove every day with an expired registration to a minimum wage job. He was trying to make ends meet for his new family. Unable to afford the bills for both the home and the car, something had to be sacrificed.

One day while driving, he saw a red light behind him. He was being pulled over. When the officer asked for his license and registration, Hayden immediately came clean. "Officer, I need to either feed my family or pay for registration. I chose food. I am guilty. It's been hard." The officer took Hayden's license and returned after a few minutes with the ticket.

Now we probably would have shown mercy and not given him the ticket. But Hayden broke the law; he deserved the ticket. He needed to pay for it but could not. With his head down, he opened the ticket. The policeman had cited him for driving with an expired registration. But the reason the story went viral is because with the citation, the officer had included a $100 bill to pay for it!

The offense: He broke the law. The problem: He could not pay for his trespass. The blessing: It was paid for him.

This entire world has received a citation from God. The offense: We are all sinners. The problem: We cannot pay for it, nor can we fix ourselves. Therein lies the dilemma—what God furiously hates is in those He passionately loves. How does God deal with the people He loves in the condition He hates? How does He deal with the citation?

It is not a $100 bill but a crucified Savior who paid the price for you and me. At the cross, the citation was dipped in the blood of Jesus as our payment! Oswald Chambers, the great devotional writer and missionary, said this about the cross: "All heaven is interested in the Cross of Christ, all hell terribly afraid of it, while men are the only beings who more or less ignore its meaning."[2] We will certainly not ignore the cross in this book. How fitting that the first letter in our study of *What Does God Have to Say?* is the letter *A* for *atonement*.

The atonement is the cross. The word *atonement* means "taking action to amend a wrong that has been done." When you apologize for doing something wrong, that is an act of atonement. The cross is the action taken by God to fix the wrong that was done. The cross proves that we matter to God.

The great British writer G. K. Chesterton said, "It has never been quite enough to say that God is in his heaven and all is right with the world; since the rumor that God had left his heavens to set it right."[3] Let's talk about the rumor that is, in fact, a reality, starting with the offense.

THE OFFENSE

There is an old hymn with the line, "By God's Word at last my sin I learned." It is so important to study the Scriptures, for that is how we discover the truth of our condition. The Bible tells us, "For all have sinned and fall short of the glory of God" (Romans 3:23) and "As it is written, there is none righteous, no, not one" (Romans 3:10 KJV).

Why is sin such an offense?

A verse we are all familiar with, John 3:16, says, "For God so loved the world . . ." Yet the God who so loves us hates sin and evil. "Your eyes are too pure to look on evil; you cannot tolerate wrongdoing" (Habakkuk 1:13 NIV). God deeply loves the world, but He cannot tolerate sin. See what sin has done between God and humanity:

But your iniquities have separated you from your God;
And your sins have hidden His face from you,
So that He will not hear.
(Isaiah 59:2 NKJV)

The condition of God's beloved people has separated them from Himself. So how do we pay for the offense and bridge that separation? Perhaps it will be helpful to first look at some ways *not* to go about it.

THE PROBLEM

When I was growing up, I couldn't exactly define what a rhetorical question was; I just knew there were certain questions you should not answer because they were not meant to elicit a response. Here are some of the big rhetorical questions I heard from my parents growing up: *Are you still awake? How many times do I have to tell you? Who's making all this noise? Are you deaf?* I quickly learned that a rhetorical question is asked for a purpose other than obtaining information.

In Proverbs 20, Solomon asked the biggest rhetorical question anyone has ever asked. Since God is Father and God wrote the Bible, this is essentially God the Father speaking to His children, asking a massive rhetorical question:

Who can say, "I have cleansed my heart,
I am pure from my sin?"
(Proverbs 20:9)

He was *not* looking for an answer. He was making a huge statement, basically creating an exclamation point with a question mark! The Apostle John said it this way:

If we say that we have no sin, we are deceiving ourselves and the truth is not in us. If we confess our sins, He is faithful and righteous, so that He will forgive us our sins and cleanse us from all unrighteousness. If we say that we have not sinned, we make Him a liar and His word is not in us. (1 John 1:8–10)

Both John and Solomon were declaring that no man can fix his sin issue by himself. A third party is needed. When defining the "he" in 1 John 1:9, if "he" is not God, then *you* must come up with your own cleanser. Many people are trying to do just that. Some compare themselves with people who are worse than them, thereby considering themselves clean. Others attempt to use the scales of good deeds over bad deeds. In fact, all religions apart from Christianity teach that heaven or the afterlife is what we get as a result of our good works. There are also those who try to cleanse only the outside—attempting to look good without actually being good. And then there are people who create a whole theology that everyone is basically good anyway, so we all go to heaven no matter what. However, the Bible tells us in Mark 10:18 that "only God is truly good"(NLT)!

One of the worst crimes of humanity is to try to fix this separation from God on our own. If any of these other cleansers that people have come up with were indeed true, then Jesus coming to die for our sin was a scandal, and God is a fool.

We must come to the conclusion that we *cannot* fix our own sin condition. The Bible refers to this condition as a debt we owe. In other words, we must declare bankruptcy!

There is an old chorus that goes:

> *He paid a debt He did not owe.*
> *I owed a debt I could not pay.*
> *I needed Someone to wash my sins away.*

That is the message of the cross, but the only way for it to be effective is if we do not mitigate sin. The disease is sin; the remedy is the cross. The remedy means little if the disease is denied.

Perhaps you are wondering: Why did Jesus have to die on the cross to forgive my sin? Why is sacrifice necessary for the atonement of sin? Simply put, justice demands it. A debt cannot be forgiven without a payment; it is not settled with a mere "I'm sorry."

I am sure very few people have owned a credit card without dipping into debt at some point or another. Now imagine you ended up in debt yet decided to change your spending habits. You call up Visa and tell them, "Please forgive me. Yes, I racked up $5K in undisciplined spending, but I'm fixing my ways. From this point on, I will only charge what I can pay for at the end of the month." What will they say? "Great . . . but what about what you owe?!" In the same way, some people are making promises to God, saying, "I'm going to be a better person. I'm going to start coming to church." God says, "Great . . . but what about the debt you owe?"

Some people try to pay their debt to God with the wrong currency. Take note of three payments that God will not accept:

1. Sincerity: assuming because you mean well, it is sufficient.
2. Service: believing God owes you something because of your basic decency—you provide for you family, you give to charity, you haven't hurt anybody.
3. Sorry: concluding that God is content as long as you feel guilty enough.

None of those currencies actually deal with the debt.

THE BLESSING

A true Christian addresses the debt issue by acknowledging he cannot pay it. But the good news is that all along, God had a plan. More than 700 years before Christ came, the prophet Isaiah told us why Jesus would die:

He was despised and abandoned by men,
A man of great pain and familiar with sickness;
And like one from whom people hide their faces,
He was despised, and we had no regard for Him.

However, it was our sicknesses that He Himself bore,
And our pains that He carried;
Yet we ourselves assumed that He had been afflicted,
Struck down by God, and humiliated.
But He was pierced for our offenses,
He was crushed for our wrongdoings;
The punishment for our well-being was laid upon Him,
And by His wounds we are healed.
All of us, like sheep, have gone astray,

> Each of us has turned to his own way;
> But the LORD has caused the wrongdoing of us all
> To fall on Him.
> (Isaiah 53:3-6)

The key word in Isaiah 53 is *our*—our griefs, our sorrows, our transgressions, our iniquities. Not *His* but *ours*, all put upon Jesus! We must recognize that we are responsible for putting Jesus on the cross. In fact, a word that is often associated with the cross is *substitution*. Substitution refers to the fact that Jesus was literally doing everything on our behalf. Jesus was punished for my sin because sin had to be punished. If my sin was not transferred to Jesus, then I would still have to pay for it. That is why I am so grateful for the cross!

John described Jesus' sacrifice this way:

> My little children, I am writing these things to you so that you may not sin. And if anyone sins, we have an Advocate with the Father, Jesus Christ the righteous; and He Himself is the propitiation for our sins; and not for ours only, but also for the sins of the whole world. (1 John 2:1–2)

R. T. Kendall reminded us that the blood of Jesus does two things: expiation and propitiation. Expiation is called atonement. It is what the blood does for *us*—it washes away our sin. Propitiation is called satisfaction.[4] It is what the blood does for *God*—it turns away His wrath from us, for the blood of His Son satisfies His justice.

Let's take a moment to ponder the power of the cross. What happened when Jesus died for our sins?

> "And Jesus cried out again with a loud voice, and gave up His spirit. And behold, the veil of the temple was torn in two from top to bottom; and the earth shook and the rocks were split. Also the tombs were opened, and many bodies of the saints who had fallen asleep were raised; and coming out of the tombs after His resurrection, they entered the holy city and appeared to many. Now, as for the centurion and those who were with him keeping guard over Jesus,

when they saw the earthquake and the other things that were happening, they became frightened and said, "Truly this was the Son of God!" (Matthew 27:50–54)

Notice some key things that occurred the moment Jesus died. The temple veil was rent in two. This temple veil had separated every man from God, with the exception of only one man—the high priest. Once a year, that priest was allowed to pass beyond the veil to ask God for mercy upon the sins of Israel. In essence, the temple veil was a boundary between heaven and earth. Yet when Jesus died and the veil was torn in two, every man was given access to God. In other words, God was removing religion. Then there was a great earthquake, displaying God's lordship over the earth. The tombs were opened; God was proclaiming His victory over death. Put another way, religion is not in charge, the earth is not in charge, and death is not in charge . . . Jesus is in charge, and His blood sets us free!

I have had one vision in my life, and I remember it clearly to this day. I don't know if it is what happened while Jesus was in the grave for three days. All I know is that I had a vision of the caverns of hell.

I saw demons too numerous to count, and in the center of the bowels of hell was a wooden platform. Lucifer would ascend to the stage and bring up people from the body of Christ, placing them one by one on an auction block, asking, "Who will be my highest bidder for this one?" A myriad of demonic figures would erupt with sounds too dark to speak of as the bidding went on. Depression, suicide, addiction, divorce, sexual perversion, anger, hatred, racism—all bid on the body of Christ. One after another, people were dragged out in chains to the highest bidder.

Then suddenly, under the black steel doors, a brilliant light shot through, causing all hell to retreat. The doors slapped open as if kicked down, and in walked the Lamb of God. He declared, "I will be the highest bidder!"

Hell cowered. Hell screamed. One by one, Jesus broke off the chains and claimed every single person who belonged to Him. "They are Mine! My blood has paid for them!"

Christ "led captivity captive " (Ephesians 4:8 NKJV). He is the victory!

The How-To

So how do we live in all that the atonement affords us?

Confession is the starting place for freedom. There can never be a relationship between you and God until your debt is acknowledged. Consider once again this verse in 1 John:

> If we confess our sins, He is faithful and righteous, so that He will forgive us our sins and cleanse us from all unrighteousness.
> (1 John 1:9)

Confess is the key word. The word *confess* means "to say the same thing" or "to agree with." In other words, you must agree with what God says; you must say the same thing He does. You must call sin "sin." As you begin to say the same thing God says, the cleansing comes.

This is where some of us get stuck. Did you know that the lyrics to the classic hymn "Amazing Grace" are being changed in some hymnals? "Amazing grace, how sweet the sound that saved a wretch like me." Some are removing "that saved a wretch like me" and replacing it with "that saved and set me free." Why? Man is trying to evade the uncomfortable idea of his sinfulness and need for a Savior. Pull out sin, and the gospel is no longer amazing.

Let's confess and agree with God. What does He say about our relationship with Him? According to the book of Romans, if we want peace with God, it cannot be up to *us*. Jesus must be in the equation.

> We were reconciled to God through the death of His Son.
> (Romans 5:10)

> We have peace with God through our Lord Jesus Christ.
> (Romans 5:1)

Through Jesus' death, the debt has been paid and our separation from God has been bridged. Jesus' death was our payment—*in full!*

I came across the story of a young woman who accepted Jesus as her Savior one day during a church service. Though she had a very rough past involving alcohol, drugs, and prostitution, the change in her was evident. She became a faithful member of the church and soon caught the eye of the pastor's son, and they eventually got engaged. However, problems arose when the father retired and announced that he wanted his son to take over the church. Half of the church did not consider a woman with such a past to be a suitable pastor's wife. The church began to argue about the matter. Finally, they decided to hold a meeting. As the people presented their arguments, the young woman became upset about all the things being brought up about her past. She began to cry, so the pastor's son stood and made this statement: "My fiancée's past is not what is on trial here. What you are questioning is the ability of the blood of Jesus to wash away every sin. Today you have put the blood of Jesus on trial. Does it wash away sin or not?" The whole church began to weep as they realized that they had been slandering the blood of the Lord Jesus Christ.

If the blood of Jesus does not cleanse the other person completely, neither can it cleanse us completely. In which case, we are all in a lot of trouble! Thank God that Jesus' death was our full payment and cleansing!

Now while confession may be difficult, sometimes receiving what Jesus has done for us can be the hardest part. It reminds me of a time when my family and I were eating at a restaurant. As we were finishing our meal, I noticed that the waitress brought our check, took it away, and then brought it back again. She placed it on the table, smiled, and said, "Somebody in the restaurant paid for your meal. You're all set." And then she walked away. I was left with the strangest feeling sitting there—a feeling of helplessness. There was nothing I could do; it had all been taken care of. To insist on paying would have been pointless. I was faced with two choices: to live like it was true or to create my own reality in which the bill was not paid.

The wrong that was done: My family, with our four children who ate like wolves, certainly did some damage! The atonement: The bill was paid. The miracle: It was someone else who paid for it. We had to trust that we no longer owed anything.

That is the challenge—trusting that something has already been done on our behalf, believing that grace paid the bill in full. In *Mere Christianity*, C. S. Lewis reminded us of the greatness of God and the work of the cross: "Christ offers something for nothing: He even offers everything for nothing. In a sense, the whole Christian life consists in accepting that very remarkable offer. But the difficulty is to reach the point of recognizing that all we have done and can do is nothing."[5]

God's incredible solution to amend what was wrong—that is the atonement. He did it *all*, for He knew we would never be able to. Now *that* is amazing grace.

QUESTIONS

1. Is there an area of your life where you are still trying to pay a debt to God with the wrong "currency" (sincere promises, guilt, etc.)?

2. How would you explain the cross to somebody who does not know Jesus?

3. Read the parable Jesus told in Matthew 18:21–35. In light of the atonement, what ought to be our response toward those who are indebted to us?

THE BIBLE

If It's Living, Active, and Sharp, Then Don't Make It Dead, Dull, and Blunt

"A Bible that's falling apart usually belongs to someone who isn't."
CHARLES SPURGEON[1]

Across the decades, Billy Graham has preached the gospel in person to more people than anyone in church history, reaching over 210 million people in 185 countries. In 1949, just before his first crusade in Los Angeles—one that would reach 350,000 people—Graham had a crisis of faith. He began questioning whether the Bible truly was the inspired Word of God.

Graham said in his autobiography, *Just as I Am*: "If I could not trust the Bible, I could not go on. It was not too late to become a dairy farmer." He walked the San Bernardino Mountains, wrestling with God. In the middle of the night, he fell to his knees and, laying the Bible on the ground, cried out, "Oh God, there are many things I don't understand in this book. There are many problems I don't have the solution for!" At last, the Holy Spirit freed him to shout in those mountains, "Father, I am going to accept this as Thy Word by faith. I'm going to allow faith to go beyond my intellectual questions and doubts, and I will believe this is Your inspired Word!"[2]

That night, God filled the greatest evangelist with the words that would ring across the world to millions of souls: "The Bible says . . ." It became his most famous line every time he preached. If you look at pictures of that first crusade in Los Angeles, in the center of the stage stood a large replica of an open Bible—twenty feet high and twenty feet wide. Billy wanted the Bible behind him as he preached, and the Bible would remain at the center during of his fifty-eight years of preaching.

When you say, "The Bible says," you are saying, "God says." The Bible is the Word of God; it is God speaking to humanity. The Bible is also the *heart* of God. It contains the words of God, and words reveal the heart: "For out of the abundance of the heart the mouth speaks" (Matthew 12:34 NKJV). So every time you read the Bible, you are hearing God's heart.

With that in mind, let's look at something that happened in the book of Jude. Jude was about to write on one topic until something else suddenly captured his attention:

> Dear friends, although I was very eager to write to you about the salvation we share, I felt compelled to write and urge you to contend for the faith that was once for all entrusted to God's holy people. For certain individuals whose condemnation was written about long ago have secretly slipped in among you. They are ungodly people, who pervert the grace of our God into a license for immorality and deny Jesus Christ our only Sovereign and Lord. (Jude 1:3–4 NIV)

Jude was saying, "I was going to write about salvation, but based on an alarm I am hearing in the church, I made a U-turn and am now writing about contending for the faith." He felt compelled to change his message because people and ideas had "secretly slipped in" among the church.

That Greek phrase "slipped in" has three interesting meanings: to slip into water without making a ripple; to slip through a side door into an event where everyone uses the front door; what a devious lawyer does in a court of law when he slips in a phrase for the jury to hear that is inadmissible. The judge says, "Strike this from the record," but it is already in the jury's mind.

In other words, the ungodly had slipped in stealthily, and by the time they were noticed, their false doctrine had already infiltrated the church. Jude knew it had to be dealt with immediately. I believe the same thing is happening in our day. In fact, there is a prophecy in the book of Malachi that is currently being fulfilled:

> Then shall ye return, and discern between the righteous and the wicked, between him that serveth God and him that serveth him not. (Malachi 3:18 KJV)

Return and *discern*. There is a great return in America today with thousands of students crying out for revival. We are witnessing one of the most incredible outpourings of the Holy Spirit across college campuses. Yet as revival is sweeping across the next generation, God is also causing us to discern between the righteous and the wicked. He is exposing false doctrine and any preacher who will not hold to what the Scriptures say. For example, there are pastors today who are muddying the Scriptures by regarding the Bible's clear message on identity and sexuality as "clobber passages" through which people who identify as LGBTQ are unfairly discriminated against. However, what they preach directly contradicts what the Bible states in 1 Corinthians 6:9–11.

It is incredibly dangerous to muddy what God has made clear. When we do, we pollute and corrupt the Scriptures. As theologian Søren Kierkegaard once said, "The Bible is very easy to understand. But we Christians are a bunch of scheming swindlers. We pretend to be unable to understand it because we know very well that the minute we understand, we are obliged to act accordingly."[3]

A pastor in the Southeast has even gone viral convincing his congregation to grow cannabis on church property in order to teach the community how to farm and make an income. He is using his pulpit and position so that the church can grow marijuana!

What is going on? I believe what is happening today is what the psalmist called "broken-down hedges."

> Why have You broken down her hedges,
> So that all who pass by the way pluck her fruit?
> (Psalm 80:12 NKJV)

A hedge is a protective wall against enemies. The Word of God is our hedge of protection around the harvest. But our hedge is broken, our walls are down. And if the hedge is broken, then all who pass by can steal the fruit of the harvest.

Sadly, the hedge is being destroyed, not by people on the outside but by the vineyard keepers! Picture for a moment the Great Wall of China—an incredible structure built over 2,500 years ago, extending more than 10,000 miles long and ranging in height from fifteen to thirty feet. It can even be seen from space! Yet three times it was breached—not externally, but *internally*—when guards were bribed to let the enemy walk through the gates. Though the Chinese government invested a great deal of money and manpower to protect their country, they failed to invest in the moral character of their gatekeepers, rendering the Great Wall worthless!

Likewise, our hedge is being broken down from within as pulpits are being bribed with money, notoriety, likes, and sales. There is a famine of the Word of God today, just as the prophet Amos spoke of:

> "Behold, days are coming," declares the Lord GOD,
> "When I will send a famine on the land,
> Not a famine of bread or a thirst for water,
> But rather for hearing the words of the LORD.
> People will stagger from sea to sea
> And from the north even to the east;
> They will roam about to seek the word of the LORD,
> But they will not find it."
> (Amos 8:11–12)

It also says in Amos, "Take away from Me the noise of your songs; I will not even listen to the sound of your harps" (Amos 5:23). Songs were increasing, but the Word was decreasing—just like we see in many churches today. We are masking Wordless pulpits with stirring songs.

We begin to understand the gravity of our situation when we read in the book of Revelation: "[Jesus] is clothed with a robe dipped in blood, and His name is called The Word of God" (Revelation 19:13). Isn't it interesting that God gave the same name to the Bible as He did Jesus? They are not identical, but they are inseparable. In other words, losing the Word is losing Christ in His Church!

Paul asked in the book of Romans, "And how are they to hear without a preacher?" (Romans 10:14). He didn't say, "How will they hear without all of the crazy optics on stage?" No! How will they hear without a *preacher*? We have focused so much on all the other things that we have lost the hedge. We need preachers—not "communicators," as some are calling them today. You cannot be a preacher unless your only content is the Bible. If you try to preach your thoughts, your confusion, or your ideas, you are no longer a preacher.

Look at the description of God's Word in the book of Hebrews:

> For the word of God is living and powerful, and sharper than any
> two-edged sword, piercing even to the division of soul and spirit,
> and of joints and marrow, and is a discerner of the thoughts and
> intents of the heart. (Hebrews 4:12 NKJV)

Many pastors today are taking the living, active, and sharp Word of God and making it dead, dull, and blunt. We need to sharpen our swords today. "The sons of Ephraim were archers equipped with bows, yet they turned back on the day of battle" (Psalm 78:9). In other words, they were fully equipped with all that they needed, but when it was time to fight, they turned back. We are living in a day of battle, but many in the pulpit are turning back.

With the incoming harvest of souls, we simply cannot afford to have a broken-down hedge. Remember, the Word of God is our hedge that protects. While it is tragic to see the Word being distorted and disregarded in many pulpits, I believe it is the mercy of God exposing it. We are living in a solemn moment. God will not allow preachers to lose the fruit of this revival among next-generation students by corrupting the Word of God.

The Lord is calling His Church to rise up and rebuild what has been broken down. It is time to put back the four walls of the hedge! To better equip us to do so, let's examine four characteristics of the Bible or, in other words, four sides of a strong defense:

The Bible is *inerrant, infallible, indestructible,* and *incontestable.*

1. The Bible is INERRANT

Inerrant means that the Bible is true with no errors whatsoever. It is completely accurate and cannot be wrong. Inerrancy contends that the Bible does not contain any errors of fact nor any contradictory statements.

Many assume that because the Bible is old, it must contain errors. However, the age of the Bible and the content of the Bible are two different things. The Bible was written over the course of 1,600 years by forty different authors. It was written in thirteen countries on three different continents in three languages: Greek, Hebrew, and Aramaic. Nevertheless, the Bible is error-free in its original writing! More than 100,000 ancient manuscripts of the Bible have been excavated—far exceeding that of any other writing of antiquity—*all* of which confirm that the Bible we have is as accurate as if it came from God Himself . . . because it did come from God Himself![4]

Let's take a moment to look at three things that support the Bible's inerrancy: its historical accuracy, its consistency with science, and its fulfilled prophecies.

Historical Accuracy

Many archaeological discoveries have confirmed the Bible's accuracy. For example, in 1947, a little shepherd boy stumbled upon a cave in a rugged area on the western side of the Dead Sea. What the boy discovered was soon proclaimed to be the greatest archaeological find of the twentieth century. In the cave were jars containing well-preserved antiquity documents. These documents were Hebrew manuscripts of the Old Testament—between 800 and 900 of them.[5] It is encouraging to know that after the parchments were examined, only minimal differences were found between the Dead Sea Scrolls and the Old Testament we use today.

Another example was a stone tablet discovered in 1961 in Caesarea on the Mediterranean coast. Although much had previously been written to discredit the Gospels with regard to the existence of Pilate, this stone tablet bears an inscription mentioning the name of Pontius Pilate, the procurator of Judea. It also mentions the Tiberium, an edifice Pilate built in honor of the emperor Tiberius, who ruled from AD 14 to AD 37. The tablet says that it was from "Pontius Pilate, Prefect of Judea," verifying that he was indeed a person who lived during the time of Jesus.[6]

Many other sites have been unearthed in the Middle East that are in accordance with the Bible's description and mention of them—from the Pool of Bethesda to Jacob's Well to Hezekiah's Tunnel.[7]

Consistency with Science

While it may sometimes appear that science and the Bible contradict each other, it is usually the case that science has just not caught up with the Bible yet. For example, from the very beginning of time, people thought Earth was balanced on elephants or turtles. But in one of the earliest books of the Bible, Job said that God "stretches out the north over empty space; He hangs the earth on nothing" (Job 26:7 NKJV). Under the inspiration of the Holy Spirit, long before man understood gravity's role in keeping Earth in orbit, Job knew that it was not balanced on elephants or turtles but on "nothing"!

As late as Columbus's voyage in 1492, people thought that Earth was flat. Yet more than 700 years before the birth of Christ, Isaiah pronounced, "He sits enthroned above the circle of the earth" (Isaiah 40:22 NIV). Isaiah called it a circle before men called it a sphere. Science was still catching up to what God already said!

Or consider the fact that men have been numbering the stars for centuries. Hipparchus, who lived 150 years before Christ, was the astronomer and scientist of his day. His number of 1,022 stars was considered accurate for 250 years. Then along came Ptolemy who said, "Did Hipparchus say there are 1,022 stars? How absurd—there are 1,056 stars!" Ptolemy's count had upgraded the science of the day for a while. Around 1,300 years later, a young medical student named Galileo invented the first telescope and discovered there are more stars than can be counted.[8] Yet God revealed it to Jeremiah long before Galileo revealed it to the world: "And as the stars of the sky cannot be counted and the sand on the seashore cannot be measured, so I will multiply the descendants of my servant David" (Jeremiah 33:22 NLT). Some now conclude that there are more than 12 octillion stars (that's twenty-seven zeros). Scientists say that is more than there is sand on the earth!

How about human blood? In the old days, man's way of healing was through bloodletting. Our first president, George Washington, died not fighting for American independence but from doctors draining out almost 50 percent of his blood.[9] All the while, the Bible was saying differently: "The life of every creature is in its blood" (Leviticus 17:14 NLT).

Fulfilled Prophecies

Fulfilled prophecy is perhaps the greatest proof of the Bible's inerrancy. If you can find one place where the Bible predicts something that does not come to pass, then the whole Bible is not true! Yet even in this, God is not afraid to have His Word put under scrutiny.

Historian Alfred Edersheim found 456 Old Testament verses prophesying about Jesus—where He would be born, how He would live, what city He would grow up in, how He would die, what words He would say from the cross . . . and all 456 were fulfilled![10] For example, Micah 5:2 says, "But you, Bethlehem Ephrathah, though you are little among the thousands of Judah, yet out of you shall come forth to Me the One to be Ruler in Israel" (NKJV). It was fulfilled in Matthew 2:1: "Now after Jesus was born in Bethlehem of Judea."

In Isaiah 53, Isaiah prophesied of a Suffering Servant who would pour out His life unto death to justify many. Centuries later, Jesus came and fulfilled every single detail of that chapter. In the Old Testament, there were thirty-three prophecies made of Jesus' death alone that were all fulfilled at Calvary. All these prophecies were written hundreds of years before His birth!

2. The Bible is **INFALLIBLE**

The word *infallible* means that the Bible is trustworthy and will never fail you. Here is how Peter described it:

> We also have the prophetic message as something completely reliable, and you will do well to pay attention to it, as to a light shining in a dark place, until the day dawns and the morning star rises in your hearts. (2 Peter 1:19 NIV)

"Completely reliable" means that what the Bible says is useful and true. The Bible was not only useful and true in the day it was written—it is timeless and unchanging! God's Word does not vary based on current events.

> What you say goes, God,
>   and stays, as permanent as the heavens.
> Your truth never goes out of fashion;
>   it's as relevant as the earth when the sun comes up.
> Your Word and truth are dependable as ever.
> (Psalm 119:89–91 MSG)

> Your words all add up to the sum total: Truth.
> (Psalm 119:160 MSG)

The Bible teaches us what is true and right.

> All Scripture is inspired by God and is useful to teach us what is true and to make us realize what is wrong in our lives. It corrects us when we are wrong and teaches us to do what is right. God uses it to prepare and equip his people to do every good work.
> (2 Timothy 3:16–17 NLT)

All Scripture is inspired by God! It corrects us when we are wrong and teaches us to do what is right. We must not be afraid to be corrected by the Word. The Bible is like the manufacturer's instruction manual found in the glove compartment of every new car. God is our Maker, and He knows that things work best when done according to His guidelines!

Because the Bible is infallible, it is therefore our rightful standard.

Can you imagine a world without standards and measurements? What if there were no alphabet, no metric system, no currency exchange, no hours or minutes, no 1+1=2? Alex McFarland said, "A world without standards is not a world without standards but a world with many standards defined by whomever you are speaking to."[11] We need standards for life to function properly. Without standards, we are left with anarchy. Everyone accepts standards as being necessary in math, medicine, currency, language, science . . . but few people want standards for morality and right living!

Yet David said in his psalm:

> I love Your commandments
> Above gold, yes, above pure gold.
> Therefore I carefully follow all Your precepts concerning
>   everything,
> I hate every false way.
> (Psalm 119:127–128)

We, too, ought to "carefully follow" God's Word concerning *everything.* In other words, God always has the final word. When men do not give God the last word, it is as E. Paul Hovey said: "Men do not reject the Bible because it contradicts itself. Men reject the Bible because it contradicts them."[12]

3. THE BIBLE IS **INDESTRUCTIBLE**

Throughout history, men have tried to destroy the Bible. In the eighteenth century, the French philosopher Voltaire said, "A hundred years from my death, the Bible will be a museum piece." Yet a hundred years after his death, the French Bible Society set up its headquarters in Voltaire's old home in Paris, and they even used Voltaire's printing press to print Bibles![13]

No matter how hard people try, no one can seem to get rid of this Book! It's popularity just keeps growing. An estimated 60 to 100 million Bibles are printed each year. No other book even comes close! Presently, there are more than 6 billion Bibles in the world.[14] Let me give you some perspective. To be in the top five on Amazon's bestseller list, you have to sell about 300 books a day,[15] which brings you to about 100,000 copies by the end of the year. Taking the median of the estimated number of Bibles printed each year, 80 million, would mean 219,178 are sold each day—making the Bible an Amazon bestseller *twice* a day!

How about another crazy statistic? There are 6,900 spoken languages in the world at present.[16] The Bible has been translated in 2,846 languages in 157 countries.[17] That means the staggering number of Bibles printed annually is *only* considering the 2,846 languages that the Bible is currently translated into! Can you imagine how many *more* will be printed when we start translating the Bible into the other 4,000 languages?

No other book in history is even in the same class as the Bible! That tells me there is something supernatural about this Book. It's God's Book!

> For you have been born again not of seed which is perishable, but imperishable, that is, through the living and enduring word of God. For,
>
> > "ALL FLESH IS LIKE GRASS,
> > AND ALL ITS GLORY IS LIKE THE FLOWER OF GRASS.
> > THE GRASS WITHERS,
> > AND THE FLOWER FALLS OFF,
> > BUT THE WORD OF THE LORD ENDURES FOREVER."

And this is the word which was preached to you.
(1 Peter 1:23–25)

The Bible endures forever. It is indestructible!

4. THE BIBLE IS **INCONTESTABLE**

The Bible's impact is undeniable: 2.4 billion people on the planet serve Jesus Christ.[18] It is very hard to argue against lives that have been changed! Jesus Himself told a parable illustrating the fact that when the Word of God enters someone's heart, it changes them forever.

> The seed that fell into good, fertile soil represents those lovers of truth who hear it deep within their hearts. They respond by cling-ing to the word, keeping it dear as they endure all things in faith. This is the seed that will one day bear much fruit in their lives.
> (Luke 8:15 TPT)

We clearly see the Bible bearing much fruit in the story of the Walamo tribe in Ethiopia. Before World War II, two missionary ladies went to Ethiopia to begin work there. However, in 1936, Mussolini's army took over Addis Ababa and subsequently expelled all missionaries from the country. The only thing the missionaries could do was leave some Bibles with the people they were ministering to—about 150 Christians. With all the missionaries and preach-ers gone, the only thing left with the Walamos was the Word of God. But when the missionaries returned six years later, they were astounded to discover that 48,000 Walamos had come to Christ![19] Churches were planted; blood feuds be-tween the tribes ceased . . . all because they left the Word of God!

Throughout history, there have been people who began to read the Bible to try to find a way to discredit it—only to end up being transformed by it! There was even a young man in our church in Detroit who had tried every Eastern religion. Christianity was going to be last. Unaware that an audio version of the Bible already existed, he decided to make his own. In the middle of recording the Bible, he got saved!

How can you argue with changed lives?

LET THE LION OUT

The Bible is inerrant, infallible, indestructible, and incontestable. It is within this hedge that God wants to grow His Church and bring in an incredible harvest!

Now if you happen to find yourself witnessing to someone and feel like it is going nowhere, here is my suggestion: Just give them a Bible! I love how Charles Spurgeon put it: "How do I defend the Bible? I treat it like a lion. I let it out of its cage, and it defends itself!"[20] God's Word, with its inherent power, will surely accomplish all that He pleases.

> For as the rain comes down, and the snow from heaven,
> And do not return there,
> But water the earth,
> And make it bring forth and bud,
> That it may give seed to the sower
> And bread to the eater,
> So shall My word be that goes forth from My mouth;
> It shall not return to Me void,
> But it shall accomplish what I please,
> And it shall prosper in the thing for which I sent it. . . .
> Instead of the thorn shall come up the cypress tree,
> And instead of the brier shall come up the myrtle tree.
> (Isaiah 55:10–11, 13 NKJV)

God's Word will not return empty! It is likened to rain that causes things to grow. Instead of thornbushes and briers will come cypress and myrtle trees. That means that even in the toughest places where nobody can bring growth, God's Word bears fruit.

It is time to let the lion out of its cage. The challenge is not necessarily "Why don't you believe it more?" but rather "Why don't you read it more?" Consider the words of John in the book of Revelation:

> Happy is the one who reads this book, and happy are those who listen to the words of this prophetic message and obey what is written in this book! (Revelation 1:3 GNT)

Don't miss the first part: "Happy is the one . . ." Your happiness is connected to the Bible. Your happiness increases when your Bible habits increase. Read it, listen to the words, and obey what is written. God promises that His Word will never return void!

QUESTIONS

1. Give an example of how your life has been impacted by the Bible.

2. Has anyone ever challenged your belief in the Bible? How did you respond? How would you respond today?

3. What are some practical ways you can further incorporate God's Word in your life?

THE CHURCH

The Body, the Bride, and the Army: The Church of Jesus Christ

"When it comes to my salvation, all I need is Jesus; after my salvation, everything is Jesus plus the church . . . When people preach that all you need is Jesus, they cut you and I off from one of the greatest sources of healing, which is the body of Christ. Don't go it alone—you won't make it."

JOSH MCDOWELL[1]

I have often been asked the question: Can I be a Christian and *not* go to church? My answer is simply, yes, you can be a Christian . . . but not a growing Christian. As former pastor and author R. Kent Hughes said, "On the most elementary level, you do not have to go to church to be a Christian. You do not have to go home to be married either. But in both cases if you do not, you will have a very poor relationship."[2]

Even a recent study conducted by a professor at the Harvard School of Public Health discussed the benefits of attending church. It found that married couples who attend church services together are 30 to 50 percent less likely to get divorced than those who do not. Such couples are also nearly 30 percent less likely to be depressed and, over a sixteen-year follow-up period, were shown to have a significantly lower risk of dying.[3]

There are obviously many more benefits of going to church that we could discuss. It is important, however, that we first define what the church is as well as what it is not. When you make the church something that it is not, you make it ineffective.

The church is not a hall of fame with perfect people who always bat a thousand. The church is not a museum; it should not be a place where all people talk about is the good old days. The church is not a night-club meant to resemble a comfortable place for the next generation. The church is not an alternative to a worldly lifestyle; it is a *contrast*. It is not meant to be in lieu of your former life or a close substitute; the church is antithetical to your former life!

D. Martyn Lloyd-Jones said in his book *Studies in the Sermon on the Mount*: "The glory of the gospel is that when the Church is absolutely different from the world, she invariably attracts it. It is then that the world is made to listen to her message, though it may hate it at first."[4] Unfortunately, the church has tried to be so current that it has become irrelevant. For example, on Valentine's Day 2022, when war between Russia and Ukraine was imminent, most churches still preached on date nights and relationships. All the while, the world was on the cusp of utter destruction with 250,000 deaths and counting.

A number of church strategists have recently informed me that churchgoers are now only showing up to church an average of 1.8 times a month.[5] These experts have been offering me strategies on how to help the 1.8'ers. However, I think the problem is that they have diagnosed the wrong thing. They are trying to fix the 1.8'ers, but it is the *church* that needs the help!

If the church truly was what God intended it to be, I guarantee you that people would not come only 1.8 times a month. If the church was where God's presence, healing, and deliverance could be found, people would be coming whenever the doors are open!

You see, the church is meant to be a hospital to get you healthy, an army barrack to prepare you for battle, a school to instruct you, a lighthouse in a dark world. I love the title of a sermon that Charles Spurgeon preached many years ago: "The Church, the World's Hope."[6] *That* is what we are meant to be. Jesus left His church on this earth to complete His mission.

I was reading a story about a pastor who was in Atlanta and noticed a restaurant called Church of God Grill. The peculiar name aroused his curiosity, so he dialed their number. A man answered, "Hello, Church of God Grill!" The pastor asked how the restaurant had been given such an unusual name, and the man answered, "Well, we had a little mission down here, and we started selling chicken dinners after church on Sunday to help pay the bills. People liked the chicken, and we had such good business that eventually we cut back on the church services. After a while, we just closed down the church altogether and kept on serving chicken dinners. But we kept the name we started with, and that's Church of God Grill."[7]

This church had clearly lost its way, but what I love about the story was their honesty. If you are not going to be what God has asked you to be, then don't be a church, be something else! If you are not going to be a lighthouse, a hospital, or an army barrack, then at least sell good chicken!

So what is the church that God is calling His people to be? Answering this question is critical to our biblical worldview. I find it best to use the Word of God to define the church for us.

The book of Ephesians gives us three images that we will examine in this chapter:

1. The church is the body of Christ: an extension of Him.
2. The church is the bride of Christ: intimacy with Him.
3. The church is the army of Christ: warfare for Him.

1. THE CHURCH IS THE BODY OF CHRIST

> And He put all things in subjection under His feet, and made Him head over all things to the church, which is His body, the fullness of Him who fills all in all. (Ephesians 1:22–23)

What does it mean to be the body of Christ? Jesus is the head that leads us, and we are an extension of Him. Around the world, we are His hands and feet. The mind of Christ dictates where we are to go; He tells us to know Him and make Him known. Just as almost everything you know about me is through my body, the body of Christ reveals who Jesus is. That is how the world will know Him!

Unity is critical in the body of Christ. The body cannot have its own agenda; it cannot be effective independently. Think of it this way: An airplane is a machine 100 percent made up of non-flying parts. The seats do not fly. An engine cannot fly. But when you assemble it and all the parts are working together, they can lift 175,000 pounds. Likewise, many members of the church can accomplish collectively what the same members cannot do individually. There is power in the unified body of Christ to do the unimaginable!

The Apostle Paul described the body of Christ this way:

> For just as the body is one and yet has many parts, and all the parts of the body, though they are many, are one body, so also is Christ. For by one Spirit we were all baptized into one body, whether Jews or Greeks, whether slaves or free, and we were all made to drink of one Spirit. For the body is not one part, but many. (1 Corinthians 12:12–14)

It is very dangerous when we begin to exalt a part of the body instead of the Person. When we tout our denomination, our choir, our style of preaching . . . it is a surefire way to be grounded rather than flying. The body must work together in order to be effective. Paul went on to say:

> If the whole body were an eye, where would the hearing be? If the whole body were hearing, where would the sense of smell be? But now God has arranged the parts, each one of them in the body, just as He desired. If they were all one part, where would the body be? But now there are many parts, but one body. And the eye cannot say to the hand, "I have no need of you"; or again, the head to the feet, "I have no need of you." (1 Corinthians 12:17–21)

I need the other parts of the body to be effective, even in the natural realm. If I stub my toe on the corner of the bed, my hurt toe tells my brain to tell my hands to grab the toe. Then it tells my other leg to prepare itself to bear the weight of my entire body as it bounces up and down. Then my mouth knows it is time to yell, "Help me, Jesus!" I cannot be effective with just a toe. When my toe gets hurt, it needs the whole body to express it!

We as the body of Christ must be ready to do what God wants us to do . . . together! Ebony and Ivory were the names given to two elderly women in New Jersey, one white and one black, who played classical piano. Both had experienced a stroke in 1982 and become partially disabled. Ruth Eisenberg and Margaret Patrick were introduced to each other the following year and began playing piano together, one hand each. A reporter covering their story dubbed them "Ebony and Ivory" after the 1982 hit song by Paul McCartney and Stevie

Wonder.[8] Together they ended up doing something they never could have done on their own! I need you to help me play a masterpiece; you need me to help you play a masterpiece. What God is doing requires a symphony, not a soloist! That symphony is the body of Christ.

2. The Church Is the Bride of Christ

I have done a lot of marriage counseling in my life. Why? Because marriage means two totally different people living together in the same house, both trying to change each other.

To this day, Cindy and I still laugh about the dumbest thing I ever did in our marriage. We were married just less than a year when we stopped for pizza at Sbarro in the Pittsburgh airport. I wanted to tell Cindy everything she was doing wrong in the marriage, so I concocted a brilliant scheme. I would look humble and say, "Cindy, tell me how I can be a better husband. What do I need to change?" Of course, she would then ask me in return, "Is there anything I need to do?"—for which I had a list ready to go.

However, when I asked her, she went on and on about me. When she was finally done, she just ate her pizza. She never asked me about her! My plan completely backfired. Of course, I wasn't interested in me getting fixed; I was interested in her adjusting to me!

God chooses to describe the relationship that He has with His people as that of a bride and groom. Jesus is the groom, and the church is His bride. We get a glimpse of the bride of Christ as we read God's instructions for husbands and wives:

> Husbands, love your wives, just as Christ also loved the church and gave Himself up for her, so that He might sanctify her, having cleansed her by the washing of water with the word, that He might present to Himself the church in all her glory, having no spot or wrinkle or any such thing; but that she would be holy and blameless. (Ephesians 5:25–27)

I pray this over our marriage every night: "Help me to love my wife as Christ loved the church." This is the part where Cindy always adds, "*and . . . gave Himself up for her.*" It is the part we somehow always leave out—the dying-to-self part. Marriage on the husband's part is most like the crucifixion of Jesus. Men are shown a cross for leadership, not a throne. Christlike leadership in a marriage means embracing crucifixion, not dictatorship.

Now after forty years of marital counseling, let me give you the top three issues that cause problems in a marriage. They are: (1) selfishness, (2) selfishness, and (3) selfishness! I believe the same holds true for the bride of Christ. Can you imagine if Jesus and His bride came to marriage counseling? The issue would not be Jesus at all but the selfishness of His bride!

Amos 3:3 says, "Can two walk together, unless they are agreed?" (NKJV). In order for the church to walk with her groom in unity, she must agree with Him! It is not Christ who must agree with us and adjust to our lifestyle. If we do not like what the groom says, then we, too, are given a cross.

As a perfect groom, Jesus loves His bride—which means we must as well. Over the years, I have seen individuals get frustrated with the church, finding a reason to leave because of the people. "I have nothing in common with them!" they insist. But the issue here is that God does. The church is His bride, His choosing! Have you noticed that God does not preselect people who have a natural ability to get along? Why do you think all these people got saved in the first place? In fact, if you knew the pasts of some of the people you sit next to in church, you would be scared to death!

If you choose a church based on finding people with whom you have a lot in common, you do not want a church—you want a club. Remember, the church is not a natural community comprised of people with common interests; it is a *supernatural* community of people all saved by the grace of God!

Matthew 10 is one of the best ways to explain how Jesus brings His bride together. Before we look at the passage, let me give you a brief history of two groups of people found in the New Testament—tax collectors and Zealots. The tax collectors were Jews who collected taxes from their fellow Jews on behalf of the Roman Empire. They made their living by charging an extra amount, some of them making much more than a living. They exacted any amount they could and thus became well-to-do. Tax collectors were therefore considered traitors who became wealthy by collaborating with Roman authorities at the expense of their own people.

The Zealots were the radical loyalists. They basically carried out acts of terrorism against the Romans in the name of religion. The Zealots passionately hated traitors—more specifically, tax collectors. Put the tax collectors and Zealots together? Get ready to call 911!

With that in mind, look at this list in Matthew 10:

> Jesus summoned His twelve disciples and gave them authority over unclean spirits, to cast them out, and to heal every disease and every sickness. Now the names of the twelve apostles are these: The first, Simon, who is called Peter, and his brother Andrew; and James the son of Zebedee, and his brother John; Philip and Bartholomew; Thomas and Matthew the *tax collector*; James the son of Alphaeus, and Thaddaeus; Simon the *Zealot*, and Judas Iscariot, the one who also betrayed Him. These twelve Jesus sent out after instructing them. (Matthew 10:1–5, emphasis added)

Matthew put a tax collector and a Zealot close to each other in the disciple list—Matthew the tax collector and Simon the Zealot! What I love about Jesus' list is that it does not say: "Peter a fisherman, John a fisherman, Simon a fisherman." He chose people who could not be further opposites!

Our tendency is to hang out with people who are just like us. But God will put a person who irritates you in the seat right next to you! Some marriages may feel like a tax collector and a Zealot together. But that is how sandpaper works—you get rubbed so that your rough edges come off. You do not grow by being with people who are just like you. Oswald Chambers summed it up well: "We say, 'If God would only use His own fingers and make me broken bread and poured-out wine in a special way, then I wouldn't object!' But when He uses someone we dislike . . . then we object."[9]

So the next time your Zealot nature sits next to an irritating tax collector—or your "I was raised in a Christian home all my life" sits next to a brand-new saved person who smells like his struggle—don't say, "That person bothers me." Instead, try saying, "That person sanctifies me!" If you look back at the passage in Ephesians 5, you will see that Jesus' goal is a church "having no spot or wrinkle" (verse 27). So all of this is part of the work that Jesus is doing in His bride!

Have you ever been around a married couple who finishes each other's sentences? They are in tune with one another's needs. In the same way, the Scriptures tell us that "the Spirit and the bride say, 'Come'" (Revelation 22:17).

When we are in right relationship with Him, the church and heaven say the same thing at the same time.

We are saying a lot of things today but not necessarily what the Spirit is saying. I want to say what the Spirit is saying—not what some strategist or denomination or preacher is saying. We must be in alignment with heaven, where the Spirit and the bride are walking and speaking in unison. And then one day that glorious celebration that John spoke of in the book of Revelation will come:

> And I heard, as it were, the voice of a great multitude, as the sound of many waters and as the sound of mighty thunderings, saying, "Alleluia! For the Lord God Omnipotent reigns! Let us be glad and rejoice and give Him glory, for the marriage of the Lamb has come, and His wife has made herself ready." And to her it was granted to be arrayed in fine linen, clean and bright, for the fine linen is the righteous acts of the saints. Then he said to me, "Write: 'Blessed are those who are called to the marriage supper of the Lamb!'" (Revelation 19:6–9 NKJV)

3. THE CHURCH IS THE ARMY OF CHRIST

After Paul talked about the body of Christ in Ephesians 1 and the bride Christ gave Himself up for in Ephesians 5, he then moved on to talking about the armor of God in Ephesians 6. In other words, the bride of Ephesians 5 has to put on her armor in Ephesians 6! So don't hang out too long in that wedding gown . . . the church is the army of Christ, and we are constantly in warfare.

I was reading about a man living in the second century named Polycarp who definitely needed to put his armor on. He was the bishop of Smyrna—the same church Jesus addressed in the book of Revelation—which at that time was undergoing terrible persecution. Emperor Tiberius required that all citizens sprinkle incense on his statue once a year and confess to him, "Caesar is lord."

In AD 156, Polycarp refused and was therefore sentenced to die. When given a chance to recant on account of the powerful church he had, Polycarp said, "For eighty and six years I served Him and He has done me no wrong; how then can I blaspheme my King Who saved me?"

While Polycarp was at the stake about to be burned, one church official stood up and said, "From the church militant and the church triumphant, we excommunicate you, Polycarp!"

Yet right before he was martyred, Polycarp lifted his head and spoke, "From the church militant, maybe. But from the church triumphant, never!" Only the army of God is triumphant forever![10]

Like Polycarp, we will always be considered out of step with culture. Whenever we are building for God, there will always be enemies trying to hinder the work. That is why we as His bride must always have our armor on, ready to fight. However, all too often, that is where the challenge lies. The church is trained to fight, but if we do not fight the enemy, we end up fighting each other! If we are not fighting against selfishness, sin, the spirit of this age, lust, or the chains that want to come and hold us . . . that is when offenses build, and we are defeated from within. So not only must we have our armor on, we also must focus on fighting the right battle!

Interestingly, in the four Gospels, the word *church* came out of the mouth of Jesus twice—both times in the context of a fight. More specifically, He used the word *church* in regard to hell and offense. Two things keep people from church—deception and offense. One comes from without and the other from within. Therefore, we must constantly be on guard. However, remembering what Jesus declared about His church gives us courage for the fight:

> And I say also unto thee, That thou art Peter, and upon this rock I
> will build my church; and the gates of hell shall not prevail against
> it. (Matthew 16:18 KJV)

"The gates of hell shall not prevail" may seem like an odd phrase. Gates prevailing does not make sense, for gates do not fight, they protect. An attacking force never carries its own gates up to besiege a city. We therefore understand that Jesus' point was not that the church is invincible against hell's attack; rather, the church is unconquerable when she goes *on the offensive*. This is a picture of a church moving into hell's region. As the church attacks, the gates of hell will yield before her, unable to prevent God's army from infiltrating hell's fortified camps and recovering all that was held in chains and bondage!

Smith Wigglesworth once said, "Great faith is the product of great fights. Great testimonies are the outcome of great tests. Great triumphs can only come out of great trials."[11] The church has a great story to tell because of the great fights it has won through Jesus.

How do we win this fight? Ephesians 6 is known as the spiritual warfare chapter of the New Testament.

> Finally, my brethren, be strong in the Lord and in the power of His might. Put on the whole armor of God, that you may be able to stand against the wiles of the devil. For we do not wrestle against flesh and blood, but against principalities, against powers, against the rulers of the darkness of this age, against spiritual hosts of wickedness in the heavenly places. Therefore take up the whole armor of God, that you may be able to withstand in the evil day, and having done all, to stand. (Ephesians 6:10–13 NKJV)

This passage contains a few interesting contrasts. We do not fight against flesh and blood but against principalities and powers of darkness. However, the contrast we often miss is that of wrestlers versus soldiers. Notice that Paul said in verse 12, "We do not wrestle." And then he said in verse 13, "Take up the whole armor of God." He was saying that we are not wrestlers, we are soldiers. Wrestlers used to go mano a mano—oiling up their bodies and fighting to the death, one individual against another. But Paul reminded us that we do not fight that way. We are not wrestlers, fighting by ourselves for ourselves. We are soldiers—fighting together as part of an army! We fight the enemy by locking arms, just as the Roman army used to lock shields before moving forward in battle.

There is a scene in the movie *Gladiator* where Maximus—former Roman army general played by Russell Crowe—is in the Colosseum fighting for his life with other gladiators. He exhorts the men: "Whatever comes out of these gates, we've got a better chance of survival if we work together. Do you understand? If we stay together, we survive!"[12] And they did. Maximus gave them the key to winning the fight, just as Paul gave us the key in Ephesians 6. You are a soldier, and you are in an army. If you fight alone, you will die. If we fight together, we will win!

I am reminded of the lyrics from an old song we used to sing:

God's got an army
Marching through the land
Deliverance is their song
And there's healing in their hand
Everlasting joy and gladness in their heart
And in this army I've got a part

You have a part! You play a critical role in the body, the bride, and the army of Christ. As the body works together, as the bride walks in unity with her groom, and as the army links arms and moves forward—the gates of hell cannot prevail against us! We are part of the church triumphant . . . not going down but going up, by the grace of God!

QUESTIONS

1. When have you seen the body of Christ accomplish something collectively that its individual members could not have done alone?

2. How have you been impacted by someone in the church who was a "tax collector" or "Zealot" to you?

3. What are some ways the church can go on the offensive against hell?

4. How does this chapter challenge your perception and attitude toward your role in the church?

DISCIPLESHIP

Turning Multitudes into Disciples

"The man with a cross no longer controls his destiny; he lost control when he picked up his cross. That cross immediately became to him an all-absorbing interest, an overwhelming interference. No matter what he may desire to do, there is but one thing he can do; that is, move on toward the place of crucifixion."

A. W. TOZER[1]

If you wanted to start a worldwide movement, how would you go about it? What if you only had thirty-six months to do it?

Fortunately, we don't have to figure it out. Jesus did it.

During the last three years of His life on earth, Jesus poured into twelve disciples who would, in turn, change the world. Considering the fact that discipleship was the last thing Jesus spoke about before He left this earth, it probably ought to be the first thing on our agenda today.

Now when you were born again, you became heaven bound. And since you are heaven bound, you are called to display heaven's birthmarks. The Apostle John used the phrase "born of God" several times in 1 John, giving examples of birthmarks that show we belong to God's family:

> No one who is born of God will continue to sin, because God's seed remains in them; they cannot go on sinning, because they have been born of God. (1 John 3:9 NIV)

Christians are not sinless, but we will sin less and less because we are born of God.

> Dear friends, let us love one another, for love comes from God. Everyone who loves has been born of God. (1 John 4:7 NIV)

A love for people comes to those born of God.

> Everyone born of God overcomes the world. This is the victory that has overcome the world, even our faith. (1 John 5:4 NIV)

People born of God experience victory in their lives.

A life marked by love and victory rather than being dominated by sin proves that one is growing. Growth is the evidence of life; we must always be going further in our faith. That is why I am challenging you today to move from belief in God to *discipleship*.

Let me describe it this way: Red Seas lead to Jordan Rivers. Both the Red Sea and the Jordan River played an important part of Israel's journey out of bondage and into their future in the Promised Land. Their freedom journey is similar to our salvation journey. The Red Sea is leaving the past behind, and the Jordan River is stepping into a new future.

God parted both bodies of water, making a way through where no path existed. Each miracle marked the entrance into a new season. But each miracle happened a different way. The Red Sea miracle came from thousands of people doing nothing but watching God from the shore.

> And Moses said to the people, "Do not be afraid. Stand still, and see the salvation of the LORD, which He will accomplish for you today."
> . . . Then Moses stretched out his hand over the sea; and the LORD caused the sea to go back by a strong east wind all that night, and made the sea into dry land, and the waters were divided. So the children of Israel went into the midst of the sea on the dry ground, and the waters were a wall to them on their right hand and on their left. (Exodus 14:13, 21–22 NKJV)

The Jordan River miracle was different. The priests needed to stand in the middle of the river rather than watching from the shore.

> When the people set out from their tents to cross the Jordan, with the priests carrying the ark of the covenant before the people, and when those who were carrying the ark came up to the Jordan and the feet of the priests carrying the ark stepped down into the edge of the water . . . then the waters which were flowing down from above stood and rose up in one heap . . . and those which were flowing down toward the sea of the Arabah, the Salt Sea, were completely cut off. So the people crossed opposite Jericho.
> (Joshua 3:14–16)

The Israelites did not get wet in the Red Sea crossing, but they did have to get their feet wet to cross the Jordan River. Similarly, in order to go forward into the future God has for us, we are going to have to step in and get our feet wet. The longer you walk with God, the more He will ask you to jump in, and the less He will allow you to just stand and watch the miracle. God got you out of the slavery of sin, and now He wants to lead you into your victorious future. That is discipleship.

Here is what the Apostle Paul said we must do to become heaven born and heaven bound:

> That if you confess with your mouth Jesus as Lord, and believe in your heart that God raised Him from the dead, you will be saved; for with the heart a person believes, resulting in righteousness, and with the mouth he confesses, resulting in salvation.
> (Romans 10:9–10)

Yet once you have confessed Jesus as Lord, you are faced with a challenge to your confession. It is found in the most embarrassing question Jesus ever asked:

> Why do you call Me, "Lord, Lord," and do not do what I say?
> (Luke 6:46)

To call Jesus "Lord" means you do what Jesus says. If Jesus is your Lord, He is now calling you to get your feet wet with discipleship. There is no such thing as cheap discipleship. Christianity works when we are *all in!* Yes, you can come to Jesus while you are addicted to drugs, addicted to porn, using horrible language, living a sexual life that is not pleasing to God, lying, or cheating. But you cannot walk with Jesus and stay the same. Salvation is free, but discipleship costs. If Jesus is truly your Lord, I guarantee He will speak things to you that you will not immediately agree with.

Sadly, not everyone will fully submit to Jesus. Notice what happened at the Last Supper:

> Now when evening came, Jesus was reclining at the table with the twelve. And as they were eating, He said, "Truly I say to you that one of you will betray Me." Being deeply grieved, they began saying to Him, "Surely it is not I, Lord?" And He answered, "He who dipped his hand with Me in the bowl is the one who will betray Me. The Son of Man is going away, just as it is written about Him; but woe to that man by whom the Son of Man is betrayed! It would have been good for that man if he had not been born." And Judas, who was betraying Him, said, "Surely it is not I, Rabbi?" Jesus said to him, "You have said it yourself." (Matthew 26:20–25)

Judas said "Rabbi" while all the other disciples said "Lord." Judas enjoyed Jesus the teacher, but he did not want his life changed. If Jesus is Lord, we must do things His way. C. S. Lewis put it well: "I didn't go to religion to make me happy. I always knew a bottle of Port would do that. If you want a religion to make you feel really comfortable, I certainly don't recommend Christianity."[2]

Jesus clearly laid out what is required of anyone who is going to be His disciple. At the time, great multitudes were following Him. However, Jesus was about to thin out the crowds with lordship. Preachers today will water down the message as the crowds get bigger, but Jesus did the opposite. His message got stronger as the crowds grew larger. He turned to the multitudes and issued a discipleship challenge:

> If anyone comes to Me and does not hate his own father, mother, wife, children, brothers, sisters, yes, and even his own life, he cannot

be My disciple. Whoever does not carry his own cross and come after Me cannot be My disciple. For which one of you, when he wants to build a tower, does not first sit down and calculate the cost, to see if he has enough to complete it? Otherwise, when he has laid a foundation and is not able to finish, all who are watching it will begin to ridicule him, saying, "This person began to build, and was not able to finish!" Or what king, when he sets out to meet another king in battle, will not first sit down and consider whether he is strong enough with ten thousand men to face the one coming against him with twenty thousand? Otherwise, while the other is still far away, he sends a delegation and requests terms of peace. So then, none of you can be My disciple who does not give up all his own possessions.

Therefore, salt is good; but if even salt has become tasteless, with what will it be seasoned? It is useless either for the soil or the manure pile, so it is thrown out. The one who has ears to hear, let him hear. (Luke 14:26–35)

Three times Jesus said that if you do not subscribe to this, you cannot be His disciple. Jesus spoke to the multitude and cut it down to disciples. Today the church is full of crowds but not many disciples.

In this passage, we see that disciples are identified by five traits:

- A strange **comparison**
- A daily **crucifixion**
- A calculated **construction**
- A constant **conflict**
- A distinct **contrast**

I am not questioning your Red Sea decision—the day you prayed to be born again. But I do want to challenge you with a Jordan River future—the decision to go further. I want you to cross both bodies of water. Many of those who prayed the born-again prayer have dry feet. It is time to get your feet wet and enter discipleship.

What exactly will that entail? Let's examine each of the traits that mark a true disciple of Jesus.

1. A STRANGE **COMPARISON**: HAVING SUCH A STRONG LOVE FOR GOD THAT PEOPLE THINK YOU HATE THEM

I have told my wife that she is the second most-important voice in my life next to Jesus. It is not because I dislike Cindy that I tell her she is second. Her voice matters, but it is not first. What the Bible says is first. If we are discussing painting our apartment and she wants New York Jets green, I may argue, but I will let her win. We get a green living room, and I pretend we are camping in a forest every day. But if she were to say, "I don't want us to tithe anymore," she loses. God's Word wins.

When Jesus said that to be His disciple, you must hate your father, mother, and so on, this "hate talk" is not actually hate. Rather, He was giving His disciples a challenge to love God so much that it would be interpreted by others as "you don't love us anymore." It is preparation for the accusations that will arise when second voices want to be first voices. I like the word *comparison* used here:

> If you want to be my disciple, you must, by comparison, hate everyone else—your father and mother, wife and children, brothers and sisters—yes, even your own life. Otherwise, you cannot be my disciple. (Luke 14:26 NLT)

You will be labeled as one who hates your family, your roots, your people, your fraternity brothers. If you become a Christian and you are currently living with your boyfriend or girlfriend, when you tell them you cannot live with them anymore, they will say, "You don't like me." But you can respond, "You're right. I don't like you. Now I love you with Christ's love, so that is why I am moving out!"

If you want to be a disciple, Jesus comes before any relationship. Your upbringing, parents, and ethnicity all play second chair to Christ. If anything is contrary to His Word, it must be set aside.

2. A DAILY CRUCIFIXION: REALIZING THERE ARE OLD THINGS THAT DON'T NEED TO BE FIXED BUT NEED TO DIE

Jesus used the cross to speak about discipleship: "Whoever does not carry his own cross and come after Me cannot be My disciple" (Luke 14:27). The cross was an instrument for capital punishment, not an ornament to be worn around the neck. Today it would be as reprehensible as wearing an electric chair on a chain as jewelry. Whenever Jesus speaks about our carrying a cross, it is an invitation to die to self and selfishness. I heard a pastor once say that "the cross can be thought of as any discomfort that comes to my life as a result of my nonnegotiable commitment to follow after Christ."

The more a man dies to himself, the more he lives for God. Today we have a Christianity that caters to your opinions and self. However, true Christianity is dying to self. The reason so many Christians have no forward progress is because they have not come to the end of themselves yet. God will not allow you to bring "you" into the future—only the new and transformed "you!"

In her classic book *Through Gates of Splendor*, Elisabeth Elliot recounted the story of her husband, Jim Elliot. On January 8, 1956, Jim and four other missionaries were bringing the gospel for the very first time to an Indian tribe in Ecuador known then as the Aucas, only to be speared to death by the tribe. When Elisabeth was informed by radio that Jim had died, she told them that Jim did not die there. They repeatedly told her Jim had died, and she kept insisting that Jim did not die there. They thought it was denial from the shock. But Elisabeth went on to say this: "Jim did not die in the Curaray River. Jim died at an altar at Wheaton College a few years ago when he surrendered everything to Jesus." He died before he even started his missionary journey! How fitting that Jim Elliot was the one who had written these famous words: "He is no fool who gives what he cannot keep to gain what he cannot lose."[3]

The Scriptures show us that the Christian life is a series of deaths and funerals—from beginning to end.

> I have been crucified with Christ: and I myself no longer live, but Christ lives in me. And the real life I now have within this body is a result of my trusting in the Son of God, who loved me and gave himself for me. (Galatians 2:20 TLB)

> So look upon your old sin nature as dead and unresponsive to sin,
> and instead be alive to God, alert to him, through Jesus Christ our
> Lord. Do not let sin control your puny body any longer; do not give
> in to its sinful desires. Do not let any part of your bodies become
> tools of wickedness, to be used for sinning; but give yourselves
> completely to God—every part of you—for you are back from death
> and you want to be tools in the hands of God, to be used for his
> good purposes. (Romans 6:11–13 TLB)

The picture the Bible gives is that we are now unresponsive to sin; we are legally dead. Many of us are fighting to stay alive when we really should just die! Watchman Nee explained, "God sets us free from the dominion of sin, not by strengthening our old man but by crucifying him; not by helping him to do anything, but by removing him from the scene of action."[4] In other words, dying to self is coming to the conclusion that you are no longer the most important person in the world . . . Jesus is!

3. A Calculated CONSTRUCTION: Building a Life for the Glory of God Regardless of What It May Cost Me

There is a famous story that when Hernán Cortés landed at Veracruz in 1519 to begin his conquest of Mexico with a small force of 600 men, he purposely set fire to his fleet of eleven ships.[5] His men on the shore watched their ships sink to the bottom of the Gulf of Mexico. With no means of retreat, there was only one direction to move—forward. Likewise, in order for us to go forward, we must burn the ships that want to take us back to our old life. It says in the book of Hebrews:

> And if their hearts were still remembering what they left behind,
> they would have found an opportunity to go back. But they couldn't
> turn back for their hearts were fixed on what was far greater, that
> is, the heavenly realm! (Hebrews 11:15–16 TPT)

Jesus Himself spoke about the importance of making a calculated construction so that we do not end up turning back:

> For which one of you, when he wants to build a tower, does not first sit down and calculate the cost, to see if he has enough to complete it? Otherwise, when he has laid a foundation and is not able to finish, all who are watching it will begin to ridicule him, saying, "This person began to build, and was not able to finish!" (Luke 14:28-30)

True discipleship involves going through the plans and counting the cost. I knew what it would cost my marriage, my family, and my personal life to move to New York City and pastor Times Square Church. Cindy and I counted the cost. We anticipated a lot of the battles that we would face, though, of course, there were some we did not expect. Nevertheless, we knew it would not be easy. Red Sea people asked us what we were doing in the Jordan. All we could say was, "We know it's going to part at some point; we just don't know when!" It has been one of the hardest yet most fulfilling things I have ever done. Sometimes my mind goes back to a line Tom Hanks said in the movie *A League of Their Own*: "It's supposed to be hard. If it wasn't hard, everyone would do it. Hard is what makes it great."[6] That is why Jesus implores us to count the cost of discipleship before we say "yes" to our Jordan River crossing. The life of faith is amazing, but it is one that is hard and costly.

William Borden, heir to the Borden Dairy Estate, is an example of a disciple who had counted the cost. In 1904, William graduated from a Chicago high school a millionaire. His parents gave him a trip around the world. Traveling through Asia, the Middle East, and Europe gave William a burden for souls. Writing home, he said, "I'm going to give my life to prepare for the mission field." When he made that decision, he wrote in the back of his Bible two words: "No Reserves." He later turned down high-paying job offers upon graduating from Yale University, at which point he entered two more words in his Bible: "No Retreats." When he had completed his studies at Princeton Seminary, William sailed for China to do missionary work, stopping first in Egypt for some preparation. While there he was stricken with cerebral meningitis and died within a month. When his family went through his Bible after his death, they found a final entry underneath the words "No Reserves. No Retreats." William had written: "No Regrets."[7] He had counted the cost!

4. A Constant **CONFLICT**: A Willingness to Fight Enemies of the Cross

We saw in the previous chapter that to live the Christian life is to be in constant warfare. You will fight the devil, the flesh, the world. You will fight to pray, to tithe, to read the Bible. You will fight for your children's salvation, for peace, for joy, for your marriage. Jesus told us that a disciple must be ready to fight even when it looks like the odds are against him.

> Or what king, when he sets out to meet another king in battle, will not first sit down and consider whether he is strong enough with ten thousand men to face the one coming against him with twenty thousand? (Luke 14:31)

In this passage it is a two-to-one fight, but God plus you is still a majority! Even when everything feels like a fight, remember that it is a good fight. Consider the words of Paul:

> Fight the good fight of faith; take hold of the eternal life to which you were called. (1 Timothy 6:12)

> I have fought the good fight, I have finished the course, I have kept the faith. (2 Timothy 4:7)

It is a fight you will win with the help and grace of God. The crowds will make you cowardly, compromising and cautious. But discipleship puts you in constant battles with promised victories.

In his book *The Signature of Jesus*, Brennan Manning shared about a copy of a note that he was given. This note was found in the office of a young pastor in Zimbabwe, Africa, following his martyrdom for his faith in Christ:

> I'm part of the fellowship of the unashamed. I have the Holy Spirit's power. The die has been cast. I have stepped over the line. The decision has been made—I'm a disciple of his. I won't look back, let up, slow down, back away, or be still. My past is redeemed, my present makes sense, my future is secure. I'm finished and done with low living, sight walking, smooth knees, colorless dreams,

tamed visions, worldly talking, cheap giving, and dwarfed goals.

I no longer need preeminence, prosperity, position, promotions, plaudits, or popularity. I don't have to be right, first, tops, recognized, praised, regarded, or rewarded. I now live by faith, lean in his presence, walk by patience, am uplifted by prayer, and I labor with power.

My face is set, my gait is fast, my goal is heaven, my road is narrow, my way rough, my companions are few, my Guide reliable, my mission clear. I cannot be bought, compromised, detoured, lured away, turned back, deluded, or delayed. I will not flinch in the face of sacrifice, hesitate in the presence of the enemy, pander at the pool of popularity, or meander in the maze of mediocrity.

I won't give up, shut up, let up, until I have stayed up, stored up, prayed up, paid up, preached up for the cause of Christ. I am a disciple of Jesus. I must go till he comes, give till I drop, preach till all know, and work till he stops me. And, when he comes for his own, he will have no problem recognizing me . . . my banner will be clear![8]

That is a disciple—one who not only stepped in but made it to the other side of the Jordan!

5. A Distinct CONTRAST: Living a Life of Distinction

Jesus told His disciples that they were the salt of the earth (see Matthew 5:13). In those days, salt was used to preserve food and prevent it from spoiling. God's people are meant to be the preservative agent in a corrupt society. However, salt becomes useless when it is not distinct.

> Therefore, salt is good; but if even salt has become tasteless, with what will it be seasoned? It is useless either for the soil or the manure pile, so it is thrown out. The one who has ears to hear, let him hear. (Luke 14:34–35)

Unfortunately, the church has diminished her influence by her compromise. Churches are trying to rescue the world by being like the world, from cursing pastors to sipping saints. As Jesus' disciples we are called to live lives of distinction—in direct contrast to the spirit of this age.

TIME TO GET YOUR FEET WET

And now the question remains: Are you ready to be a disciple?

It means getting your feet wet in the Jordan River. It requires a love for God so strong that it makes all other attachments seem like hate. It calls for a daily dying to self. It means building a life for the glory of God regardless of the cost. You must be willing to fight enemies of the cross and live a life of distinction.

When I was seventeen years old, my youth pastor gave me a book about an incredible missionary to the South American Indians. However, it was not the book that challenged me to be a disciple but the inscription my youth pastor had written on the first page: "The world has yet to see what God can do through one man wholly committed to Him. Tim, you can be that man."

That was the beginning of discipleship for me.

No reserves.

No retreats.

No regrets.

QUESTIONS

1. Is there an area of your life that Jesus does not have lordship over?

2. When counting the cost, what reservations do you have about being all in?

3. What changes have you made (or do you need to make) in order to live a *life of distinction*?

4. What is the Jordan River God is asking you to cross that you have been avoiding? Maybe it is time to get your feet wet. Only wet feet walk into the future!

ETERNITY

Life After Life

*"There are a good many things which
would not be worth bothering about if
I were going to live only seventy years,
but which I had better bother about very
seriously if I am going to live forever."*
C. S. LEWIS[1]

On one occasion, the great nineteenth-century preacher Charles Spurgeon did something astonishing: He came to the pulpit to preach without his Bible. The prince of preachers with no open Bible? It had never been seen before. He began by saying to the congregation that some have found fault with him, claiming that he is too old fashioned, always quoting the Bible and not saying enough about science and culture.

Spurgeon went on. "Well, there is a poor widow today in our church who just lost her only son—a fine Christian boy—to a tragic accident. We buried him yesterday. So let's turn to science for some answers on this issue. Science, will she see him again? What do you have to say, Science?" There was a long pause.

"Science, will he be in eternity? Is there life beyond the grave to hope for?" Another long pause.

"This woman is anxious to know something. Science, we need answers about eternity. What? Nothing for this woman who is grieving? Then I shall turn to the Book that *does* have something to say." Spurgeon then retrieved his Bible and read Jesus' wonderful promises concerning eternal life.

When it comes to the big questions of life, experts in government and science can tell you *what* but not *why*. They can describe the situation, but they cannot tell you what you ought to do, nor give you the power to do it. Every expert has his limits. That is why we must turn to a limitless God to find the answers our souls are longing for. Only an eternal God and the eternal Scriptures can speak about eternity. So let's see what He has to say.

The book of Ecclesiastes contains a little phrase that is huge:

> He has also set eternity in their heart. (Ecclesiastes 3:11)

This explains a lot to me. We are creatures of time. Our bodies live by it. We see it in our hands, our faces, our hair, our legs, our eyes. Things eventually start breaking down. We get gray, we get slow, we get achy. Yet all the while, there is something in every heart called eternity. It is because God has set forever—this thinking of life after life—inside of us.

This brings up an important question: What is the length of every man's life? *Forever.* Once born, the existence of man becomes as everlasting as the existence of God. His length *on earth* may be seventy or eighty years, which the Bible calls a vapor.[2] But his existence will be for all eternity. That means your departed friends still exist right now.

Now there is constant warfare between time in our bodies and eternity in our hearts. The battle is whether you will choose time or eternity to make you happy. If you search for happiness here in time without God, who is eternal, you will inevitably hit a dead end.

Eternity may not be immediate, but it is imminent. You can take vitamins, drink green tea, and bathe in essential oils every night to prolong time, but you will still face eternity. Around the world, approximately three people die every second. That means 250,000 go to heaven or hell every day.[3] Death is unavoidable and undeniable; statistics tell us that one out of one will die. So, whether you eat tofu or Twinkies, you will die.

However, there is something about our mortality and death that we do not want to talk about. We try to keep death far from us—out of sight, out of mind. Years ago, people would die in their home; today it is in the hospital or in a nursing home. We do not even let our pets die; we put them to sleep. Your kid is asking where Spot is, and you say he has been put to sleep . . . and then you wonder why your child does not want to take a nap.

We try to sanitize the topic and use nice phraseology to deal with death. He is "no longer with us." She has "passed away." Funeral homes are now Eternal Management Care Centers. Undertakers or morticians have become "death managers." People also try to avoid death through any means possible. The division of the National Institute on Aging in the U.S. spends about $325 million a year on researching the biology of aging.[4] Now in Saudi Arabia, the Hevolution Foundation plans to spend up to $1 billion per year indefinitely supporting research on aging and finding ways to extend the number of years people live in good health.[5] And then there are cryonics in California where the rich have their dead bodies put in liquid hydrogen, hoping one day they will wake up again.

Yet none of this changes the definitiveness of death and the fact that there is life after life.

The Apostle Paul reminded us that "the things we see now are here today, gone tomorrow. But the things we can't see now will last forever" (2 Corinthians 4:18 MSG). The things we cannot see now—that is eternity! Always remember that our life on earth is the first page of a never-ending story!

You will see on cemetery headstones a little dash between the date you are born and the date you die. Within that dash is what you do with your life on earth—every decision, every impact, every hurt, every good time, and every bad time. Everyone must consider what they are doing with their dash, for on the other end of that dash is heaven or hell. Heaven and hell are real places; they are places on the map.

So let's talk about these places—life after life. We will begin with . . .

A GLIMPSE OF HEAVEN

Heaven is mentioned 500 times in the Bible. The Bible talks about three "heavens." The first we see by day; the second we see by night. The third we see by faith—which is the one we are talking about today. I believe John 14 gives the best definition of heaven: "My Father's house." It is our eternal home. The saved go to heaven immediately at their death:

> Now we look forward with confidence to our heavenly bodies, realizing that every moment we spend in these earthly bodies is time spent away from our eternal home in heaven with Jesus. We know these things are true by believing, not by seeing. And we are not afraid but are quite content to die, for then we will be at home with the Lord. (2 Corinthians 5:6–8 TLB)

Look at this description of heaven in Revelation 7:

> After these things I looked, and behold, a great multitude which no one could count, from every nation and all tribes, peoples, and languages, standing before the throne and before the Lamb, clothed in white robes, and palm branches were in their hands. (Revelation 7:9)

"A great multitude"—that's us! Every nation, tribe, people, and language. No black line, white line, Indian line, Hispanic line, Chinese line, Arabic line . . . we are all there. People are fighting for diversity today. If you want diversity, go to heaven! The biggest fight is not getting diversity in our churches here, though that is a noble fight. Rather, it is fighting to get the soul to heaven where true diversity finally exists!

> And they cried out with a loud voice, saying, "Salvation belongs to our God who sits on the throne, and to the Lamb." And all the angels were standing around the throne and around the elders and the four living creatures; and they fell on their faces before the throne and worshiped God. (Revelation 7:10–11)

When we get there, we will join a worship service already in progress. There are angels and elders already worshipping: "Amen, blessing, glory, wisdom, thanksgiving, honor, power, and might, belong to our God forever and ever. Amen. (Revelation 7:12)

By the time you get to this verse, worship has been mounting. It has been revving up throughout the book of Revelation. Notice how it increases over the following verses through four movements of praise:

Revelation 1:6 with two notes of praise:

> To Him be the glory and the dominion forever and ever. Amen.

Revelation 4:11 increases to three notes of praise:

> Worthy are You, our Lord and our God, to receive glory and honor and power.

Revelation 5:13 rises further to four notes of praise:

> To Him who sits on the throne, and to the Lamb be the blessing, the honor, the glory, and the dominion forever and ever.

Revelation 7:11–12 is at perfection with seven notes of praise:

> And they fell on their faces before the throne and worshiped God, saying, "Amen, blessing, glory, wisdom, thanksgiving, honor, power, and might, belong to our God forever and ever. Amen."

Then all of a sudden, right in the middle of this crescendo of worship with seven notes of praise, heaven stops!

> Then one of the elders responded, saying to me, "These who are clothed in the white robes, who are they, and where have they come from? (Revelation 7:13)

The worship stops, and someone asks, "Who are the new guys? Where did they come from?"

Who are these Nigerians, Russians, Ukrainians, Indians, Italians, and Mexicans? Who are these people in white clothing?

> I said to him, "My lord, you know." And he said to me, "These are the ones who come out of the great tribulation, and they have washed their robes and made them white in the blood of the Lamb." (Revelation 7:14)

In Revelation 7, John showed us three things that will be discovered in glory:

1. An Invitation You Never Deserved

> They have washed their robes and made them white in the blood
> of the Lamb. (Revelation 7:14)

You really have no idea what you are about to experience . . . but you will
know it has nothing to do with you! Christianity is the only identity received
and not achieved. It is not based on your performance or failures. It does not
exclude anyone. It is all because you have been washed in the blood of the
Lamb!

There are two ways whereby God punishes sin: the fires of hell or the blood
of Jesus. It is not a question of whether your sin will be punished; it is a question of how. As we saw in the first chapter on the atonement, God's justice has
been completely and eternally satisfied by what Jesus did for us on the cross.
The blood of Jesus alone can get you into heaven.

2. A Gratitude You Will Never Have Enough Words to Express

Years ago, someone gave Cindy and me tickets to Yankee Stadium. Now
whenever we get free tickets, they are usually in the nosebleed sections. We are
grateful, just exhausted walking up into heavenly places. So when we received
these tickets to Yankee Stadium, we had no expectations. However, when we
arrived at the game, the ushers kept bringing us closer and closer to the field
until we were directly behind home plate! What a difference—the view was
better, the food was better, even the air was better!

You may arrive late in heaven, but just wait for where they seat you.
Revelation 7 gives us the seating chart. We saw how verse 9 talked about the
multitude from every nation, tribe, people, and language. Verse 15 tells us
where they will be:

> Therefore they are before the throne of God, and serve Him day
> and night in His temple. And He who sits on the throne will dwell
> among them. (NKJV)

You are going to be before—or right in front of—the throne! The angels are
"around the throne" in verse 11. You will be ushered past them, past those who
have been in heaven for millennia, straight down to the front. Verse 15 continues: "and He who sits on the throne will spread His tabernacle over them"

(AMP). The angels have creature righteousness, but we have Jesus' righteousness! The righteousness of Jesus is our covering, making us more beautiful than angels.

Not only that, when they bring you down to your seat, they will give you something to worship with. It is like when you are seated at a sporting event and you receive something to cheer with—perhaps a towel to wave or thundersticks to bang together. As you are seated before the throne, you will receive a palm branch to worship with (see verse 9).

The Jews used to have palm branches at the Feast of Tabernacles. When the harvest was over, they would come to a community party and wave their palm branches. The motion of waving symbolized a process from beginning to end, saying: "We started working here. We have gone through difficult times, but the harvest has come!" So when you get to heaven, you get to wave a palm branch that says, "The journey is complete. I am here by nothing else but the grace of God!"

Notice that only humans get palm branches; the angels do not. Angels have not been through any battles. They don't know what it is like to fight the fight of faith, resist temptation, stand firm with the armor of God, weep in prayer and pray through, sing a song with a diagnosis of cancer, or lift their hands with arthritis in them. That is why God sees songs on earth as greater than songs in heaven! No pain, then no palm; no cross, then no crown. White robes mean "it's through Jesus," and palm branches mean "through the battle." No one tells sad stories there. They simply cry, "Salvation to God!"

3. A Life Like You Never Imagined

They will no longer hunger, nor thirst anymore, nor will the sun beat down on them, nor any scorching heat; for the Lamb in the center of the throne will be their shepherd, and will guide them to springs of the water of life; and God will wipe every tear from their eyes. (Revelation 7:16–17)

When we were living in Detroit, we ended up purchasing a XXX theater and converting it into a church. The very first person I talked to there was the theater prostitute. As I shared the gospel with her, I told her about heaven and read to this young lady the Revelation 7 passage. At that moment she stopped me and said, "Are you telling me that there is a place that I don't have to cry anymore?"

Many people fight with the eternity God has set in their hearts. It keeps telling them they were made for better things . . . which is the truth. There could be a white robe, a box seat, and a palm branch waiting for them. God offers us a life in eternity that is beyond anything we could ever imagine. That is why Paul said:

> For I consider that the sufferings of this present time are not worthy
> to be compared with the glory that is to be revealed to us.
> (Romans 8:18)

These were Paul's fighting words. No matter what he had to endure for the sake of Christ, his eyes were fixed on the glory to be revealed in him. He would say to his present battles: "Not worthy! Can't compare!"

Now that we have seen a glimpse of heaven from the Scriptures, consider this quote from Leon Morris: "Some say, 'I believe in heaven but not in hell.' I answer that if there is no hell, then there is no heaven. Your only authority for believing in heaven is the Bible—which also teaches there is a hell. It is not always realized that Jesus spoke more often of hell than of heaven. For Him the consequences of unforgiven sin were terrible to contemplate."[6]

It is only right that we now take some time to ponder . . .

A GLIMPSE OF HELL

Hell is the only possible response for a holy God. What would you think of a judge who looks at a child molester or murderer and says, "I forgive you, just don't do it again." We would be outraged! We would certainly never want that judge to have authority. Something in us knows that justice is right. Wrongs need to be made right. Yet here is our dilemma: We want justice, but we don't want hell.

Hell is the final justice of God. Hell does not deal with wicked people. It deals with *all* people. It is one of the most profound things when you see in the book of Psalms that the psalmist begins to rejoice over judgment. He is praising judgment because it is God making things right.

Hell was my bill. If there is no hell, then Sunday church has respectable people who shake God's hand and say, "Thank you." But if there is a hell, then Sunday church has a bunch of people who fall at God's feet and worship Him, knowing what they have been rescued from.

What if you could hear from someone who has died and can tell you about hell? That is Luke 16. In this chapter, Jesus gave us a glimpse of what is beyond death. I have heard and read the stories of those who said that they saw a light and visited heaven, and I have been skeptical. But now we do not have a person we can challenge—this is Jesus, who has come from beyond!

> Now there was a rich man, and he habitually dressed in purple and fine linen, enjoying himself in splendor every day. And a poor man named Lazarus was laid at his gate, covered with sores, and longing to be fed from the scraps which fell from the rich man's table; not only that besides, the dogs also were coming and licking his sores. Now it happened that the poor man died and was carried away by the angels to Abraham's arms; and the rich man also died and was buried. And in Hades he raised his eyes, being in torment, and saw Abraham far away and Lazarus in his arms. And he cried out and said, "Father Abraham, have mercy on me and send Lazaru,s so that he may dip the tip of his finger in water and cool off my tongue, for I am in agony in this flame." But Abraham said, "Child, remember that during your life you received your good things, and likewise Lazarus bad things; but now he is being comforted here, and you are in agony. And besides all this, between us and you a great chasm has been set, so that those who want to go over from here to you will not be able, nor will any people cross over from there to us." And he said, "Then I request of you, father, that you send him to my father's house—for I have five brothers—in order that he may warn them, so that they will not come to this place of tormentas well." But Abraham said, "They have Moses and the Prophets; let them hear them." But he said, "No, father Abraham, but if someone goes to them from the dead, they will repent!" But he said to him, 'If they do not listen to Moses and the Prophets, they will not be persuaded even if someone rises from the dead." (Luke 16:19–31)

This is life after life. First of all, is this history or a parable? History means that it actually happened, and I believe we are reading history. Jesus often taught in parables, but when He did, the passage clearly states that it is a parable, or you see the words "like" or "can be compared to."

Let me show you some parable introductions from Matthew 13:

> Listen then to the parable of the sower. (verse 18)

> Jesus presented another parable to them, saying, "The kingdom of heaven is like . . ." (verse 24)

> He presented another parable to them, saying, "The kingdom of heaven is like . . ." (verse 31)

> He spoke another parable to them: "The kingdom of heaven is like . . . " (verse 33)

Jesus also repeated, "The kingdom of heaven is like . . ." in verses 44–47. Matthew 22 and Luke 13–15 give us more examples of parables clearly depicted as such. So now look at our introduction one more time . . . parable or history?

> Now there was a rich man, and he habitually dressed in purple and fine linen, enjoying himself in splendor every day. (Luke 16:19)

There *was*. This tells us that there is a man who was. It does not say, "Hell will be like . . ." The next verse also backs this up as history:

> But there was a certain beggar named Lazarus, full of sores, who was laid at his gate. (verse 20 NKJV)

There is not one parable where Jesus used a specific name. Yet here He spoke of a *certain* beggar named Lazarus. When the Bible uses this language, it is distinguishing one man against many others so that they would not be confused. In Jerusalem there were many beggars, but this one had a name. Look at some other "certain" passages:

> But a certain man named Ananias, with Sapphira his wife, sold a possession. (Acts 5:1 NKJV)

But there was a certain man called Simon, who previously practiced
sorcery in the city and astonished the people of Samaria, claiming
that he was someone great. (Acts 8:9 NKJV)

There was a certain man in Caesarea called Cornelius, a centurion
of what was called the Italian Regiment. (Acts 10:1 NKJV)

If Ananias, Simon, and Cornelius are real, then Lazarus must be real. We
should expect to meet this Lazarus when we get to heaven.

Now do not be confused assuming that the point of this passage is that the
rich go to hell or that poor people are the only ones saved, for neither is true.
Their earthly position did not make the difference. When life is done, the joys
and sorrows of life have no further power. The issue is that whether poor or
rich, you will die and be judged. And at that point, your destination is fixed.

And just as it is destined that men die only once, and after that
comes judgment. (Hebrews 9:27 TLB)

When the rich man and the poor man were born, they were both born
without Christ. When they died, Lazarus had Christ and the rich man had
nothing. The rich man had everything but God. The beggar had nothing but
God. Just as the believer dies and is in the presence of the Lord, there was no
lapse of time between the rich man's death and him being in the flames of hell.

Now it is important to understand that there are only two choices of desti-
nies here. This is not the devil's teaching, so it becomes offensive to people. The
devil desires to create more options—especially a group that says, "I'm not a
bad person, so I don't need Christ. Surely I will not end up in hell."

But what was the sin of the rich man that sent him to hell?

His sin was contentment without God. The rich man lived his life without God. Perhaps to you this rich man did not seem bad enough to end up in
hell. There is nothing in these verses about cursing, murder, or adultery. Yet
he chose the world and the things of the world, making contentment without
God his sin.

What is Jesus telling us in this sobering story? *Hell is truth seen too late.* He
who never longs for a Savior on earth will desperately long for one in hell. The

rich man was content without a Savior in this life, but as soon as he was in hell, he realized his need.

> And being in torments in Hades, he lifted up his eyes and saw Abraham afar off, and Lazarus in his bosom. (verse 23 NKJV)

How agonizing for those in hell to see beyond the river! The rich man not only saw the flames but also what might have been—heaven. But he saw heaven too late.

> Then he cried and said, "Father Abraham, have mercy on me, and send Lazarus that he may dip the tip of his finger in water and cool my tongue; for I am tormented in this flame." (verse 24 NKJV)

Here we see that hell has a prayer meeting. The rich man not only sees what he never saw on earth, but his very first act in hell is to do what he never did on earth—pray! He was not in hell for more than a verse before he started praying. But he prayed too late.

Those who are unsure about their salvation or who have been putting it off can be sure that the first thing they will do in hell is pray. Jesus said, "He saw . . ." and then "he cried out." Whenever a man sees the kingdom, whether on earth or in hell, he will cry out. Why? He is seeing something satisfying, something the heart thirsts after. If it happens on earth, that prayer will be heard and that man's thirst will be satisfied. But if it occurs in hell, the prayer will be too late. Man's need can only be satisfied by Christ, and Christ is not in hell. This rich man has been praying in vain for the last 2,000 years.

If the rich man would have prayed on earth, God would have given him rivers of living water. But he was thirsty too late. On earth he felt no need for what he longed for in hell. There is no mercy in hell; he could not even get a drop of water on his tongue. I believe the torment of thirst that this rich man felt in hell is what Jesus paid for on the cross.

> After this, Jesus, knowing that all things had already been accomplished, in order that the Scripture would be fulfilled, said, "I am thirsty." (John 19:28)

When Jesus said, "I thirst," on the cross, it was not a physical need to help

Him make it through. Rather, it was Him carrying our torments of hell in His body. Jesus bore it so that you and I would never have to. Jesus said in John 6:35, "I am the bread of life. He who comes to Me shall never hunger, and he who believes in Me shall never thirst" (NKJV).

Not only did the rich man get thirsty too late and pray too late, but when he did pray, he prayed to the wrong person!

> And he cried out and said, "Father Abraham, have mercy on me." (verse 24)

He prayed to Father Abraham. Even if this prayer were offered up on earth, it could never have been answered. This is the only instance in the Scriptures of a man praying to a saint, and it bore no fruit. We see here where praying to the saints originated from—hell itself! Prayers to the saints began by a lost soul praying in his agony.

Was the too-late, misdirected prayer answered? Not answered, but he did get a response.

> But Abraham said, "Child, remember that during your life you received your good things, and likewise Lazarus bad things; but now he is being comforted here, and you are in agony. And besides all this, between us and you a great chasm has been set, so that those who want to go over from here to you will not be able, nor will any people cross over from there to us." (verses 25–26)

Abraham called him "child." What a horrible thing to be called, for it meant that this was a son of Abraham in hell. A son of Abraham to us would be a son of the church. He likely had morals and was very religious—but all without Christ. He learned the hard way that being associated with a religious system did not get him into heaven. It will take more than morality to keep you out of hell.

Abraham not only said "child" but also said to remember the "good things." Remember the things that satisfied you on earth—that can now do you no good in hell. Now you realize the value of Christ, but He is lost to you forever. The rich man lost Christ not for drugs and sex and pornography but for "good things."

Notice as well that in hell, the rich man possessed all five senses: He recognized Lazarus when he lifted up his eyes. He opened his mouth and cried to Abraham. He knew what water was and craved a drop of it. He had feelings because he said he was being tormented. He remembered his father's house and his brothers. Memory and the senses are wicked things in hell. Think of the tormenting memories in hell—what must now be the memories of Achan, Balaam, Herod, Felix, Agrippa, Ananias and Sapphira, Judas, Demas, and the rich young ruler.

The rich man then prayed a second prayer:

> Then I request of you, father, that you send him to my father's house—for I have five brothers—in order that he may warn them, so that they will not come to this place of torment as well. (verses 27–28)

What would you write back to planet Earth if you were in hell? You would not care about how your stocks are doing or about what college your children are going to. This man is wanting to get a message to his family not to come to where he is. Hell made this man an evangelist, but he was an evangelist too late.

I do not believe that the rich man's prayer for his brothers was out of concern for them, for there is no love or compassion in hell. Then why this prayer? He wanted to be delivered from the torment of feeling the responsibility of having led others to hell with him. This man knew that he had set for his brothers an example of a man content without God, and it was agonizing. While he is praying for them in hell, they are living like him on earth. If you live and die and take no interest in the souls of family members, you can be sure you will take an interest once you are in hell. You can pray for them now or attempt to pray for them in hell.

The first prayer of the rich man, denied.

The second prayer, denied. But he was told of the power of the Word of God.

> But Abraham said, "They have Moses and the Prophets; let them hear them." (verse 29)

The Word of God is enough to get a man to salvation; you do not need the spectacular. Those who are not saved today yet hear the Word are like one of these brothers. Abraham went on to say to the rich man:

> And besides all this, between us and you a great chasm has been set, so that those who want to go over from here to you will not be able, nor will any people cross over from there to us. (verse 26)

First, this man was called to think in retrospect about the good things he sold his soul for. Now, he is called to look forward and understand the fact that a great chasm is set, and he cannot change his fate. In the end, Abraham could not give the rich man any hope. Hell has no hope. If there were any hope, then hell would cease to be hell, and the rich man may have comforted himself with the fact that relief will eventually come. But in Mark 9, where Jesus preachedthe hottest sermon on hell found in the Bible, He was clear that hell is eternal:

> And if thy hand offend thee, cut it off: it is better for thee to enter into life maimed, than having two hands to go into hell, into the fire that never shall be quenched: Where their worm dieth not, and the fire is not quenched. (Mark 9:43–44 KJV)

Five times Jesus says that the fires will never be quenched (see also Mark 9:45–48). The word used here for "not quenched" is the same word used for "everlasting life." That means if hell is not eternal, neither is heaven. If the wicked do not suffer forever, the righteous do not rejoice forever.

Leonard Ravenhill once gave me a book called *The Lost Soul's First Day in Eternity* by J. M. Humphrey. Here is a sobering excerpt:

> Our lost friends are lost forever; we recollect that there is no shadow of hope for them. When the iron gate of hell is once closed upon them it shall never be unbarred again to give them free exit. . . . Nature's last anesthesia, death, fails in hell. It would have been a happy release. A man can count the weary hours till death shall give him rest; but oh, remember there is no death in hell. Death, which is a monster on earth, would be an angel in hell. If death could go there, all the damned would fall down and worship him; every tongue would sing, and every heart would praise, each cavern then

would echo with a shout of triumph, till all was still, and silence brood where terror reigned. But no, the terrible reality is this: Their worm dieth not and the fire is not quenched. In hell there is no hope. They have not even the hope of dying—the hope of being annihilated. They are forever, forever, forever lost. On every chain in hell there is written, 'forever.' In the fires, there blazes out the word "forever."[7]

Let me take a few moments to address the famous question: If God is a loving God, how can He send people to hell?

First, posing it that way is already an incriminating question, making God the villain and humanity the victim. Why don't we ever ask, "How can a holy God send sinful people to hell?" We must understand that God judges criminals, not victims. Man wants to be considered a victim, not an offender. We must also realize that God did not make hell for man:

> Then He will also say to those on His left, "Depart from Me, you accursed people, into the eternal fire which has been prepared for the devil and his angels." (Matthew 25:41)

> In the beginning God created the heavens and the earth. (Genesis 1:1)

It does not say that God created the heavens, the earth, and hell. Hell was not created for man, because in the beginning, there was no need for it. It was created for Satan and those who did not want God but wanted to be god of their own life. If you go to hell, you go there against the will of God.

> The Lord is not slow about His promise, as some count slowness, but is patient toward you, not willing for any to perish, but for all to come to repentance. (2 Peter 3:9)

> Say to them, "As I live!" declares the Lord God, "I take no pleasure at all in the death of the wicked, but rather that the wicked turn from his way and live. Turn back, turn back from your evil ways! Why then should you die, house of Israel?" (Ezekiel 33:11)

God has done everything a loving God could do to keep men out of hell. He is restraining Himself on account of those who have not yet repented; He is holding back the end because He does not want anyone lost. Ultimately, people who want nothing to do with Christ during their lifetime on earth will end up with exactly that . . . for all eternity. Hell is the final exit of a journey of choosing oneself over God.

That is our glimpse of heaven and hell. We began with Solomon's words in Ecclesiastes 3 telling us God has set eternity in our hearts. Solomon also issued another important plea:

> Remember your Creator before the silver cord is broken and the golden bowl is crushed, the pitcher by the spring is shattered and the wheel at the cistern is crushed; then the dust will return to the earth as it was, and the spirit will return to God who gave it. (Ecclesiastes 12:6–7)

Remember God! Remember Him before all these things happen—all of which are images of death. And death can certainly happen suddenly. I am reminded of a time when I was invited to speak at my alma mater's Christian Medical Association. It was a privilege to do a Bible study with this group of future nurses and doctors. As soon as I was finished, I received the oddest invitation of my life. One soon-to-be doctor said, "Let me take you to the basement and show you the bodies that are donated to science." I was a little nervous, but we were soon in the bowels of that medical building where they work on the cadavers. He showed me a human heart and pointed out what looked like a yellow thread going through it.

"That's it—the number one killer in the country," he told me. "When that gets clogged, you have a heart attack. It has ended more lives than any other thing in America." It is by a thread that we are here today! Yet some of us are toying with forever. Heaven and hell are not faraway places. It is time *now* to consider life after life.

Eternity is too long to be wrong.

QUESTIONS

1. Do you know where you will spend eternity? How do you know you are going to heaven?

   If you are unsure, please see the section "How Do You Get to Heaven?" at the back of this book.

2. Who in your life needs to hear about eternity? When will you share it with them?

3. What would your response be to someone who questions the existence of heaven and/or hell?

4. How can you maintain an eternal perspective in your daily life?

FORGIVENESS

Acting Like God

Acting Like God

"If our greatest need had been information,
God would have sent us an educator; if our greatest need
had been technology, God would have sent us a scientist; if
our greatest need had been money, God would have sent us
an economist; if our greatest need had been pleasure, God
would have sent us an entertainer; but our greatest need was
forgiveness, so God sent us a Savior."

AUTHOR UNKNOWN

In March 2023, America was horrified again as twenty-eight-year-old Audrey Hale, dressed in camouflage and a red hat, walked into a Christian elementary school in Nashville, Tennessee, and shot three nine-year-old students, a substitute teacher, a custodian, and the head of the school. The attack was the deadliest school shooting since the 2022 attack in Uvalde, Texas, which left twenty-one dead. In 2022, there were fifty school shootings in America.[1]

We are living in a powder keg society. It seems as if all over the country, someone is waiting to explode. What happened to Audrey Hale, this former student of The Covenant School? What is happening with all these school shootings? How should we as the church respond? What is our message to a volatile society that can seemingly snap at any moment?

I believe we are experiencing the repercussions of an unforgiving population. A violent world is the result of people living with unforgiveness that is consuming them. However, the glory of Christianity is to conquer its "enemies" through forgiveness. A spiritual problem cannot be fought with political legislation and laws. We may rescue some, but ultimately, we leave things unfixed, making it only a matter of time before another horrible tragedy occurs. Someone said it like this: "If we all live by 'an eye for an eye,' the whole world will be blind."

The only way out is forgiveness. Forgiveness is giving up my right to hurt you for hurting me. Unforgiveness is revenge in the flesh. But as C. S. Lewis said, "To be a Christian means to forgive the inexcusable because God has forgiven the inexcusable in you."[2]

One of the most astounding stories on the struggle of forgiveness is that of Corrie Ten Boom, author of the Christian classic *The Hiding Place*. Corrie and her Christian family housed Jews during the Holocaust. The Nazis found out and put Corrie and her entire family into concentration camps, and all of them died except for Corrie. After being miraculously released from the Nazi concentration camp Ravensbruck, she preached the gospel around the world for three decades.

One day, many years after being released from the concentration camp, Corrie was preaching at a church in Munich. From the pulpit, she noticed a familiar face in the audience—the guard from the concentration camp who would mock and instill fear in the prisoners, making them believe they were going to be exterminated momentarily. He was the very one who was responsible for the death of Corrie's sister Betsy. Although Corrie recognized the guard, he did not recognize her. He later came up to her and said, "Fräulein, I heard you mention Ravensbruck. I was a guard there, but since those days I have become a Christian. I know that God forgives me, but would you forgive me?"

Corrie recounted that she stood there paralyzed. This man was a monster; he had filled her with shame and misery every day, and he had killed her sister Betsy. But how could she preach forgiveness while staring into the face of the one she needed to forgive yet finding herself unable to? She said she did the only thing she knew to do: She prayed right there on the spot, "Forgive me,

Father, for the inability to forgive!"

Immediately, power surged through her. She felt her hand go out and clasp this man's hand, and out of her mouth came the words, "You are forgiven."[3] The man was set free. But Corrie acknowledged that even more on that day, *she* was set free!

Sadly, we live in a culture where we hold on to unforgiveness until it consumes us. We must learn to let go. You see, being offended is a choice. You cannot choose what people do to you, but you do have a choice whether to be offended after it happens. When you forgive, you do not change the past, but you do change the future.

Forgiving others is part of God's curriculum in maturing us. It is especially painful when God uses someone we do not particularly like. It is much easier to forgive the forgivable and the repentant, but none of us like forgiving arrogant people who do not think they did anything wrong.

However, it may be helpful to put things into perspective by considering the last three things Jesus did before He died on the cross: He prayed, He witnessed, and He forgave. He prayed to the Father, He witnessed to the thief next to Him, and then He forgave those on the ground.

Jesus was teaching us a lesson from the cross on forgiving the unapologetic. I call that forgiveness moment "Calvary forgiveness." Jesus was answering a very important question with this act of forgiveness: How do you forgive someone who does not think they did anything wrong?

From the cross, Jesus looked at the men who beat and scourged Him, who mocked Him and were gambling for His clothes, and said, "Father, forgive them; for they know not what they do" (Luke 23:34 KJV). No one asked Jesus for forgiveness. No one was repenting. Yet while they were crucifying Him, He was forgiving them! Forgiving the unrepentant is one of the hardest things to do. Yet Jesus was demonstrating that you can and must forgive even those who feel no guilt or responsibility for what they have done to you. You release them, and as a result, you are not held captive either.

I can guarantee you that at some point you will be offended by someone—a spouse, a pastor, a deacon, a choir member, a church member, a colleague, an associate, a firm partner, a dorm supervisor, a professor, and so on. Why? Because where there are people, there are problems. People have problems because they are all broken. When people interact, they do and say wrong things. What may be surprising is that it will even happen in the church. I have been on both sides. I have been offended, and I have been the offender.

It only takes a minute to cause hurt but sometimes a lifetime to repair it. The hardest hurt to repair is when it involves those you love, trust, and would never expect it from. According to youth evangelist Winkie Pratney, "Hurt is proportional to intimacy."[4] That means the closer you are to someone, the deeper the hurt that comes. I have preached on streets all over America, and I have been shot at, spit on, had bottles and rocks thrown at me, and none of that affects me. But if my wife, Cindy, looks at me the wrong way, it is worse than all that put together! The closer you are to a person, the less they have to do to hurt you.

Even the psalmist David spoke about this:

> For it is not an enemy who taunts me,
> Then I could endure it;
> Nor is it one who hates me who has exalted himself against me,
> Then I could hide myself from him.
> But it is you, a man my equal,
> My companion and my confidant;
> We who had sweet fellowship together,
> Walked in the house of God among the commotion.
> (Psalm 55:12–14)

Since you are going to be hurt, you must learn what to do with the offense. Hurt that is not dealt with will turn into bitterness, and that is when the chaos happens. Hurt wants to morph into confusion. A hurt heart is never stagnant; it lives at a crossroads.

How does hurt morph? When hurt is not dealt with, a third party enters the equation:

> Don't let the sun go down while you are still angry, for anger gives
> a foothold to the devil. (Ephesians 4:26–27 NLT)

When you sleep on hurt, you wake up with the devil! According to these verses, you have until sundown to deal with offenses. What if the person does not come to you and apologize before then? You turn to Calvary forgiveness. If Jesus could forgive the unrepentant from the cross, you can declare forgiveness over your offender from wherever you are.

When dealing with hurt and offense, we must learn to start from a very neglected place—the only place freedom can come from. However, we typically start with what has been done to us and forget to start with what has been done *for* us. We mistakenly believe that freedom is found when the person admits their wrong and sincerely apologizes. But that is not where freedom from the deepest hurts is found. We have a hard time forgiving people because we have focused on the horrible event that hurt us instead of the epic event that changed us! We see the wound done to us, not the healing given to us.

In order to know how to forgive, you must first know how God forgave you. Forgiveness is hard, if not impossible, when you do not feel forgiven by God. Karl Menninger, the famed psychiatrist, once said that if he could convince the patients in psychiatric hospitals that their sins were forgiven, 75 percent of them would walk out healed![5]

There are so many passages on God's forgiveness, but I will pick just one verse for us to look at.

I, even I, am He who blots out your transgressions for My own sake;
And I will not remember your sins.
(Isaiah 43:25 NKJV)

From this verse, we understand some important things about God's forgiveness.

1. GOD HAS NEVER TURNED DOWN ANYONE'S REQUEST TO BE FORGIVEN

God's record is 100 percent! If you ask Him, He will forgive you. Isaiah said that it is a shocking forgiveness. Name any sin—God has a perfect track record of forgiving that sin. How do we know? Because it is not based on what you did but on who is forgiving you.

"*I, even I,* am He who blots out your transgressions."

"I, even I" is a Hebraism for "Let's be clear, no one but God can give you forgiveness." "I, even I" is important because God is the One who must forgive you, for it is God whom we have sinned against. As it says in Psalm 51:4, "Against You, You only, I have sinned." We have offended God, but the good news is that the same offended God is a forgiving God.

A pastor friend of mine recently told the true story of one of his church members who is an attorney. After meditating on several scriptures, this attorney had a Zacchaeus moment and decided to cancel the debts of all his clients who'd owed him money for more than six months. He drafted a letter explaining his decision and its biblical basis, and he sent seventeen debt-canceling letters via certified mail.

One by one, the letters began to return, unsigned and undelivered. Sixteen of the seventeen letters came back to him because the clients refused to sign for and open the envelopes—fearing that this attorney was suing them for their debts. Only one person opened the letter and received full forgiveness! How profound! We owe a debt for our sin, and God is willing to cancel it. Yet too many people refuse to even open the letter which explains it all!

2. God Forgives So Thoroughly That He Sees You as If You Never Offended Him

I, even I, am He who *blots out your transgressions.* (Isaiah 43:25 NKJV)

The Hebrew word "wipes" or "blots" is in the present tense. It is not in the future. "He who blots out" does not mean "He gets all the details and then decides." Not at all! We ask Him to forgive, and He does it right then and there. And how thorough is His forgiveness?

> He has removed our sins as far from us
>   as the east is from the west.
> (Psalm 103:12 NLT)

David also described God's thorough forgiveness:

> According to the multitude of Your tender mercies,
> Blot out my transgressions.

Wash me thoroughly from my iniquity,

And cleanse me from my sin.

(Psalm 51:1–2 NKJV)

To be satisfied with God forgiving 99 percent of our sins would be like say-ing we should be satisfied with near completeness in other areas. For example, should we be happy that Chicago O'Hare lands 99 percent of their planes?[6] That means only two crash every day. Or that the Postal Service successfully deliv-ers 99 percent of all the mail,[7] which means 176,000 letters are lost every hour?[8]

That would certainly not be acceptable! How much more with God's for-giveness? The good news is that because of Christ, God forgives *all* our sins. When you, as a Christian, wallow in guilt, imagining that the weight of God's wrath bears down on you and not on Christ, you have forgotten your status in Christ.

God's forgiveness is so huge, He looks at you as if you have never done any-thing wrong! If someone did something to hurt you, would you be able to look at them as if they never did anything wrong? We do not forgive people; we put them on probation. We say, "I forgive you, but it better not happen again!" But when we say, "I can forgive but I cannot forget," it is just another way of saying, "I will not forgive."

Think about it: Have you asked God for forgiveness regarding the same thing more than once? And did God ever reply, "Fool Me once, shame on you. Fool Me twice, shame on Me"? Of course not! God blotted it out, striking it from the record. It was paid for in full; nothing is owed. God sees the Christian as if he had never sinned . . . *ever*! That is why the gospel is good news.

3. GOD FORGIVES BECAUSE *WHO HE IS* IS GREATER THAN WHAT WAS DONE TO HIM

Read that again and let it sink in. God is greater than the sin. He is greater than the offense. There is more grace in God's heart than there is sin in your past. And why does God forgive?

I, even I, am He who blots out your transgressions *for My own sake.*

(Isaiah 43:25 NKJV)

Those are big words . . . "for My own sake." I love the way The Message words it:

> But I, yes I, am the one
>   who takes care of your sins—that's what I do.
> (Isaiah 43:25 MSG)

He does this because of who He is. It is not based on the amount of sin, the repetition of sin, or the enormity of sin. Forgiveness is based on who God is! God was saying, "This is not hard for Me because this is what I do. It is My character."

There is a phrase found throughout the Bible: "There is no one else" or "none beside Me" or "true God." It is God saying, "Be careful of getting a knockoff god." A knockoff is the guy on the street corner in New York City with a big blanket selling Louis Vuitton, Prada, and Chanel purses for $30. If you are ever in Manhattan and come across them, let me help you out . . . they are not real! We call them knockoffs. God was saying, "I am the only One that does forgiveness by grace. That's what I do!"

Consider the words of Charles Spurgeon:

> "For mine own sake." No man has his sins forgiven because they are little, for the smallest sin will ruin the soul, and every sin is great, however little it may seem to us. Each sin has the essence of rebellion in it, and rebellion is a great evil before God. No man, therefore, will have God say to him, "I have blotted out thy sins because of the littleness of them." Never. . . . Neither does our text tell us that God forgives men's sins because He trusts that after they are forgiven, they will do better. By His grace, forgiven men are made to do better; but it is not the foresight of any betterness on their part which leads God to the forgiveness. That cannot be a motive, for if they do better, their improvement is His work in them. . . . No, the only motive which God has for pardoning sinners, according to the text, is one which lies within Himself: "for mine own sake."[9]

4. GOD HAS NEVER GOSSIPED ABOUT ANYONE WHOM HE FORGIVES.

In his book *A Forgiving God in an Unforgiving World*, Ron Lee Davis told a story about God's complete forgiveness involving a priest in the Philippines. This priest was a much-loved man of God, but he carried the burden of a secret sin he had committed many years before. He had repented but still had no peace, no sense of God's forgiveness. In his parish was a woman who deeply loved God and claimed to have visions in which she spoke with Christ and He with her. The priest, however, was skeptical. To test her he said, "The next time you speak with Christ, I want you to ask Him what sin your priest committed while he was in seminary." The woman agreed. A few days later the priest asked, "Did Christ visit you in your dreams?"

"Yes, He did," she replied.

"And did you ask Him what sin I committed in seminary?"

"Yes."

"Well, what did He say?"

"He said, 'I don't remember!'"[10]

The final part of Isaiah 43:25 says: "And I will not remember your sins" (NKJV). It is just as Corrie Ten Boom said: "When God forgives, He forgets. He buries our sin in the sea and puts up a sign on the bank saying, 'No fishing allowed!'"

I want you to think for a moment about the trigger switches of offense—when you see someone and instantly think about what they did to you in the past. What if God were to do that? He would be triggered every time He hears our voice as we pray!

The other day I got blindsided on my phone. I was listening to something online, and a voice from my past came on and started speaking. It triggered pain and hurt in me. I was literally reaching to turn it off when God reminded me of Jesus' challenge—one that has been my go-to when triggered.

The challenge involves the math equation that Jesus once mentioned: 70 x 7. This equation has to do with forgiveness. The disciples had presented a question to Jesus:

> Then Peter came to Him and said, "Lord, how often shall my brother
> sin against me, and I forgive him? Up to seven times?" Jesus said
> to him, "I do not say to you, up to seven times, but up to seventy
> times seven." (Matthew 18:21–22 NKJV)

It sounds like everyone has an account of 490 offenses with each other. But I don't think that's it. This is a trigger-switch weapon to fight against the anger that tries to seep into your soul. C. S. Lewis gave the best insight on 70 x 7: "We forgive, we mortify our resentment; a week later some chain of thought carries us back to the original offense and we discover the old resentment blazing away as if nothing had been done about it at all. We need to forgive our brother seventy times seven not only for 490 offenses but *for one offense!*"[11]

We are left with the choice to either *forgive* or *relive*. God sees the people who cursed Him every day, those who blasphemed His name, yet He does not say, "Oh yeah, you are the guy who said this about Me." Not once. Never. When we ask for forgiveness, He chooses to never remember what we did!

Think for a moment of the biggest sinner you know who has repented. What has God done for them? God never turns down anyone who asks to be forgiven. There are no limits to what He will forgive. How amazing is that kind of forgiveness!

Now think of the biggest sin that has been committed against you. What has been the hardest thing for you to forgive? Have you ever turned down someone's request to be forgiven?

Then consider this verse:

> Be kind to each other, tenderhearted, forgiving one another, just as
> God through Christ has forgiven you (Ephesians 4:32 NLT)

Forgive each other *just as God through Christ has forgiven you!* We are to base our forgiveness on what God has done for us, not on what another person has done to us. This verse is telling us to act like God! In other words, if God would forgive it, we must forgive it!

But it was adultery. It was sexual abuse. That man hit me every day. She betrayed my confidence. He raped me. He stole thousands of dollars and put my family at risk. They fired me. They posted lies. Still, the bottom line is that if

God would forgive them, you must forgive them. This is not a suggestion; it is a command. What Paul went on to say later in Ephesians sealed the deal:

Therefore be imitators of God. (Ephesians 5:1)

In other words, mimic Him! When it comes to imitating God, we would love to imitate sovereignty so no one can boss us around. We would love to imitate power so we are in control, healing so we can be adored, teaching so we can have everyone follow and listen to us, holiness so we can be admired . . . but not His forgiveness. There is not enough praise in that.

However, you are never more like God than when you are forgiving someone. There is a story that beautifully illustrates this. The year was 1948 and the place was Yeosu-Suncheon, near the thirty-eighth parallel. A group of communists had taken over the town and executed Pastor Son Yang-Won's two sons. The boys died as martyrs, calling on the persecutors to have faith in Jesus. When the communists were later driven out, Chai-Sun, a young man of the village, was identified as the man who fired the murderous shots at the pastor's sons' heads, killing them. Chai-Sun was convicted and sentenced to be executed.

Amazingly, Son Yang-Won requested that the charges be dropped, and that Chai-Sun be released to him as his adopted son. Son Yang-Won's thirteen-year-old daughter, Rachel, the boys' sister, testified and supported her father's request. The court agreed to turn over Chai-Sun to the family whose members he had murdered just a few months before.[12] Chai-Sun became the adopted son of the pastor—and also became a believer. Did he have a choice? How could one respond to that demonstration of forgiveness in any other way?

I want you to always remember: Your reason to forgive is not because the person is forgivable or because the offense is forgivable. Stop waiting for the person to apologize. You are to forgive because you have been forgiven, and you are called to imitate God. Forgiveness is not just *for us* but must come *through us*. If you need to, pray Corrie Ten Boom's prayer: "Father, forgive me for the inability to forgive," and the Lord will empower you. Just as God has forgiven us, we shall forgive others thoroughly, swiftly, and surely—in remembrance of what has been done for us!

QUESTIONS

1. Why is it so hard for people to forgive?

2. Why does God require us to forgive others?

3. Is there anyone in your life who you still associate with a wrong done to you? How will you deal with this "trigger"?

GOD

A Horrible Misunderstanding Has Occurred . . . You Thought I Was Just Like You

"It's not great faith you need; it is faith in a great God."
N. T. WRIGHT[1]

"I believe in God" is perhaps one of the most meaningless statements one can make today. Opinion polls tell us that 80 percent of Americans believe in God. The number goes up to 84 percent when considering how many people in the world believe in God. Contrary to popular belief, we do not have a godless world but rather a god-filled world. However, this does not necessarily mean that the God of the Bible is the god that people believe in.

The thing I am most concerned about right now is what the church believes about God. A. W. Tozer's words ring particularly true in our day: "The Church has surrendered her once lofty concept of God and has substituted for it one so low, so ignoble, as to be utterly unworthy of thinking . . . This she has not done deliberately, but little by little and without her knowledge, and her very unawareness only makes her situation all the more tragic . . . What comes into our minds when we think about God is the most important thing about us."[2]

So what does the church today believe about God? I remember many years ago reading this piece of prose that might challenge us:

> I would like to buy $3 worth of God, please, not enough to explode my soul or disturb my sleep, but just enough to equal a cup of warm milk or a snooze in the sunshine. I don't want enough of

Him to make me love someone of a different color or work with a
migrant. I want excitement, not transformation; I want the warmth
of the womb, not a new birth. I want a pound of the Eternal in a
paper sack. I would like to buy $3 worth of God, please.[3]

The $3 god is being preached all over America. This was even clearly seen
on Easter Sunday when large churches in our nation were celebrating by playing secular music! How absurd to think that the resurrection needs help from a
secular song. It is the strange fire spoken of in Leviticus (see Leviticus 10:1–3).
It is a low view of God, a $3 god. If you think that Jesus—who defeated death—
needs your props, then you have a $3 god.

The greatest sin of the twenty-first-century church is the trivialization of
God, the depreciation of the One of immeasurable value. We prefer the illu-
sion of a safer deity, so we have pared God down to more manageable proportions. Idolatry is not a group of people from some remote part of the jungle
dancing around an image they carved out. It is constructing a mental idea of a
deity that bears little resemblance to the God who has revealed Himself in the
Bible. Idolatry is fashioning an idea of God according to our own opinions and
preferences. Ultimately, it is the worship of self, for we are worshiping what we
created.

In the Old Testament, we see that in order to protect a new nation called
Israel, God gave them ten commandments. What was the first commandment
He gave to His people after they left Egypt and were beginning their new lives
of freedom?

Then God spoke all these words, saying, "I am the Lord your God,
who brought you out of the land of Egypt, out of the house of
slavery. You shall have no other gods before Me." (Exodus 20:1–3).

God said, "You shall have no other gods" to Israel, not to a heathen nation!
He was warning people who believed in Him: "Be careful not to make up a
god." Believing in God never guarantees the worship of the true God. In fact,
today we are more susceptible to the forsaking of the living God for one we
have fashioned. I heard someone say this: "Genesis 1:27 says that God created
man in His own image. Today, man has returned the favor. We have created
God in our own image."

How does this happen? God answers the question in Psalm 50.

> And now I speak to the wicked. Listen to what I
> have to say to you!
> What right do you have to presume to speak for me
> and claim my covenant promises as yours?
> For you have hated my instruction and disregarded
> my words,
> throwing them away as worthless!
> You forget to condemn the thief or adulterer.
> You are their friend, running alongside them into
> darkness.
> The sins of your mouth multiply evil.
> You have a lifestyle of lies;
> you are devoted to deceit as you speak against others,
> even slandering those of your own household!
> All this you have done and I kept silent,
> so you thought that I was just like you. . . .
> This is your last chance, my final warning.
> (Psalm 50:16–22 TPT)

God essentially says, "A horrible misunderstanding has occurred . . . you thought I was just like you!" Therein we see the root of the problem and the indictment by God. We have created a god that believes in everything we believe in. We do not want to be told what is right and what is sin. We want a theology that evolves with our culture. For instance, deciding one's gender was never about gender identity but about God's authority. We live in a society that believes in the autonomy of man. People deciding whether they are male or female is nothing else but rebellion against God, who already decided it in the womb!

If we say we believe in God, we had better get God right! Jeremiah 10 is critical. Jeremiah was writing to believers in God who had been found guilty of recreating Him. Look at their indictment:

> "'Go west and look in the land of Cyprus;
>   go east and search through the land of Kedar.
> Has anyone ever heard of anything

> as strange as this?
> Has any nation ever traded its gods for new ones,
> even though they are not gods at all?
> Yet my people have exchanged their glorious God
> for worthless idols!
> The heavens are shocked at such a thing
> and shrink back in horror and dismay,"
> says the LORD. (Jeremiah 2:10–12 NLT)

Jeremiah then began to speak to this horrible god trade Israel made and the church is making today. Notice that he used the phrases "there is none like You" and "true God" a number of times:

> There is none like You, LORD;
> You are great, and Your name is great in might.
> Who would not fear You, O King of the nations?
> For it is Your due!
> For among all the wise men of the nations
> And in all their kingdoms,
> There is none like You.
> But they are altogether stupid and foolish;
> The instruction from idols is nothing but wood!
> Beaten silver is brought from Tarshish,
> And gold from Uphaz,
> The work of a craftsman and of the hands of a goldsmith;
> Their clothing is of violet and purple;
> They are all the work of skilled people.
> But the LORD is the true God;
> He is the living God and the everlasting King.
> The earth quakes at His wrath,
> And the nations cannot endure His indignation.

> This is what you shall say to them: "The gods that did not make the heavens and the earth will perish from the earth and from under these heavens."

It is He who made the earth by His power,
Who established the world by His wisdom;
And by His understanding He has stretched out the heavens.
(Jeremiah 10:6–12 NASB)

How did it get to this point? Jeremiah went on to say:

"The shepherds of my people have lost their senses.
They no longer seek wisdom from the LORD.
Therefore, they fail completely,
and their flocks are scattered."

(Jeremiah 10:21 NLT)

Look at what God said in the chapter just prior:

Thus says the LORD:
"Let not the wise man glory in his wisdom,
Let not the mighty man glory in his might,
Nor let the rich man glory in his riches;
But let him who glories glory in this,
That he understands and knows Me,
That I am the LORD, exercising lovingkindness,
judgment, and righteousness in the earth.
For in these I delight,' says the LORD.
(Jeremiah 9:23–24 NKJV)

"Let him who glories glory in this, that he understands and knows Me!" I think we can see why churches today are afraid to take a stand for truth—they do not know God. Pastors are refraining from speaking truth because they are afraid of public opinion and public sentiment. But as Leonard Ravenhill once said, "A man who is intimate with God will never be intimidated by men." We must be intimate with God because intimidation is everywhere. We cannot be what we are supposed to be without knowing God. The Bible tells us:

But the people who know their God shall be strong and do great things. (Daniel 11:32 TLB)

This verse is introduced by the conjunction *but*. That means it is a response to something—the second half of a bigger picture. What comes before the conjunction *but* is the antichrist with his last-days system and corruption. Verse 21 calls him the "despicable person" who sets up the abomination that causes desolation and corrupts by smooth talk those whose loyalty to God's covenant has failed (Daniel 11:31–32). This shows us that the *action* of the people of God is a *reaction* to the antichrist. The people who know their God are not afraid of the most wicked man who will soon walk this planet!

We have been fighting the greatest battle of our time with the most untrained army on earth—untrained because we have lost sight of who God is and instead made God like us. However, I believe a new courage is coming to Christians who know their God. They will not be intimidated by mobs, courts, laws, or picketing. The darker the times, the braver they become.

Do you now see how vital it is to know God? Knowing God will prepare you to stand. Of course, the challenge is to serve the living and *true* God—not the American god or the Republican god or the Democratic god, or the god of Africa or Asia . . . but the God of heaven! Only God can reveal God; otherwise, it becomes man's imagination—a made-up version.

Therefore, it would be wise for us to start with what God has revealed about Himself in His Word. Now when God reveals Himself, it is called revelation. He is making known divine mystery. If God reveals Himself to us, that means He gives us the grace and capacity to receive that revelation. He reveals Himself because we could not figure Him out unless He made the first move.

God gave us the Holy Spirit so we can respond to revelation. Our response to revelation is called faith. Faith is believing that God tells the truth, believing what God says about Himself. What God reveals about Himself are called His attributes—His character, His reliable patterns that make Him who He is. Here are three attributes to know in order for us to take action and do exploits.

1. Our God Is Omnipresent

Omnipresent **means God is everywhere, always.** He can hear prayers in New York and in India at the same time. God has the ability to listen to every single person, every single moment, every single day, every single prayer, all at the same time. He never hushes someone, saying, "Quiet, I'm trying to listen to someone else right now!" He hears them all.

> "Am I a God near at hand," says the LORD,
> "And not a God afar off?
> Can anyone hide himself in secret places,
> So I shall not see him?" says the LORD;
> "Do I not fill heaven and earth?" says the LORD.
> (Jeremiah 23:23–24 NKJV)

No space and no place is without God.

> I can never escape from your Spirit!
> > I can never get away from your presence!
> If I go up to heaven, you are there;
> > if I go down to the grave, you are there.
> If I ride the wings of the morning,
> > if I dwell by the farthest oceans,
> even there your hand will guide me,
> > and your strength will support me.
> I could ask the darkness to hide me
> > and the light around me to become night—
> > but even in darkness I cannot hide from you.
> (Psalm 139:7–12 NLT)

God is in touch with every part of creation. He cannot be excluded from any part of your life. You can never accuse Him of being an uninvolved Father. But here is the catch: Though God is present everywhere, God's presence is not experienced in the same way everywhere.

Cindy and I recently experienced one of the toughest moments for us as parents. My daughter, Grace, plays volleyball for a junior national team, and she had just completed five months of recovery after knee surgery. Excited to be back to play in a qualifying tournament in Philadelphia, Grace was diving for a ball when the knee of another player hit her right in the mouth. It was horrific. I just watched my girl cry, "Dad!" At that moment, I just prayed, "God, don't break her spirit!" She had just come back after five months, and now we didn't know what was happening—if her teeth were even still there. Blood was everywhere. I think I'm the only man in America who still carries a handkerchief in his back pocket. I pulled it out; it was all we had to hold the blood. We rushed to the hospital, which was only eight minutes away, and we were taken into the operating room because they needed to do oral surgery.

As they were operating, Cindy held Grace's arm and I held onto her leg. I couldn't even look. All I did was pray in tongues. I began to ask, "God, where are You? This little girl fought hard, and now she's sitting here. Where are You?" I was really angry with God at that moment. Now I am a pastor who knows the theology of all this, yet I kept crying out to the omnipresent God, "Where are You? Where are You?"

All of a sudden, God started bringing to mind every little detail that showed He was there the whole time. He reminded me, "The director was there, her car was there, the best children's hospital in the country was there. They brought you in immediately. There was no wait. You got in, they did the surgery. They were able to get the teeth. Where was I? I've been orchestrating this whole thing to be with this little girl!" Right there in Children's Hospital of Philadelphia, I got this revelation: Gratitude finds omnipresence. Ungrateful people never notice God. When you start thanking God, you recognize His presence. You see Him working through it all. I started thanking God for each item that seemed unconnected but in reality was the tapestry of God who is present with us all the time.

2. Our God Is Omniscient

Omniscient means God is all-knowing. There is no mystery for Him. He never scratches His head. He never has to google something to figure it out. He knows every language. God knows everything perfectly and exhaustively; nothing is hidden from Him.

When Daniel's life was in the balance, this is one of the things Daniel prayed: "He knows what is in the darkness" (Daniel 2:22 NKJV). Only God knows what is in the darkness. It also says in the New Testament: "For if our heart condemns us, God is greater than our heart, and knows all things" (1 John 3:20 NKJV).

If you are in politics and say that you believe in God, remember that the true God is omniscient—which means He knows what is best. To all judges and congressmen who believe in God . . . remember that when God defines something, we are to go with His definition. Definitions do not come from politics, a court ruling, or a majority—they come from God, who is omniscient!

> Great is our Lord and mighty in power;
> his understanding has no limit.
> (Psalm 147:5 NIV)

When the United Nations headquarters was being built in New York City, there was some controversy over whether a place of worship should be included in the building. One New York newspaper carried a brilliant cartoon depicting a huge hand—God's hand—and in the center of the hand was a small globe. On top of the globe stood a group of tiny little men from the United Nations in a heated argument. The caption read: "Do we have to invite Him as well?"[4]

Yes, we should! Considering what we are facing in our world today, we desperately need an omniscient God. It is time for us to invite Him back into our government, the United Nations, our schools, and our courts!

3. Our God Is Omnipotent

Omnipotence means God is all-powerful. God never looks at a situation and thinks, "That's above My pay grade. It is too big to fix. I don't have the proper tools." With our God all things are possible!

I was standing in line at Barnes and Noble some years ago, looking at the rack of random books they try to entice you with as you wait. One book full of crazy facts caught my attention—particularly the section on the Roman Caesars. The Caesars had their busts all over their residence. But what was amazing was that they would lose power so fast that eventually they started just using the same bust with detachable heads! If you lost power, they simply popped your head off and replaced it with another head. The Caesars claimed to be gods that were all-powerful . . . yet had removable heads![5]

In contrast, we have a Head that is not going anywhere! He is omnipotent. This is how Revelation shouts it out:

And I heard, as it were, the voice of a great multitude, as the sound of
many waters and as the sound of mighty thunderings, saying, "Alleluia!
For the Lord God Omnipotent reigns!" (Revelation 19:6 NKJV)

God has all power. He is the only being in the universe who can handle this
kind of power. He can do far more than we can even conceive.

Now glory be to God, who by his mighty power at work within
us is able to do far more than we would ever dare to ask or even
dream of—infinitely beyond our highest prayers, desires, thoughts,
or hopes. May he be given glory forever and ever through endless
ages. (Ephesians 3:20–21 TLB)

God has revealed Himself and His attributes to us, which we receive by
faith. This revelation also elicits another response: worship. Worship is responding to the revelation of God. Without revelation, we start worshiping
worship. We are responding to good music and all the peripherals. Look at this
response to the revelation of God in Psalm 95:

Come, let us sing for joy to the Lord;
    let us shout aloud to the Rock of our salvation.
Let us come before him with thanksgiving
    and extol him with music and song.

For the Lord is the great God,
    the great King above all gods.
(Psalm 95:1–3 NIV)

We shout and sing aloud because God is great—not because the music is
great. If we just stay on the topic of who God is, worship happens.

You who fear the Lord, praise Him. . . .
From You comes my praise in the great assembly . . .
Those who seek Him will praise the Lord.
(Psalm 22:23, 25–26)

Where does praise come from? Those who fear the Lord, those who know the Lord, those who seek the Lord! It does not say anything here about music or instruments. When you know God, your hands automatically go up, your knees go down, your voice cries out. Yet when God is lost in the church, then praise turns into manipulation. You need lights and smoke to praise when you are not preaching the greatness of God. But the true God is enough for true praise.

As we consider these attributes of God, we can only conclude, "How great is our God!" Think about the fact that God is omniscient and omnipotent, yet He is also omnipresent. In other words, greatness does not imply distance. One day I saw something in the book of Psalms that overwhelmed me. It was this massive bridge between greatness and closeness, immensity and intimacy:

> He heals the brokenhearted
> And binds up their wounds.
> He counts the number of the stars;
> He gives names to all of them.
> Great is our Lord.
> (Psalm 147:3–5)

As soon as you finish the words "He heals the brokenhearted," the verse then catapults us to outer space, speaking about how God counts the stars and knows their names. Think of the distance between verses 3 and 4. While you are so moved that God heals your heart, before you can get out a "hallelujah," the psalmist tells you that God is in control of the universe.

The closest star to us in our solar system is the sun, which is 93 million miles away.[6] Yet God can take care of a star and a cry from your bedroom at the same time! He has His eye on everything and everyone at the same time. He can wipe away tears and make sure the sun rises. We see God's active compassion in the small circles of human experience as well as His unmeasured power in the great realms of creation. The universe and the person, stars and broken hearts—our God is concerned about them both!

May we know and worship the one true God. He is omnipresent; He is with you all the time. He is omniscient; He knows your name. He knows what is right and what is best. And He is omnipotent; nothing is too difficult for Him!

QUESTIONS

1. Think of a difficult time in your life. Where was God during that time?

2. If God is omnipotent and good, how would you explain why tragedies happen in our world?

3. Can you think of an example of when gratitude made you more aware of the omnipresent God?

THE HOLY SPIRIT

The 380 or the 120:
Which Group Are You In?

*"Without the Spirit of God, we can do
nothing. We are as ships without the
wind, branches without sap, and like coals
without fire, we are useless."*
CHARLES SPURGEON[1]

Church leaders, researchers, and podcasters are all trying to figure out why Christians are only attending church an average of 1.5 times a month.[2] We have men using their own ingenuity to try to solve the problem by cutting services down to less than an hour to accommodate busy schedules, or providing food and coffee so that people can have breakfast at church. Some are putting on bigger productions to attract more people. The church experts have focused on culture and what the church lacks, but not one report that I read said, "We need the Holy Spirit to come once again."

You cannot be in the presence of God and be bored! When God comes, people will come. The great Christian writer on prayer E. M. Bounds said it like this: "What the Church needs today is not more machinery or better, not new organizations or more and novel methods, but men whom the Holy Ghost can use—men of prayer, men mighty in prayer."[3] Leaders are so busy trying to figure out what we need instead of stopping to invite the Holy Spirit to come once again.

During my installation service at Times Square Church in 2021, Pastor Carter Conlon preached and Dr. R. T. Kendall gave the charge and prayed. Dr.

Kendall's words to me were: "Honor the blood, and honor the Holy Ghost!" We must honor the Holy Ghost. We simply cannot exist as a church without His presence.

Why does the church need the Holy Spirit? Do you know what God has commissioned the Holy Spirit to do? Here are thirty-one things that the Holy Spirit does:

- He helps us. Romans 8:26
- He guides us. John 16:13
- He teaches us. John 14:26
- He speaks. Revelation 2:7
- He reveals. 1 Corinthians 2:10
- He instructs. Acts 8:29
- He testifies of Jesus. John 15:26
- He comforts us. Acts 9:31
- He fills us. Acts 4:31
- He calls us. Acts 13:2
- He strengthens us. Ephesians 3:16
- He prays for us. Romans 8:26
- He bears witness to the truth. Romans 9:1
- He brings joy. 1 Thessalonians 1:6
- He brings freedom. 2 Corinthians 3:17
- He helps us obey. 1 Peter 1:22
- He transforms us. 2 Corinthians 3:18
- He lives in us. 1 Corinthians 3:16
- He frees us. Romans 8:2
- He renews us. Titus 3:5
- He produces fruit in us. Galatians 5:22–23
- He gives gifts. 1 Corinthians 12:8–10
- He leads us. Romans 8:14
- He convicts us. John 16:8
- He sanctifies us. 2 Thessalonians 2:13
- He empowers us. Acts 1:8
- He unites us. Ephesians 4:3–4

- He seals us. Ephesians 1:13
- He gives us access to the Father. Ephesians 2:18
- He enables us to wait. Galatians 5:5
- He casts out demons. Matthew 12:28

How can we possibly improve on the work of the Holy Spirit with the props of man?

Paul ended his Corinthian letters with a doxology, "The grace of the Lord Jesus Christ, and the love of God . . ." (2 Corinthians 13:14). Now if you would have asked me what comes next—what word he associated with the Holy Spirit—I would have guessed wrong. My Pentecostal roots want to say, "and the *power* of the Holy Spirit." But the verse says, "and the *fellowship* of the Holy Spirit, be with you all."

Paul connected fellowship not with what we do with people but with the Holy Spirit. Fellowship means partnership—a walking together. He was challenging the church at Corinth to get back in step and in fellowship with the Holy Spirit.

The Scriptures tell us that when Jesus rose from the dead, He spoke to about 500 people (see 1 Corinthians 15:5–6) and gave them specific instructions that would lead to the birth of the church of Jesus Christ. What exactly was His charge to them?

> And now I will send the Holy Spirit, just as my Father promised. But stay here in the city until the Holy Spirit comes and fills you with power from heaven. (Luke 24:49 NLT)

Five hundred people got the memo from the resurrected Jesus; those 500 were going to experience the thirty-one things that the Holy Spirit does. Some forty days later, Jesus ascended to heaven, and the doors open to an upper room in Jerusalem where they were to wait for the Holy Spirit to fill them with power.

> Then they returned to Jerusalem from the mountain called Olivet, which is near Jerusalem, a Sabbath day's journey away. When they had entered the city, they went up to the upstairs room . . . All these were continually devoting themselves with one mind to prayer,

along with the women, and Mary the mother of Jesus, and with His brothers. At this time Peter stood up among the brothers and sisters (group of about 120 persons was there together). (Acts 1:12–15)

Here is my question: The resurrected Jesus told 500 to wait to be filled, but now there were only 120 in the upper room. What happened to the other 380 people?

Apparently 76 percent of the people said, "Jesus, great teaching. We got this from here." I don't think these 380 were not Christians, but I do think the 120 were filled with power and a fellowship with God that the other 380 did not receive.

And another question: Why were these *eyewitnesses* unable to be *witnesses* for Jesus? Why was Jesus telling them to wait for power?

But you will receive power when the Holy Spirit has come upon you; and you shall be My witnesses both in Jerusalem and in all Judea, and Samaria, and as far as the remotest part of the earth. (Acts 1:8)

I would think that if anyone had the qualifications to be witnesses, it would have been the eyewitnesses of the resurrected Jesus! They saw Jesus as a corpse, then they saw Jesus walking through walls and ascending to heaven. If anyone was qualified to get a church website, have an Instagram account, rent a building, and get some business cards, it should have been those 500! Yet Jesus told them, "Wait, don't start anything until you invite the power of the Holy Spirit to change you! You have seen it all, but you have not received the Holy Spirit yet."

Five hundred got the message, but only 120 would be empowered.

Five hundred had a promise, but only 120 cashed in.

Five hundred had an inheritance, but only 120 claimed it.

Which group would you be in?

I was speaking with someone who shared that he recently had a distant relative die, leaving an inheritance to him and his wife that would change their lives. It was set to hit their account within the next few days. He said to me, "That relative's death and our inheritance will change everything for us!" How much more has Jesus' death, resurrection, and ascension given us an inheritance—the indwelling Holy Spirit, who changes our lives! Yet for some people, the reality of who He is and what He longs to do has not hit their bank account yet. They continue to live far below their true inheritance.

It reminds me of a time just before I left Detroit when film shoots were coming into Michigan for the Hollywood tax break. Next to my house, they were shooting a far from Oscar-worthy movie called *S.W.A.T.: Firefight*, the sequel to another *S.W.A.T.* film. My house would be in one of the scenes, and they wanted to pay me for showing my house in the movie.

"How much?" I asked the *S.W.A.T.: Firefight* staffer.

He replied, "How about $50?"

"Done! D-i-l-e-n-a is how you spell it." And a check was written out to me just like that.

That night on the set, they invited me to come watch since my house would be in the shot. Curious, I posed this question to one of the assistant directors: "You guys started setting up my neighbor's house way before you asked me. What if I had said 'no'?"

"We would have offered more money," he answered matter-of-factly "Sometimes we go up to $6 or 7K, but you said yes so quickly. You were the easiest person we've ever negotiated with!"

There was more?! Some of you said the born-again prayer, cashed your $50 check, and took off.

But there's more! I want you to be part of the 120. Somehow 76 percent, the majority, felt they could do it without an upper-room experience. We are not much different. A. W. Tozer said it like this: "If the Holy Spirit was withdrawn from the church today, 95 percent of what we do would go on, and no one would know the difference. If the Holy Spirit had been withdrawn from the New Testament church, 95 percent of what they did would stop, and everybody would know the difference."[4]

The first church at Ephesus in Acts 19 faced that problem. They had church services and accurate teaching, but without the presence of the Holy Spirit. They were of the 380 disciples who had not experienced the 120's upper-room power.

> Now a Jew named Apollos, an Alexandrian by birth, an eloquent man, came to Ephesus; and he was proficient in the Scriptures. This man had been instructed in the way of the Lord; and being fervent in

spirit, he was speaking accurately and teaching things about Jesus, being acquainted only with the baptism of John. (Acts 18:24–25)

Paul came to town and realized here were some of the 76 percent.

Now it happened that while Apollos was in Corinth, Paul passed through the upper country and came to Ephesus, and found some disciples. He said to them, "Did you receive the Holy Spirit when you believed?" And they said to him, "On the contrary, we have not even heard if there is a Holy Spirit." And he said, "Into what then were you baptized?' And they said, "Into John's baptism." (Acts 19:1–3)

"We have not heard if there is a Holy Spirit." Who said this? These were disciples! The problem was the preacher, Apollos. He did the church of Ephesus a disservice by keeping the disciples in the dark about the Holy Spirit. I am not going down the path of Apollos. We need the Holy Spirit!

Now the best place for us to start is by looking at how God first introduces the Holy Spirit in the Word. It is the "law of first use" or the "law of first mention"—studying a Bible topic by finding its first appearance in the Scriptures.

The Holy Spirit is first mentioned in Genesis 1 at creation. What do we learn about the Holy Spirit at creation?

He is *moving*.

In the beginning God created the heavens and the earth. And the earth was a formless and desolate emptiness, and darkness was over the surface of the deep, and the Spirit of God was hovering over the surface of the waters. (Genesis 1:1–2)

When you first see Him, He is moving. He is not stagnant or sitting around. This is an active Holy Spirit. Don't tell me that this moving Spirit is inside of you, but you won't move during worship, or that the active Spirit has come into your life, yet you do not alter your behavior. The moving Spirit moves men.

He is *speaking*.

Then God said, "Let there be light"; and there was light. (Genesis 1:3 NASB)

The Holy Spirit moves, then the Word comes. When we worship, we invite the Word of God. Worship should not be the thing that takes over the church service so that we miss what the Word of the Lord is. Where the Spirit is moving, the Word of God will be spoken and . . . He is *defining*.

> God saw that the light was good; and God separated the light from
> the darkness. God called the light "day," and the darkness He called
> "night." And there was evening and there was morning, one day.
> (Genesis 1:4–5)

The Word of God brings definition. When there is definition, there will often be separation. And as God's Spirit moves, He brings order. We see here that God starts naming things. At creation, He separated light from darkness and named day and night. He put things in their proper place.

When C. S. Lewis became a Christian and started writing Christian books, he was asked about his writing of erotic material. His response went something like this: "I can't write like that anymore. It's the difference between soil and dirt. If you are planting seed in the garden, you put it in soil. But if you take that soil out of the environment it was meant to flourish in, and you put it on your dinner table, then it is dirt."[5]

Once you become a Christian, the Holy Spirit starts renaming things. What you may have called soil is now dirt if it is not in the right context. For example, sex outside of marriage is not love. God names it fornication and sin. Money under the table—God calls stealing and tax evasion. My body, my choice—God calls murder of the unborn. The first creation is much like the new creation; the Holy Spirit will define what is light and what is darkness.

The Holy Spirit is constantly moving, speaking, and defining. We all need the Holy Spirit, for what lies ahead cannot be fought without Him. Paul exhorted us:

> Through the power of the Holy Spirit who lives within us, carefully
> guard the precious truth that has been entrusted to you.
> (2 Timothy 1:14 NLT)

The Holy Spirit lives in you! Let's look at four truths about the Holy Spirit that we are called to carefully guard. It will help prepare us for the fight that lies ahead of us—a fight that we will be unable to face unless we cry out for that forsaken fellowship.

1. He Is My Seal

> In Him, you also, after listening to the message of truth, the gospel
> of your salvation—having also believed, you were sealed in Him
> with the Holy Spirit of the promise. (Ephesians 1:13)

A seal was an emblem or logo that expressed ownership. You knew who manufactured the item because their seal was on it. Did you know that there was a seal on the most famous grave in history?

> And they went and made the tomb secure with the guard , sealing
> the stone. (Matthew 27:66 NASB)

It was the seal of Rome—the most powerful place on the planet at the time. This seal was saying, "You cannot touch that body of Jesus; it is Rome's property." Of course, we all know how the story goes, but let me add a nuance to the resurrection story that is often overlooked:

> Now after the Sabbath, as it began to dawn toward the first day of
> the week, Mary Magdalene and the other Mary came to look at the
> tomb. And behold, a severe earthquake had occurred, for an angel
> of the Lord descended from heaven and came and rolled away the
> stone, and sat upon it. (Matthew 28:1–2)

Heaven sat on the seal to show that Rome was not in charge, the guards were not in charge, God was in charge!

In his book *Emblems of the Holy Spirit*, F. E. Marsh discussed the significance of the seal. In Bible times, a seal was the way a person identified something that he owned. For example, businessmen would purchase timber in Lebanon. When they purchased it, many times they could not take the timber with them. If that were the case, they would stamp it with their family seal. The logs would sit there and later be put on a ship in the Mediterranean Sea to sail to the port where the buyers could collect their logs. Any log with their mark of ownership on it belonged to them. The seal was ownership.[6]

How incredible to realize that the Christian is sealed with the Holy Spirit! We have God's mark of ownership, and God does not give up His own! Our owner said, "I cannot take them with Me now, but they belong to Me. Keep your hands off; I will be back for them." If you are saved, then you are sealed.

2. HE IS MY PLEDGE

Having also believed, you were sealed in Him with the Holy Spirit of the promise, who is a first installment of our inheritance, in regard to the redemption of God's own possession, to the praise of His glory. (Ephesians 1:13–14)

A pledge is a down payment—earnest money. When I was growing up, we did not get into debt with credit cards; we put stuff on layaway. If you wanted something in the store that you could not afford, you put $20 down, and they would hold it for you. You would come back every week to put some more money down until you could pay it off. Of course, what you probably didn't realize is that by the time you finally paid it off, it was out of style! But that down payment meant it was already promised to someone, so nobody else could purchase it from the store.

The Greek word for "pledge" is *arrabona*, which is defined by *Vine's Complete Expository Dictionary* as "an engagement ring." When I put a ring on Cindy's finger at Rockefeller Center in New York City, what it said to her was: "You are taken. We have a future date and future lives together." In other words, "This is not all there is!"

When I am saved, I am pledged. The Holy Spirit in me says, "This is not all there is. There is a marriage supper and a place being prepared for you!" So don't get comfortable with the ring because we have a date set called the rapture of the church, when He is going to bring His bride home! The best is yet to come!

3. HE IS MY COMFORTER

And I will pray the Father, and he shall give you another Comforter, that he may abide with you for ever. (John 14:16 KJV)

The word *comforter* makes me think of my mom. "Don't sleep on the comforter; get your feet off the comforter!" But it's not that word. This was a proximity word which meant "to walk alongside." But it was not just for walking; it was also for fighting.

Four times in the book of John, the Greek word *paraclete* is used to describe the Holy Spirit. According to Gordon Dalbey's *Healing the Masculine Soul*, *paraclete* was an ancient warrior's term. Greek soldiers went into battle in pairs so that when the enemy attacked, they could draw together, back-to-back, covering each other's blind side.[7] God does not send us to fight the good fight alone. We have a battle partner, the Holy Spirit, who covers our blind side and fights for us!

> Jesus, full of the Holy Spirit, returned from the Jordan and was led around by the Spirit in the wilderness for forty days, being tempted by the devil. (Luke 4:1–2)

Jesus, our forerunner, gave us this lesson during His temptation in the wilderness. Jesus, full of the Holy Spirit, faced Satan himself and left in victory. Notice what happened to Jesus as He exited His fight with Satan: "Jesus returned to Galilee in the power of the Spirit" (Luke 4:14). When we are full of the Holy Spirit, we, too, can face any battle that is ahead. Not only that, but we can also leave stronger than we went in!

Knowing that the Holy Spirit is back-to-back with me became particularly meaningful after a fight involving my family that I was not even initially aware of. Just before we left Detroit, a young man came to my office. He had previously served well in the church. However, something had happened with him in an area of sin, so I had to remove him from his position in ministry. I explained that this was his church, but he could not continue to serve here until God did a work inside of him. He became so embittered against me that he left the church.

I was surprised when this young man showed up in my office, for I had not seen him in years. He came in and put a braided tassel on my desk, saying, "I want to give this to you so that you will always remember God is fighting for you—battles that you are not even aware of." It was the tassel he received upon graduating from the Army Rangers. He was part of a special forces unit.

He continued, "I have to tell you what happened after you removed me from ministry. I became so angry with you that I went home and put on all my army fatigues. I took out all my weapons—all the assault rifles that I used in the army. I was packing it all up, and I knew where you lived. I was going to your house to kill you and your family."

Now during that season, I was already fighting things in the church, raising four kids, trying to be the best husband and pastor that I could be . . . and I did not know any of this had happened! But thankfully I have a Comforter who is fighting on my behalf, saying, "Don't worry about this; I got this for you."

This young man continued the story: "I loaded everything in the car. I sat in the car, and then I heard a voice. I'm telling you, it was an audible voice. It said, 'If you put this car in reverse and leave the driveway, I will kill you. Pastor Tim, it was so real that I started weeping and repenting. I knew you were a protected man."

At that point, all I could think was, "Thank You, Holy Spirit, that You are fighting battles I don't even know about!" God has our backs!

4. He Is My Helper

In the same way the Spirit also helps our weakness; for we do not know what to for pray as we should, but the Spirit Himself inter-cedes for us with groanings too deep for words. (Romans 8:26)

The greatest Christian on the planet said that he did not know how to pray. If the Apostle Paul did not know how to pray, then we certainly must not know how to pray either!

Our first prayer meeting when we planted our church in Detroit consisted of five people—me, two ladies, one guy who never prayed but would just read the Bible, and a demoniac from the street. Worst prayer meeting in the nation. One day, the two ladies brought in a man who had been beat up on the streets and had three broken ribs. He had just gotten out of the hospital, and they told him to come with them to a prayer meeting where we would pray for healing.

I did not have a good track record when it came to praying for healing. If I prayed for you, there was a good chance that nothing would happen. Yet at the time, it never dawned on me to say, "I don't know how to pray, but the Holy

Spirit will help me." I now know that Paul didn'ts only give us the bad news: I don't know how to pray. He also gave us the good news: God takes our ask and makes it better and bigger!

> Now to Him who is able to do far more abundantly beyond all
> that we ask or think, according to the power that works within us.
> (Ephesians 3:20)

Paul was saying, "Go ahead, say something—say anything—and the Holy Spirit will get it right. He goes beyond your ask." I love those words. He takes our ask and goes further. You can be saved for ten minutes and still be powerful in prayer because it is not you, it's God!

So the guy with the broken ribs was standing there, waiting for the pastor with the terrible healing record to lay hands on him. I prayed and made sure to throw in the blame-it-on-God fine print: "God, You can heal him, but if You don't, then it must not be Your will."

All of a sudden, he started ripping off his bandages and hitting his ribs, crying, "I'm healed!"

"No, you're not, this takes time," I said in disbelief.

"Punch me in the ribs," he insisted. "I'm healed!"

"I'm not going to punch you," I told him, certain that would guarantee me an appearance on *Judge Judy*.[8] All the while, I was wondering to myself how this happened with that prayer I just prayed!

But you see, it wasn't me. God took my feeble ask and made it go further. I have since learned to live by Brennan Manning's powerful words: "The only way to fail in prayer is to not show up."

Let me explain how God makes our words better and bigger. Elijah was an Old Testament prophet who was being hunted down by a demon-possessed woman named Jezebel. When he found out that she was trying to kill him, look at his response:

> And he was afraid, and got up and ran for his life and came to
> Beersheba, which belongs to Judah; and he left his servant there.
> But he himself went a day's journey into the wilderness, and came
> and sat down under a broom tree; and he asked for himself to die,

and said, "Enough! Now, Lᴏʀᴅ, take my life, for I am no better than my fathers.'" (1 Kings 19:3–4)

He essentially said, "Kill me, Lord; I'm done with this!" That was his prayer. How did God answer it?

He lay down and fell asleep under a broom tree; but behold, there was an angel touching him, and he said to him, "Arise, eat." And he looked, and behold, there was at his head a round loaf of bread baked on hot coals, and a pitcher of water. So he ate and drank, and lay down again. But the angel of the Lᴏʀᴅ came back a second time and touched him, and said, "Arise, eat; because the journey is too long for you." (1 Kings 19:5–7)

Elijah said, "God, kill me." The Holy Spirit took those words and said, "Father, he doesn't mean *kill* me, he means *cake* me."

How great is this? We pray, and the Holy Spirit says what we should have prayed in the first place. It takes the pressure off us! Look at Paul's bad news verse again but pay attention to the second part:

In the same way the Spirit also helps our weakness; for we do not know what to pray for as we should, but the Spirit Himself intercedes for us with groanings too deep for words. (Romans 8:26)

The Spirit Himself intercedes for us—that's the good news. The Holy Spirit is committed to taking our simple, silly prayer words and adding power to them. He is our editor! He says, "Father, this is what they really meant to say."

I say things that are so dumb sometimes, but thank God that the Holy Spirit edits prayers! If He didn't, many of us would have married the wrong person. "I love her and want to marry her. I know that's my wife." The Holy Spirit comes in and says, "Father, what he means is that he is lonely and that is the only one who said yes to him for a date. No wedding bells."

When someone prays, "I wouldn't care if they died!" the Holy Spirit says, "What she means is: Help me to forgive them; they have hurt me, and I need to love them." Or when someone cries out, "I hate You, God!" the Holy Spirit interprets, "He doesn't understand You right now and is just frustrated." When we pray, it is our words but the Holy Spirit's editing that makes it powerful!

Oh, how we need the Holy Spirit today! He is our seal, our pledge, our comforter, and our helper. It is up to you to guard these truths about the Holy Spirit, for He has been entrusted to you. Remember, the grace of the Lord Jesus Christ, the love of God, and the fellowship of the Holy Spirit are always available. Every day you are given the choice to be part of either the 380 or the 120. Which will you choose?

QUESTIONS

1. Look over the list of thirty-one things that the Holy Spirit does. How have you experienced Him in some of these ways?

2. If the Holy Spirit were taken away from you, how would your life be different?

3. What is one thing you can do to involve the Holy Spirit more in your everyday life?

ISRAEL

The Nation of Israel and the End Times

*"The land of Israel without the
God of Israel will be here today and
gone tomorrow."*
ABRAHAM JOSHUA HESCHEL[1]

Honoring the nation of Israel is not a Times Square Church value; it must be the value of the body of Christ. If Israel is important to God, then Israel must be important to us. There is no doubt that God blesses the nation of Israel, and what God blesses is what He loves. It is our privilege as God's people to love what He loves. When I fell in love with Cindy, there were two things I did not understand about her: She loved dogs and hockey. But when you are in love, you are not afraid to change your preferences. I happen to like both now. And if you love Jesus, you love what He loves.

The story of Ruth in the Bible is more than a love story. Ruth is the symbol of every Gentile who has ever come to salvation through Israel's God. The words of this Moabitess to her Jewish mother-in-law, Naomi, "Your people shall be my people, and your God, my God" (Ruth 1:16), still ring in the hearts of non-Jews today. This ought to be the covenant each of us makes with God.

Now the two greatest things that Bible critics hate are miracles and prophecy. Prophecy is when God foretells the future, or God's interference by His *Word*. Miracles are when God interferes in the present by His *acts*. If we believe in God, then we believe in both. The climax of miracles and prophecy came at the incarnation of Jesus, but their beginnings were found with Israel. Modern-day Israel is alive and thriving today because of miracles and prophecy.

In fact, there is no other nation in existence whose beginning and future we know with such clarity. God spoke to Abraham about a new nation called Israel that would be blessed and a blessing.

> Now the Lord said to Abram,
> "Go from your country,
> And from your relatives
> And from your father's house,
> To the land which I will show you;
> And I will make you a into great nation,
> And I will bless you,
> And make your name great;
> And so you shall be a blessing;
> And I will bless those who bless you,
> And the one who curses you I will curse."
> (Genesis 12:1–3)

God promised to bless those who bless Israel and curse those who curse her. Israel has always held a special place in our hearts here at Times Square Church. The first missionary couple we sent out, David and Karen Davis, went to minister in Israel. David Davis was a Broadway actor who got saved at Times Square Church. He brought his Jewish girlfriend, Karen, also a Broadway actress, to church. Though initially skeptical, Karen later became radically saved. They eventually married, and David was mentored by David Wilkerson.

David Wilkerson always had a burden for Israel, which he shared with David and Karen. Their original mission was to start a drug rehab program called House of Victory—which continues today. David Wilkerson also had a dream in his heart to start a church on top of Mount Carmel. This later transpired when Kehilat HaCarmel was cofounded by the Davises and Peter Tsukahira. The church is situated right on Mount Carmel, where Elijah stood against the prophets of Baal! For decades, TSC has supported this Messianic congregation—one of the only places in the nation with Jews, Gentiles, and Arabs meeting together to worship Jesus.

God said to Israel, "I will bless those who bless you." That sentence came directly from the lips of God and has never expired. Times Square Church has experienced this blessing of God. As soon as we started to support Israel, a flood of money began to pour in for TSC Missions and our feeding programs, ChildCry and Feed New York. We currently support more than five different programs in Israel.

God's blessings upon Israel and those who bless her have been evident from the beginning and will continue to the end. It is His supernatural hand upon the nation. How appropriate that God put Israel in the middle of the world!

> Thus says the Lord GOD: "This is Jerusalem; I have set her in the midst of the nations and the countries all around her." (Ezekiel 5:5 NKJV)

Jerusalem is the most important city on the face of the earth, and Israel the most important nation—the spiritual center of the world. We are indebted to the Jews. The Ten Commandments came from Israel. The Bible came from Israel. Even the Messiah came from Israel!

Let's now consider three things that further prove we are talking about a supernatural topic: the hatred of the Jews, the survival of the Jews, and the establishing of the Jewish nation.

1. The Hatred of the Jews

Because God is hated, Israel is hated. People hate what God loves. It is not bigotry; it is anti-Christ. People want Israel's extermination because people want God exterminated.

> We know that we are of God, and the whole world lies under the sway of the wicked one. (1 John 5:19 NKJV)

Sadly, the further this country strays from God and the Bible, the less likely it will be to support the nation of Israel.

2. The Survival of the Jews

Despite constant persecution, the Jews continue to thrive. Pharaoh tried to drown them, but he and his armies drowned. Nebuchadnezzar tried to burn them, but he ended up going insane. Haman wrote a law to eradicate them, but he ended up hanging on the very gallows he built for a Jew. Hitler tried to exterminate them, but a nation formed out of them just a few years later. Every genocide attempt against the Jews has been thwarted by God. Why? Because God gave them an everlasting covenant:

> I will establish my covenant as an everlasting covenant between me and you and your descendants after you for the generations to come, to be your God and the God of your descendants after you. (Genesis 17:7 NIV)

> This is what the LORD says,
> He who gives the sun for light by day
> And the fixed order of the moon and the stars for light by night,
> Who stirs up the sea so that its waves roar—
> The LORD of armies is His name:
> "If this fixed order departs
> From Me," declares the LORD,
> "Then the descendants of Israel also will cease
> To be a nation before Me forever . . .
> If the heavens above can be measured
> And the foundations of the earth searched out below,
> Then I will also reject all the descendants of Israel
> For everything that they have done," declares the LORD.
> (Jeremiah 31:35–37)

Has the sun stopped shining, or the moon not shown up? Until that happens, Israel is not going anywhere!

In my almost sixty years of life, I cannot remember a place where I became more emotional than when I was in Germany for the 500-year celebration of the Reformation. During my time there, I traveled a few hours away to the Buchenwald concentration camp, which was for the medical experimentation on and extermination of hundreds of thousands of Jews. The oddest thing got me emotionally—in their museum, they had a showcase of various eating utensils of the Jews. And carved into these tin cans and plates were pictures of their families and homes and fences and flowers—so that they could remember what their former life was like. Today we have our cell phones and photo albums, but for those Jews, those carvings were their only memories of a life that was mercilessly taken from them. I almost lost it. Yet as I thought about a madman trying to annihilate the people God birthed, this verse came to mind:

> For this is what the LORD Almighty says: "After the Glorious One has sent me against the nations that have plundered you—for whoever touches you touches the apple of his eye—I will surely raise my hand against them." (Zechariah 2:8–9 NIV)

When you fight against Israel, you fight against God. All the nations of the earth have persecuted the Jews, but every persecutor is gone, and the nation that God birthed is still thriving. The only way to remove the Jews is to remove God, and He is not going anywhere!

3. The Birth of the Nation of Israel

From AD 70 to 1967, the land of Palestine was ruled by forty different nations. Today it is under Israeli control. Prophecy was fulfilled on that momentous day of May 14, 1948, when Jewish leader David Ben-Gurion declared independence and established the modern State of Israel. That day, Israel was recognized as a nation by the United States, followed by many other countries. It was the fulfillment of God's promise to gather His people back to their land, and in one day a nation would be birthed (see Ezekiel 37:12–14: Isaiah 66:8).

The very next day, war broke out as surrounding Arab countries invaded Israel in attempts to take the land away from the Jews. From 1948 to the present, the Israelis have fought five national wars and, despite being vastly outnumbered, miraculously won all five!

Now there are a few things that I would like to state clearly:

To be pro-Israel is not to be anti-Arab. To be pro-Israel is not to be political but to be biblical.

The church is not Israel. Those who believe that have believed the lie of a replacement theology. Nowhere in the Bible do we see that false doctrine.

Palestine is not the name of Israel. It was a name given to the land by Rome in the second century to deliberately blot out Israel's past and claim to her land. I am praying for God to touch the Palestinians. But those who use that name are not on the side of Israel. The land was originally called Canaan and later Israel. It belongs to the Jews, according to an everlasting covenant.

I would now like to draw your attention to a story in the book of Numbers about Balaam, the Gentile prophet, and Balak, the Moabite king. This story is significant for us to know, for God is giving us a prophetic picture of Gentile believers' relationship with Israel. Most of us are familiar with the donkey part but not the Israel part.

Balak, whose name means "to devastate," was the enemy king. He represented those who wanted Israel to disappear. But in order for that to happen, they had to go after leaders who could be bribed to curse Israel.

Balak asked Balaam to curse Israel in order to gain an upper hand on them. Balaam was a non-Jewish prophet, yet he asked God if he should curse Israel. Balaam was even offered money to do this cursing, but he refuseed because of God's response:

> But God told Balaam, "Do not go with them. You are not to curse these people, for they have been blessed!" (Numbers 22:12 NLT)

The fearful Moabite king then returned again with offers of more money and prestige, and this time Balaam fell for the bait. On the way to his disobedience, God stopped him with a talking donkey who saw angelic forces that Balaam himself could not see. Therefore, Balaam said to Balak:

> "How am I to put a curse on him upon whom God has not put a curse?
> And how am I to curse him whom the Lord has not cursed" . . .
>
> Then Balak said to Balaam, "What have you done to me? I took you to put a curse on my enemies, but behold, you have actually blessed them!" (Numbers 23:8, 11)

Balak then tried to get him to look at Israel from another vantage point. He said to Balaam:

> "Please come with me to another place from where you may see them . . . and put a curse on them for me from there." So he took

him to the field of Zophim, to the top of Pisgah, and he built seven
altars and offered a bull and a ram on each altar. . . . Then the LORD
met Balaam and put a word in his mouth, and said, "Return to Balak,
and this is what you shall speak." (Numbers 23:13–14, 16)

So Balaam delivered the words God gave him:

God is not a man, that He would lie,
Nor a son of man, that He would change His mind;
Has He said, and will He not do it?
Or has He spoken, and will He not make it good?
Behold, I have received a command to bless;
When He has blessed, I cannot revoke it.
He has not looked at misfortune in Jacob;
Nor has He seen trouble in Israel;
The LORD his God is with him,
And the shout joyful of a king is among them.
(Numbers 23:19–21)

At that point, Balak wanted to give Balaam yet another point of view.

"I will take you to another place; perhaps it will be agreeable with
God that you curse them for me from there" . . . When Balaam saw
that it pleased the LORD to bless Israel, he did not go as at other
times to seek omens. (Numbers 23:27: 24:1)

Instead, Balaam turned his attention to the wilderness, raised his eyes, and
saw Israel. The Spirit of the Lord came upon him, and he said:

"Blessed is everyone who blesses you,
and cursed is everyone who curses you."
Then Balak's anger burned against Balaam, and he struck his hands
together; and Balak said to Balaam, "I called you to curse my enemies, but behold, you have persisted in blessing them these three
times!" (Numbers 24:9–10)

Today the enemy is still trying to get us to curse Israel, but when we see
things from God's vantage point, we cannot help but bless the nation! It

reminds me of driving in the days before cell phones existed. There were no real-time maps with red lines to indicate traffic up ahead. Instead, we had to tune in to the radio for traffic updates. Those in proximity of heavy traffic could even hear the traffic helicopters overhead. On the road, I needed to rely on someone who was higher than eye level—who could look at my route and say, "Stay away from that road; you won't get to where you are going." Likewise in life, we need someone who is very high up, who can see what we cannot see. That is why we need to see Israel from God's vantage point. We do not make our decisions based on the United Nations, the Democrats, the Republicans, or NATO—but based on God's Word. As it says in Isaiah:

"For my thoughts are not your thoughts,
    neither are your ways my ways,"
        declares the Lord.
"As the heavens are higher than the earth,
    so are my ways higher than your ways
    and my thoughts than your thoughts."
(Isaiah 55:8–9 NIV)

God gave us a higher view of Israel through David as well as the Apostle Paul. God used the greatest Old Testament leader, David, to challenge us to pray for the peace of Jerusalem:

And who is like Your people Israel, the one nation on the earth whom God went to redeem for Himself as a people. (1 Chronicles 17:21 NKJV)

Pray for the peace of Jerusalem: "May they prosper who love you." (Psalm 122:6 NKJV)

God then used Paul, the greatest Christian in the New Testament, to challenge us to pray for the salvation of the Jews. We see this in the book of Romans.

Now the book of Romans may very well be considered the greatest and most important letter in the New Testament. Paul journeyed through man's sinfulness in Romans 1–3, justification by faith in chapters 4–5, death to sin and victory through God in chapters 5–6, and living in the new way of the Spirit in chapters 7–8. But when we hit Romans 9–11, it is as if we come to a screeching halt, at which point most of us skip straight over to Romans 12–16.

Here is why I believe Romans 9–11 often gets skipped: Balak voices are attempting to give us different viewpoints of it. While God keeps pronouncing through each of those chapters, "I bless them . . ." every critical commentator tries to figure out a way that it is not God speaking about Israel. Balak voices try to keep these three prophetic chapters out of our understanding—deeming them too esoteric or simply irrelevant. But the reality is that Romans 9–11 is the key to understanding our connection to Israel.

ROMANS 9: THE SOVEREIGNTY OF GOD

Romans 9 calls for submission to God's *sovereignty*, which requires humility. God intentionally begins by talking about His character before talking about the nation of Israel. When you come to grips with God's sovereignty, you come to grips with the nation of Israel. *Sovereignty* is defined as God doing what He wants, when He wants, and how He wants—without asking for anyone's permission. If you ask, "Why did God choose the Jews?" then you must also ask, "Why did God choose me?" He chose the Jews because He is sovereign, just like He chose you because He is sovereign!

Paul began with the Genesis story of Rebekah and Isaac's children, Jacob and Esau:

> For though the twins were not yet born and had not done anything good or bad, so that God's purpose according to His choice would stand, not because of works but because of Him who calls, it was said to her, "THE OLDER WILL SERVE THE YOUNGER." Just as it is written: "JACOB I HAVE LOVED, BUT ESAU I HAVE HATED."
>
> What shall we say then? There is no injustice with God, is there? Far from it! For He says to Moses, "I WILL HAVE MERCY ON WHOMEVER I HAVE MERCY, AND I WILL SHOW COMPASSION TO WHOMEVER I HAVE COMPASSION." (Romans 9:11–15)

Esau is the older, and Jacob is the younger. Traditionally, the eldest son in-herited all the family's wealth. The second or third son received very little, if anything. Notice here God's sovereignty: God did not choose the oldest son to carry out His plans but the younger! That was countercultural. We should be saying, "The God of Abraham, Isaac, and Esau," not Jacob. But culture is not in charge of God. Throughout the Bible, when God chose someone to work through, He chose whomever He wanted!

The sovereignty of God is God exercising His prerogative to do whatever He pleases with His creation. What if you were to come into my home and say, "I don't like the way you decorated this room. You should move the sofa here and this picture to that wall." My response would be, "When you start buying the furniture and paying the mortgage, then we can consider your opinions. Right now, your views mean nothing, because I am the owner." God is in charge of this planet, so He can do whatever He wants. Daniel 4:35 puts it this way: "He does as he pleases" (NLT). That's sovereignty.

Why doesn't that bother me? Because God is all-wise, all-loving, and all-powerful! I don't trust any man's sovereignty because they don't have the char-acter and nature to wield that kind of power. But I can trust God's sovereignty. God chooses Israel because He is sovereign.

> For you are a holy people to the LORD your God; the LORD your God has chosen you to be a people for His personal possession out of all the peoples who are on the face of the earth.
>
> The LORD did not make you His beloved nor choose you because you were greater in number than any of the peoples, since you were the fewest of all peoples, but because the LORD loved you and kept the oath which He swore to your forefathers. (Deuteronomy 7:6–8)

Paul then finished on the sovereignty of God with these verses:

> So, what does all this mean? Are we saying that God is unfair? Of course not! He had every right to say to Moses: "I will be merciful to whomever I choose and I will show compassion to whomever I wish." Again, this proves that God's choice doesn't depend on how badly someone wants it or tries to earn it, but it depends on God's kindness and mercy. (Romans 9:14–16 TPT)

Romans 10: The Most Neglected Prayer of the Church

Once we understand that God is sovereign, we see that He desires for us to co-labor with Him in His plan. This calls for us to pray for Israel. Here is Paul's charge:

> Believe me, friends, all I want for Israel is what's best for Israel: salvation, nothing less. I want it with all my heart and pray to God for it all the time. (Romans 10:1 MSG)

Why wouldn't we pray for their salvation? We pray all the other prayers of the Apostle Paul. I found forty-three New Testament prayers of Paul, but somehow this prayer gets set aside. Here is the rest of this passage in a modern translation:

> My beloved brothers and sisters, the passionate desire of my heart and constant prayer to God is for my fellow Israelites to experience salvation. For I know that although they are deeply devoted to God, they are unenlightened. And since they've ignored the righteousness God gives, wanting instead to be acceptable to God because of their own works, they've refused to submit to God's faith-righteousness. For the Christ is the end of the law. And because of him, God has transferred his perfect righteousness to all who believe. (Romans 10:1–4 TPT)

Paul's prayer for Israel's salvation should be our prayer.

Romans 11: The Future of Israel and the World

As God's people, we must eagerly anticipate His will being accomplished. This calls for conviction. The Scriptures show us that Israel is a key and crucial timepiece in God's last-days agenda.

> I say then, Hath God cast away his people? God forbid. For I also am an Israelite, of the seed of Abraham, of the tribe of Benjamin. God hath not cast away his people which he foreknew. (Romans 11:1–2 KJV)

"God forbid" or "may it never be" is a popular phrase in the epistle of Romans. There are fourteen "God forbids" in the book of Romans where Paul was anticipating a question of the reader and answering with emphasis and passion. "God forbid" means "Of course not, are you out of your mind?" Or as one version says, "Absolutely not."

It is hard to believe that atheist Jews exist today, but it warns us that even greatly blessed religious people can walk away from God. Nevertheless, we see here that God is not through with the Jews. Although they are blind and under discipline right now, God has not forgotten His people. He asks us to co-labor with Him and intercede for Israel because this is their future:

> For I do not want you, brothers and sisters, to be uninformed of this mystery—so that you will not be wise in your own estimation— that a partial hardening has happened to Israel until the fullness of the Gentiles has come in; and so all Israel will be saved; just as it is written,
>
> "THE DELIVERER WILL COME FROM ZION."
> (Romans 11:25–26)

All Israel will be saved! How will this revival happen in Israel? Let's look at the prophecy concerning how the nation will be awakened to Jesus:

> "It will come about on that day that I will make Jerusalem a heavy stone for all the peoples; all who lift it will injure themselves severely. And all the nations of the earth will be gathered against it. On that day," declares the LORD, "I will strike every horse with confusion and its rider with insanity. But I will watch over the house of Judah, while I strike every horse of the peoples with blindness. Then the clans of Judah will say in their hearts, 'The inhabitants of Jerusalem are a strong support for us through the LORD of armies, their God.'
>
> "On that day I will make the clans of Judah like a firepot among pieces of wood and a flaming torch among sheaves, so they will consume on the right and on the left all the surrounding peoples, while [e]the inhabitants of Jerusalem again live on their own sites in Jerusalem. The LORD also will save the tents of Judah first, so that

the glory of the house of David and the glory of the inhabitants of Jerusalem will not be greater than Judah. On that day the LORD will protect the inhabitants of Jerusalem, and the one who is feeble among them on that day will be like David, and the house of David will be like God, like the angel of the LORD before them. And on that day I will seek to destroy all the nations that come against Jerusalem.

"And I will pour out on the house of David and on the inhabitants of Jerusalem the Spirit of grace and of pleading, so that they will look at Me whom they pierced; and they will mourn for Him, like one mourning for an only son, and they will weep bitterly over Him like the bitter weeping over a firstborn. On that day the mourning in Jerusalem will be great." (Zechariah 12:3–11)

On that day a fountain will be opened to the house of David and the inhabitants of Jerusalem, to cleanse them from sin and impurity. (Zechariah 13:1 NIV)

God is coming back to Jerusalem! When Israel sees the supernatural protection of God over the nation, they will acknowledge this is none other than Jesus working on their behalf!

This is only one of many prophecies concerning God's good plans for the nation of Israel. In fact, I do not think it is possible to study the end times without studying Israel. Why? Israel is the centerpiece of last-days prophecy. If you read Bible prophecy, you will discover that Israel is in some way connected to 100 percent of it. Indeed, the eyes of the entire world are upon this tiny State of Israel, and so should your eyes be. As the Jew goes, so goes the world. Israel is God's measuring rod, His blueprint. Israel is God's program for what He is doing in the world.

Here are fifteen predictions about Israel in the Bible:

- Enslavement in Egypt (Genesis 15:13)
- Take possession of Canaan (Genesis 17:8)
- Turn to idolatry in Canaan (Judges 2:11–17)
- God will establish Jerusalem as the center of worship (Deuteronomy 12:10–12)

- Captivity of northern kingdom to Assyria (2 Kings 15:29; 17:3–4, 6–7)
- Captivity of southern kingdom to Babylon (Isaiah 39:6–7)
- Destruction of the first temple (2 Kings 25:8–12; 2 Chronicles 36:19; Jeremiah 52:12–15)
- Return of the remnant from Babylon (Isaiah 11:10–16)
- Destruction of the second temple (Daniel 9:24–26)
- Scattered among all nations (Deuteronomy 28:64)
- During their dispersion they would be persecuted (Leviticus 26:36–39; Deuteronomy 28:64–68; Amos 9:4)
- The regathering from all nations; in one day a nation born (Isaiah 66:8)
- All nations gathered against Jerusalem (Luke 21:20–24)
- A supernatural revelation of Jesus to the nation (Zechariah 12:10–11)
- Messiah will return to Mount of Olives (Zechariah 14:4)

Twelve of the fifteen predictions have been fulfilled. If 80 percent of Israel's prophesies have been fulfilled, is it unreasonable to believe for the remaining 20 percent to be fulfilled? It would be unreasonable to *doubt* it.

What, then, is the response God requires? Let us heed the warning in 2 Peter:

> We also have the prophetic message as something completely reli-
> able, and you will do well to pay attention to it, as to a light shining
> in a dark place, until the day dawns and the morning star rises in
> your hearts. (2 Peter 1:19 NIV)

Certainly, the world around us reflects Peter's description of "a dark place." But in the midst of the darkness, God has provided one clear light: the prophetic message. Fulfilled prophecy is a light shining in a dark place. As the days grow darker, the light of biblical prophecy grows correspondingly brighter. We must remain alert, for the fulfillment of Israel's prophecies signals the closeness of Christ's return. And until He comes, it is our duty to submit to God's sovereignty and intercede for the nation, knowing that God's purposes for Israel—which in turn affect the entire world—will surely be accomplished!

QUESTIONS

1. How have your views of Israel been challenged through this chapter?

2. Can you think of other examples in recent history when God's blessing on the nation of Israel was evident?

3. How is God leading you to bless the nation of Israel today?

JESUS

The Knockdown Names of Jesus

"There are two hundred and fifty-six names given in the Bible for the Lord Jesus Christ, and I suppose this was because He was infinitely beyond all that any one name could express."
BILLY SUNDAY[1]

If *J* is for Jesus, then the task of writing this chapter is monumental—especially with the words of the Apostle Paul looming over me: "To me, though I am the very least of all the saints, this grace was given, to preach . . . the unsearchable riches of Christ" (Ephesians 3:8 ESV).

Unsearchable means never able to be fully explored or discovered. How do I communicate *unsearchable* in one chapter? I am faced with boundless content! Even when we think we have carried our search to the limits of possibility, in reality we have not even scratched the surface.

Who is this Jesus?

- He is the Father to the orphans;
- Husband to the widow.
- To the traveler in the night, He is the Bright and Morning Star;
- To those in a desert time, He is the cloud by day and the fire by night.
- To those who walk in the lonesome valley, He is the Lily of the Valley, the Rose of Sharon, and the honey in the rock.
- He is a table prepared in the presence of my enemies.

- He is the brightness of God's glory,
- The express image of God's person,
- The King of Glory,
- The pearl of great price,
- The rock in a weary land,
- The cup that runneth over,
- The rod and staff that comfort me,
- And the government of our life is upon His shoulders.
- He is Jesus of Nazareth,
- The Christ,
- The Son of the living God,
- My Savior, my companion, my Lord and King!

Jesus astounds and confounds every expert in every field because . . .

In chemistry, He turned water to wine.
In biology, He was born without the normal conception.
In physics, He disproved the law of gravity when He ascended into heaven.
In economics, He disproved the law of diminishing return by feeding 5,000 men with two fish and five loaves of bread.
In medicine, He cured the sick and blind without administering a single dose of drugs.
He had no servants, yet they called Him Master.
Had no degree, yet they called Him Teacher.
Had no medicine, yet they called Him Healer.
He had no army, yet kings feared Him.
He won no military battles, yet He conquered the world.
He committed no crime, yet they crucified Him.
He was buried in a tomb, yet He lives today!

I want you to be overwhelmed by Jesus. I want Him to knock you off your feet. As a matter of fact, that is exactly what Jesus did in John 18. Jesus had just finished praying in the Garden of Gethsemane. While the disciples slept, Judas was active in his betrayal. He knew where Jesus would be and led the Roman soldiers right to Him.

> So Judas, having obtained the Roman [a]cohort and officers from the chief priests and the Pharisees, came there with lanterns, torches, and weapons. Jesus therefore, knowing all the things that were coming upon Him, came out into the open and said to them, "Whom are you seeking?" They answered Him, "Jesus the Nazarene." He said to them, "I am He." And Judas also, who was betraying Him, was standing with them. Now then, when He said to them, "I am He," they drew back and fell to the ground. (John 18:3–6)

Jesus sent a tremor to the soul when He spoke those two words: "I am." If you are wondering why I say Jesus spoke two words when your Bible has three—"I am He"—it is because "I am" in the Greek is two words (*ego emi*). The English Bible added "He" because "I am" does not make sense to a non-Jew. However, it was a knockdown name to the Jews. The Jew understood "I am" from Exodus 3:14 when God spoke to Moses from the burning bush. When Moses asked, "Whom shall I say sent me?" God identified Himself as "I am." So when Jesus said, "I am," He was saying, "I am God." And at that, the Roman soldiers armed with weapons dropped like bowling pins in His presence.

Notice that verse 3 specifies it was a Roman cohort. A Roman cohort was comprised of 480 soldiers.[3] If Jesus had that kind of authority and power—knocking 481 (I added Judas to the knockdown list) to the ground at His word, He clearly did not have to surrender to them. John included this so that we would know beyond any doubt that Jesus was in control. No man took His life; He willingly laid it down as a sacrifice for you and for me.

I have personally witnessed the power in the name of Jesus. When I was pastoring my first church in Detroit, we brought in a man whom we thought had been saved. He'd even stayed with me in my apartment for a couple of days. One morning, the Holy Spirit said to me, "You need to get rid of this man; he's trying to kill you." Shocked, I called him up at his job (which we had also gotten him) and asked him to meet me at the church before coming back to the apartment. I planned to have some of my big ushers ready at the church.

When he arrived, I told him what the Holy Spirit had spoken to me.

Immediately, his eyes rolled back in his head, and a demonic spirit came out and said, "Ha! I have been commissioned to come here to kill you!" At that point, I thought the big ushers were going to help me. But as this man started advancing toward me, I looked at him and yelled, "Stand back in Jesus' name!" I watched a man who had an assignment straight from hell suddenly have to back away . . . not because of me, my degree, or my ushers, but because of the name of Jesus! There is power in His name!

I still believe His name can knock people down. When God wants to assert His dominion, He will sometimes overwhelm people with His presence. Clearly, John 18 was a demonstration of Jesus' control over the situation. That is why it was almost humorous when Peter later pulled out his dagger and cut off a soldier's ear (see John 18:10). Did he not just see 481 people fall down with two words? What did Peter think his little dagger was going to do? My big ushers were my two little daggers to help me. But the Lord said, "What do you need these men for when you have the name of Jesus to walk you through every situation?"

It is significant to note that prior to this scene in chapter 18, Jesus said "I am" seven times in the book of John, adding what is called an adjectival noun after each. Every time Jesus used one of the "I am" metaphors, He was emphatically stating that He was Yahweh—the great "I am" of Abraham, Isaac, and Jacob. Remember that "I am" is present tense. Not "I was" in the past or "I might be" in the future, but I am *right here* and *right now*.

So let's proceed in our discovery of Jesus by studying what He said about Himself. The phrases He used are much more than just figures of speech. Each of these seven "I am" sayings reveals something specific about His divine nature, His character, or His mission. It also represents a spiritual need of every individual right here and right now.

1. I am the Bread of Life. (John 6:35)
2. I am the Light of the World. (John 8:12)
3. I am the Door (John 10:7)
4. I am the Good Shepherd. (John 10:11)
5. I am the Resurrection and the Life. (11:25)
6. I am the True Vine. (John 15:1)
7. I am the Way, the Truth, and the Life. (John 14:6)

The book of John, where we find each of these names, is the most unique Gospel because it does not start out like the other three Gospels. It takes us back to the beginning . . . the real beginning. It opens with: "In the beginning was the Word, and the Word was with God, and the Word was God" (John 1:1).

That sounds very much like the beginning in Genesis at creation: "In the beginning God created the heavens and the earth" (Genesis 1:1). Yet here is what is astounding: The "in the beginning" of John takes place *before* the "in the beginning" of Genesis. This puts Jesus in a unique category—He was the only person who lived before He was born! There is certainly no one like Him! With that in mind, let's delve into these seven knockdown names of Jesus . . .

1. I AM THE BREAD OF LIFE

Jesus said to them, "I am the bread of life; the one who comes to Me will not be hungry, and the one who believes in Me will never be thirsty." (John 6:35)

Jesus had just miraculously fed 5,000 people with two fish and five loaves. He was at the apex of His popularity. In fact, the crowds wanted to take Him, by force if necessary, and make him their king and get free bread.

Jesus then called Himself the bread of life.

Bread to us is what we get in a little basket before the real meal comes. But in Jesus' day, meat was simply a side dish, and bread represented the main part of the meal. While poorer people used barley and the wealthy used wheat, most everyone had the means to make or buy bread. By using this metaphor, Jesus was saying that He is nourishment and fulfillment, available to everyone.

Jesus is not your pre-meal appetizer; He is your entrée. You do not get a little basket on Sunday and then eat all week in the world. There are many things that can fill us, but only One who can *fulfill* us. Nothing on this planet can fill you up enough so that you have no need of God. Get to the top of anything—pro sports, Broadway, Wall Street, the United Nations, education, medicine, technology—and you will still be left unfulfilled. You were not made to get your fulfillment from the success in this world. You were made for another world. Jesus must be your fulfillment each day.

2. I AM THE LIGHT OF THE WORLD

> Then Jesus again spoke to them, saying, "I am the Light of the world; the one who follows Me will not walk in the darkness, but will have the Light of life." (John 8:12)

The context here was a group of religious people getting ready to stone a woman caught in adultery. Jesus spoke His famous words, "He who is without sin, let him be the first to throw a stone at her." One by one, the men put down their stones. Jesus then said, "I am the Light of the world." Light reveals and exposes. Jesus came to a dark world and suddenly turned on the light with His presence.

I have lived in some crazy homes in the inner city of Detroit. Some of them had roaches. What made your skin crawl was when you turned on the lights all the roaches went running. The light did not create the roaches; it exposed the roaches. In this case, light exposed religion. All the roaches ran when Jesus came as the Light of the world. Religion would have stoned this woman, but Jesus gave her a second chance. Light reveals what sin is—whether an adulterer or a failing religious system.

It is interesting that Jesus did not say "I am" only once in John 8. He kept saying it:

> Then Jesus again spoke to them, saying, "I am the Light of the world; he who follows Me will not walk in the darkness, but will have the Light of life." (verse 12)

> Therefore I said to you that you will die in your sins; for unless you believe that I am, you will die in your sins. (verse 24)

> So Jesus said, "When you lift up the Son of Man, then you will know that I am, and I do nothing on My own, but I say these things as the Father taught Me." (verse 28)

> Jesus said to them, "Truly, truly, I say to you, before Abraham was
> born, I am." (verse 58)

Jesus said "I am," so many times that by the fourth time, they were ready
to stone Him (see verse 59). Every time He said, "I am," He was saying, "I am
God." It is always the case that if you do not submit to God, you have to find
some way to eliminate Him.

Bear in mind that this is the only knockdown name where Jesus insists that
we, too, must become as He is: "You are the light of the world. A city set on
a hill cannot be hidden" (Matthew 5:14). Everywhere we go, we must display
Jesus. How exactly do we shine? Let me give you a picture of this. I grew up
in a Pentecostal church and went to VBS (Vacation Bible School) every sum-
mer. We would memorize verses, for which there were various prizes available. I never won the giant Hershey bar I had my eye on, but one year I did win
a glow-in-the-dark cross. I brought it home, turned off all the lights—and it
was bogus. It did not glow at all. I finally realized that in order for it to glow, it
had to first be exposed to light. It was light—not of its own, but absorbed from
somewhere else—that allowed the cross to glow. Likewise, you cannot glow on
your own, but you can when you are exposed to the Light of the world!

3. I Am the Door

> So Jesus said to them again, "Truly, truly I say to you, I am the door
> of the sheep. All who came before Me are thieves and robbers, but
> the sheep did not listen to them. I am the door; if anyone enters
> through Me, he will be saved, and will go in and out and find pas-
> ture. The thief comes only to steal and kill and destroy; I came so
> that they would have life, and have it abundantly." (John 10:7–10)

No college uses sheep as their mascot. There are no Michigan Sheep or
Ohio State Lambs. Why? Sheep cannot attack. They are the prey. Sheep are
only as strong as their shepherd.

"Door" is a shepherd phrase. There were no doors on sheepfolds. There
would be a wall all around the sheep, except for one spot that was open. That
was where the shepherd would lie down at night and actually call himself the

door. Therefore, a door represents protection. No sheep can get out; no enemy can get in.

When I lived in Detroit, police said that the number one entry point for thieves was the front door of homes.[4] They would kick them in. We need a strong door! Anything that goes in or comes out must go through the Shepherd. I believe that when sheep wander and stray, they cannot do so without having to climb over the Shepherd's convictions and warnings. It is hard to go to hell. You have to work hard to walk away from God.

Here is the good news: My preaching and my prayers are not that strong. But I have a strong door that protects me against the enemy. Some years ago, an airline company was boasting that they were 99 percent safe when it came to flying their aircraft.[5] Not entirely reassuring! But our salvation is 100 percent safe because it is secured in the Lord Jesus Christ. We have a strong door. We have a 100 percent door!

4. I Am the Good Shepherd

I am the good shepherd; the good shepherd lays down His life for
    the sheep. (John 10:11)

In this "I am" noun name, Jesus does something different: He adds "good" to it. "Good" here is a great word. It means excellent.

Sheep are dependent animals. You never graduate from being a sheep. The older you get, the more you realize you need the Good Shepherd. Why? Sheep are prone to wander.

For you were continually straying like sheep, but now you have re-
    turned to the Shepherd and Guardian of your souls. (1 Peter 2:25)

Interestingly, the shepherd's sling was not just for wolves but also for the sheep. Whenever a sheep would start wandering, the shepherd would send a stone in the sheep's direction. It was not to hit the sheep, but the sound would scare the sheep back. At times I have found myself on the verge of making a decision when suddenly I hear a warning. It was the stone of the Shepherd. He was sending me a signal to stop moving forward. It has happened in purchases and in partnerships, in hiring and in friendships. It was the rock to back off.

The Good Shepherd is protecting us from wandering into something that we will regret later. Yield to the sound now instead of having to be rescued later!

5. I Am the Resurrection and the Life

Jesus said to her, "I am the resurrection and the life; the one who believes in Me will live, even if he dies, and everyone who lives and believes in Me will never die." (John 11:25–26)

An elderly church mother in Detroit reminded me of an old adage during one of my moments of frustration: "He may not come when you want Him to, but He's always right on time." Here in John 11, Jesus was going to be right on time. Jesus spoke this to Martha after her brother, Lazarus, died and had been in the grave for four days. What was frustrating to Martha was that Jesus did not come when they called. He did not come on their timetable.

Let me put it another way. It would have been easier for Jesus to come to sick Lazarus, not to dead Lazarus. But sometimes He delays because He would rather resurrect than heal.

Martha knew the Jesus who could heal in time but did not know the Jesus who had authority over the grave and beyond. "The resurrection and the life" means that life is not over when doctors say it's over. There is resurrection and life beyond this life. That is why we do not fear death.

I once watched an intriguing news story where they followed four individuals diagnosed with terminal cancer through to the final months of their lives. All of them grew angrier or full of regret as they were dying—except for one: an old minister from the South. The closer he came to the end, the more joyful he became. They finally asked him how he could have such joy and peace in the midst of everything. I will never forget his response. Though his voice was weak from chemo, he began quoting an old hymn:

"I'm pressing on the upward way, new heights I'm gaining every day; still praying as I onward bound, 'Lord, plant my feet on higher ground.'" He continued all the way to the fourth verse: "I want to scale the utmost height and catch a gleam of glory bright; but still I'll pray till rest I've found, 'Lord, lead me on to higher ground.'" That old preacher had peace because he knew Jesus is the resurrection and the life; He is there beyond the grave!

6. I Am the True Vine

I am the true vine, and My Father is the vinedresser. (John 15:1)

This is from the upper room discourse—the last words of Jesus to His disciples before He went to the cross. Jesus spoke about a unique relationship that He wanted to have with them.

John 15 is Jesus' plan to keep you flourishing and fruit-bearing. Jesus is the vine, and we are the branches. Just as branches are the expression of the vine, your connection to Jesus allows you to express Him. What does this look like? Fruit—the character of Jesus, which exists for the benefit of others. The closer you stay to the vine, the more fruit you bear. Branches cannot boast in and of themselves. They have nothing and can do nothing without another life acting upon them. Remember, there is a difference between work and fruit. A machine can do work, but only life can bear fruit. Work implies labor and effort while the essential idea of fruit is that it is a silent, natural, and restful production. Fruit is the glory of the vine.

Abide means the branch is connected to the vine. That means whatever destroys abiding is your enemy. When you are not abiding, men take over. But when you are abiding, you become a prayer force.

> If anyone does not abide in Me, he is cast out as a branch and is withered; and they gather them and throw them into the fire, and they are burned. If you abide in Me, and My words abide in you, you will ask what you desire, and it shall be done for you. (John 15:6–7 NKJV)

The first thing that happens to the one who is not abiding is that he dries up. Once a person becomes dry, the next step is to be gathered up by the men of this world. In other words, the danger of failing to abide in Christ is that you become flammable. On the few camping trips I have been on, when trying to build a fire, we looked for branches that were disconnected—dead ones lying apart from the tree. We would never go and find a tree and just start breaking off some of its branches. Why? Those branches still had life in them, rendering them unburnable.

Abiding is so essential that Jesus uses the word ten times in six verses (see John 15:4–10). *Abide* is an imperative. You don't have to command a child to eat dessert. You command someone to do something that does not come naturally. In order to abide, we must act. It is not doing more but doing *something*—deliberately being with Jesus.

7. I Am the Way, the Truth, and the Life

> Jesus said to him, 'I am the way, and the truth, and the life; no one comes to the Father except through Me." (John 14:6)

John 13:2 tells us that Jesus said these words during supper. I grew up where the dinner table was important. When the streetlights came on, it was time to come home. At the Dilena table, I learned life, theology, philosophy, and experience. We had debates; we heard bombshells. I saw family fights, splits, people get up and take their pizza home. I don't think it was any mistake that Jesus made the most amazing and controversial statement of His ministry over dinner: "I am the way, the truth, and the life."

Jesus did not say *a* way but *the* way.

Whether you believe it or not, let's at least make sure we know exactly what Jesus is saying here. Jesus is not just one of many ways. He is the *only* way. No one comes to the Father except through Him. The way to God is not by the Ten Commandments, the Golden Rule, ordinances, church membership—it is through Christ and Christ alone. If we can agree that this is what He is saying, that is a good place to start.

> And there is salvation in no one else; for there is no other name under heaven that has been given among mankind by which we must be saved. (Acts 4:12)

This means that Christianity cannot be reconciled with any other religion. Jesus is unique. Other religious leaders say, "Follow me, and I will show you the truth." Jesus says, "I am the truth." Other leaders say, "Follow me, and I will show you many doors that lead to God." Jesus says, "I am the door. Since I am, then follow Me."

The issue is not how many ways lead to God; the issue is that God gave us *the* way to God. We now know how to get to heaven. God made it simple. The problem is that men do not want simplicity; they want autonomy. If there were 1,000 ways to God, we would want 1,001.

When Jesus spoke those words in John 14:6, He was actually addressing Thomas—the apostle whose name, even after two millennia, is synonymous with doubt. Thomas was the last to believe in the resurrection of Jesus, simply unwilling to trust such a magnificent claim secondhand. He needed to see and feel before he would bend his knee to the Christ he knew had been crucified. Ironically, Thomas went on to preach the gospel in India—a land of more than 330 million deities and innumerable "ways to God." Ultimately, Thomas was martyred for believing in the exclusive claims of Christ!

You Get It All

As we study and ponder Jesus through the names He gave Himself, we cannot help but be spiritually disturbed in the most profound way. "What do you think about the Christ?" (Matthew 22:42) must become "What shall I do with Jesus?" (Matthew 27:22).

Years ago, I came across a story about a wealthy man who had an only son whom he loved dearly. He was a lover of art and taught his son to love fine art. Over time, he and his son amassed a valuable private collection of priceless works of art. The son eventually joined the marines and was deployed to Vietnam, where he was killed in action. The father's heart was broken. Several years later, when the wealthy man died, his estate planned to auction off his art collection, estimated to be worth millions of dollars. On the day of the auction, with art dealers anxiously waiting to bid on the Van Goghs and the Monets, the lawyer announced that the deceased had left specific instructions for the portrait of his son to be auctioned off first.

"Get that picture out of the way so we can bid on the real art!" the impatient art dealers complained.

The auctioneer held up the painting. "Who will give me $100 for the picture of the son?"

Silence. Finally, a friend of the son's who was also a soldier said, "I'll give you $20 for it."

"Twenty once," the auctioneer said, looking around the room. "Twenty twice. Sold for $20."

At that moment, the rich man's attorney stepped forward and announced, "Ladies and gentlemen, there will be no more bidding. My client left secret and specific instructions that whoever bought the painting of his son would receive all the other works of art at no additional charge. To quote the words in his last will and testament: 'Whoever chooses my son gets it all.' This concludes the auction."[6]

Whoever chooses God's Son gets it all! I want you to take Jesus. Not a Jesus that you made up, not church, not religion—but the Jesus who called Himself the Bread of Life; the Light of the World; the Door; the Good Shepherd; the Resurrection and the Life; the True Vine; and the Way, the Truth, and the Life! His name is above every other name. Along with Him, you get it all. And just as Romans 10:11 reminds us, "No one who believes in Christ will ever be disappointed!" (TLB).

QUESTIONS

1. Which "I am" name of Jesus is particularly meaningful to you?

2. After reading this chapter, in what capacity do you desire to know Jesus more?

3. Have you personally experienced a name of Jesus not mentioned in this chapter? How did He reveal Himself to you?

KNOWLEDGE

Finding Faith in the Dark

"One of the most wonderful things about knowing God is that there's always so much more to know, so much more to discover. Just when we least expect it, He intrudes into our neat and tidy notions about who He is and how He works."

JONI EARECKSON TADA[1]

My goal in this chapter is to teach you how to walk in the dark. I am sure you have noticed that the times we are living in are growing darker every day. I was recently reading a Fox News article about a popular store that is now allowing an outspoken Satanist designer to sell his clothing line with his quotes on the merchandise. The designer said, "Satan is a symbol of passion, pride, and liberty. He means to you what you need him to mean. So for me, Satan is hope, compassion, equality, and love. So naturally, Satan respects pronouns."[2]

As believers, this ought not to come as a surprise. The book of Jude already gave us an important challenge regarding the last days:

> But remember, dear friends, that the apostles of our Master, Jesus Christ, told us this would happen: "In the last days there will be people who don't take these things seriously anymore. They'll treat them like a joke, and make a religion of their own whims and lusts." These are the ones who split churches, thinking only of themselves.

There's nothing to them, no sign of the Spirit!

But you, dear friends, carefully build yourselves up in this most holy faith by praying in the Holy Spirit. (Jude 1:17–20 MSG)

We must build our faith in the last days, so the letter *K* is for faith. Yes, I can spell. Let me take you on a journey to show you why *K* is faith.

There are four places in the book of Matthew where Jesus rebuked His disciples for their little faith.

1. When they worried about provision and tomorrow

In the Sermon on the Mount, Jesus said these words:

But if God so clothes the grass of the field, which is alive today and tomorrow is thrown into the furnace, will He not much more clothe you? You of little faith! (Matthew 6:30)

2. When they got caught in a storm and felt Jesus was uninvolved in their crisis

As the storm hit, Jesus was sleeping in the boat. Of course, Jesus was there *in* the boat with them!

He said to them, "Why are you afraid, you men of little faith?" Then He got up and rebuked the winds and the sea, and it became perfectly calm. (Matthew 8:26)

3. When Peter sank after walking on water

At Jesus' word, Peter got out of the boat and began walking on the water toward Him—until he saw the wind and became frightened.

Immediately Jesus reached out with His hand and took hold of him, and said to him, "You of little faith, why did you doubt?" (Matthew 14:31)

4. When the disciples misinterpreted the words of Jesus

Jesus told them to beware of the leaven of the Pharisees, leaving the disciples confused.

Jesus, aware of this, said, "You men of little faith, why are you

discussing among yourselves the fact that you have no bread?"
(Matthew 16:8)

In all these cases, Jesus was saying to them: "You need faith to fight these battles." You need faith to fight anxiety about provision and about tomorrow. You need faith to know God cares, believing that He is attentive and present in every storm. You need faith to believe God is able to help you move forward—to take the next step even when the ground is not solid. You need faith to know God's voice—when He speaks and how He speaks. Little faith is a huge problem when you are dealing with tomorrow, provision, the future, storms, and the voice of God. All these things need strong faith.

Faith is believing God despite appearances and obeying God despite the consequences.

Now back to the big question: How is *K* faith, when faith starts with an *F*? The reason is because faith is grounded in the *knowledge* of God. Little faith is the result of believing in a little god. Great faith has a great God; small faith has a small god. Every battle is a test of faith, and every test of faith is a challenge as to how big your God is.

The knowledge of God is the key ingredient of faith. That is what determines how big your God is.

Today I believe many younger people are losing the battle for their soul because we have mistakenly built a church on discovering who *you* are instead of who *God* is. You knowing you is not going to get you through any battle. But you knowing God will lead to victory! The business of why we meet for church is not so that we can *be* somebody; we are meant to *know* somebody! Understanding this is imperative to fight the good fight. Battles are surely coming. I remember a young man who came to the Lord in our church in Detroit. He had a charismatic personality and was loved by everyone. After being saved for about six months, he came to me and said, "I've been praying, and the Lord has spoken to me. He told me that I'm done with battles. I've graduated and have no more battles to deal with."

"Are you dying?" I asked. "Because we only have no more battles when we're dead!"

In the Christian life, battles are inevitable. Look at the following battle verses. Do you see a common theme in the fight?

> Consider it all joy, my brothers and sisters, when you encounter
> various trials, knowing that the testing of your faith produces en-
> durance. (James 1:2–3)

> In all this you greatly rejoice, though now for a little while you may
> have had to suffer grief in all kinds of trials. These have come so that
> the proven genuineness of your faith—of greater worth than gold,
> which perishes even though refined by fire—may result in praise,
> glory and honor when Jesus Christ is revealed. (1 Peter 1:6–7 NIV)

Remember also how Jesus prayed for Peter before his denial:

> Simon, Simon, behold, Satan has demanded to sift you men like
> wheat; but I have prayed for you, that your faith will not fail; and
> you, when you have turned back, strengthen your brothers. (Luke
> 22:31–32)

It is evident from these verses that every battle is a faith fight. If the foundation of faith is the knowledge of God, then the goal of the demonic fight is to
twist, skew, distort, and misrepresent who God is.

When your faith is being tested, it is your knowledge of God that is being
challenged. When your vision of who God is gets blurry, the battle will be lost.
Therefore, keep this in mind: Do not just try to get more faith. Rather, pursue
knowing God more. Pursuing the knowledge of God is part of boot camp for
the battle; it will equip you to walk in dark times.

We all have a responsibility to grow in the knowledge of God. As we see in
Peter's last epistle, following fast on the heels of grace is the knowledge of God:

> But grow in the grace and knowledge of our Lord and Savior Jesus
> Christ. To Him be the glory, both now and to the day of eternity.
> Amen. (2 Peter 3:18)

Bear in mind that Peter was writing to Christians who were also living in
very dark times; many were even hunted and killed for their faith. Receiving
an exhortation to grow in the knowledge of God means that we do not know
enough about God.

So where do we get the knowledge of God? From the Bible! We simply cannot neglect the Word of God. My wife and I were recently in the Zurich Airport going through security, and in front of us was the duty-free shop with hundreds of boxes of cigarettes. Cindy looked at me and said, "Incredible. Bigger than the brand names is the warning 'SMOKING KILLS' in huge letters! Yet people don't read it. They still buy the cigarettes and run the risk of dying of cancer."

Likewise, we must read the Word, or it will be deadly to our faith! The Bible is where we get to know God. The more we read it, the more our faith is strengthened. The book of Romans tells us that "faith comes by hearing, and hearing by the word of God" (Romans 10:17 NKJV). Faith comes as you respond to God's revelation, believing what God reveals about Himself.

Notice that the Bible does not just say "believe" but "believe in the Lord Jesus Christ" (Acts 16:31). It does not just say "have faith" but "have faith in God" (Mark 11:22). Faith is not some abstract hope or attitude. Biblical faith always depends upon its object. Your faith is only as great as the God you believe in. We have a great God as the object of our faith.

WHEN IT GETS DARK

How exactly does Satan attack your faith? Remember, the demonic tactic is to twist and distort the biblical view of who God is. And the greatest attacks on our thoughts about God come when we are walking in darkness.

> Who is among you who fears the LORD,
> Who obeys the voice of His servant,
> Who walks in darkness and has no light?
> Let him trust in the name of the LORD and rely on his God.
> Behold, all you who kindle a fire,
> Who encircle yourselves with flaming arrows,
> Walk in the light of your fire
> And among the flaming arrows you have set ablaze.
> This you will have from My hand:
> You will lie down in torment.
> (Isaiah 50:10–11)

Here is what may be confusing: Look at who is in the dark. It is the one who is obedient and fears the Lord! This is not a backslider being disciplined; this is the godly having his faith challenged.

C. S. Lewis was engaged in that faith fight as his wife was dying of cancer right before his eyes. He kept a journal during that time, which was not meant to be published, and it is one of the rawest pieces of literature I have ever read. He wrote: "Not that I am (I think) in much danger of ceasing to believe in God. The real danger is of coming to believe such dreadful things about Him. The conclusion I dread is not 'So there's no God after all,' but 'So this is what God's really like.'"3

Those of greatest devotion may know the deepest darkness. So what do you do when the lights go out? There is an old hymn that gets me through those dark times when I find my faith being challenged—when God is hard to see. It is called "My Hope Is Built on Nothing Less."

My hope is built on nothing less
Than Jesus' blood and righteousness;
I dare not trust the sweetest frame,
But wholly lean on Jesus' name.

On Christ, the solid rock, I stand;
All other ground is sinking sand,
All other ground is sinking sand.

When darkness veils His lovely face
I rest on His unchanging grace;
In every high and stormy gale,
My anchor holds within the veil.4

The chorus is a declaration of the knowledge of God. When darkness seems to hide His face, we must rely on what we know about God. It reminds me of a story about the most decorated Olympic athlete, Michael Phelps. Twenty-three of the twenty-eight medals he has won are gold. Let me tell you about my favorite gold medal. His coach, Bob Bowman, went to great lengths to give Phelps extensive knowledge of the pool and his strokes—to the point of even sabotaging his equipment. He would poke a hole in the goggles but make him continue to swim. He would turn out the lights so Phelps would have to swim in the dark. The outcome? Phelps knew the strokes, the pool, and the wall like the back of his hand.

It was 9:56 a.m. at the Beijing Olympics, and Phelps stood behind his starting block, bouncing slightly on his toes. When his name was announced, Phelps stepped onto the block and swung his arms three times as he had before every race since he was twelve years old. He got into his stance and, when the gun sounded, leapt. Phelps knew that something was wrong as soon as he hit the water. There was moisture inside his goggles. He couldn't tell if they were leaking from the top or bottom, but as he broke the water's surface and began swimming, he hoped the leak would not become too bad. By the second turn, however, everything was getting blurry. As he approached the third turn and final lap, the cups of his goggles were completely filled. Phelps later said he couldn't see anything—not the line along the pool's bottom, not the black *T* marking the approaching wall. But at that moment, all the training kicked in!

On that last lap, Phelps estimated how many strokes the final push would require—twenty-one—so he started counting. At eighteen strokes, he began anticipating the wall. He could hear the crowd roaring, but since he was blind, he had no idea if they were cheering for him or someone else. Nineteen strokes, then twenty. He made a twenty-first huge stroke, glided with his arm outstretched, and touched the wall. He had timed it perfectly. When he ripped off his goggles and looked up at the scoreboard, it said "WR"—world record—next to his name. He had won another gold![5]

When we are in the dark, we must, as Isaiah said, "trust in the name of the Lord and rely on his God" (Isaiah 50:10). Trusting in the name of the Lord is trusting in His character—everything we have studied in boot camp. That is swimming with water in your goggles! Those who have been trained do not merely sit around asking, "Why are the lights out?" or "What did I do to deserve this?" No, those who have been trained move forward in the darkness, living not by explanations but by their knowledge of God and His promises they have embraced.

Let me sum up some things I have learned about those times of darkness— when you want to believe but you do not see God:

1. Let God Define God

The best place to go in dark times is the Word of God, not your own mind. Look at verse one of that hymn again:

My hope is built on nothing less
Than Jesus' blood and righteousness;
I dare not trust the sweetest frame,
But wholly lean on Jesus' name.

What does "sweetest frame" mean? Think of the phrase "frame of mind." We cannot lean on our emotions in good or bad times. Many people believe in themselves and incorrectly define who God is because of their frame of mind. We must remain in the Word and believe what God says about Himself!

2. Feed on His Faithfulness

Trust in the Lord, and do good;
Dwell in the land, and feed on His faithfulness.
(Psalm 37:3 NKJV)

Faith is trusting in God's faithfulness—or in other words, His consistency. Faithfulness does not happen from one good act. You do not call a spouse faithful in a marriage if he or she avoided temptation one time. God is who He is every moment of every day. God is reliable and constant, and we can therefore depend on Him. We rest on His unchanging grace! Since God does not change, our faith does not change if our faith is in Him. Feed on His faithfulness by finding examples of His consistency in the Word and meditating on testimonies of His faithfulness in your own life.

3. Follow the Tracks of the Past

Have you ever heard of a whiteout? It is a winter word. It is when there is so much wind and snow that you are left with practically no visibility. All you can do is follow the car tracks ahead of you. When you feel like you cannot see God at all, remember that there are others who have gone ahead of you who have laid down tracks you can follow. Just look for the people who have made it through the storm.

4. Get Ready to See Things You Have Never Seen Before

There are things you cannot see in the sunlight and can only see in the dark. The stars are always there, but we can only see them at night. Did you know that many of the stars we see are actually more than 1,000 times farther away than the sun? In the light we see clearly, but in the dark we see farthest. And if right now your sun has set, there is good news: A sunrise is coming!

Even in darkness light dawns for the upright. (Psalm 112:4 NIV)

Yes, those night fights are valuable. From dark clouds we get precious water. From dark mines we get precious stones. And from our darkest trials come the greatest discoveries of what God has placed within us. In fact, it is often the case that the deeper you go in God, the darker and more intense the pressure around you grows. Thankfully, God has well-equipped you.

In *Unhappy Secrets of the Christian Life*, the authors recountd how a nuclear submarine called the *Thresher* went too deep into the sea and collapsed under the weight of the water. The submarine was crushed into such tiny bits in the ensuing implosion that almost nothing could be identified by rescue teams. You see, a submarine needs thick steel bulkheads to withstand the pressure of the water as it descends. However, there are few walls that can be built to withstand the pressure of the deepest oceans; even steel can give way as the crew of the *Thresher* tragically discovered.[6]

Yet in the same deep waters that crush steel submarines, how is it that little fish swim without a care in the world? You never see crushed fish except in sushi. What is their secret? Are they made of some new indestructible iron we should be using for our submarines? No, they possess a layer of skin so thin that it is measured in micrometers. But what the little fish do have is an internal pressure system that perfectly corresponds to the pressure they are faced with from without. God gave them what they need to swim in deep places!

You and I can spend our lives building walls to keep out temptation, but the pressure will eventually crush us. That is why God has given us what the fish have—a power inside that corresponds to the pressure on the outside.

Greater is He who is in you than he who is in the world.
(1 John 4:4)

An ideology and worldview that removes God cannot withstand the pressure of dark times. But you cannot squeeze a Christian if God is in him! I therefore encourage you with the words of Paul: "Fight the good fight of faith" (1 Timothy 6:12). Stay in the Word, and pursue the knowledge of God. Know His faithfulness, His lovingkindness, His justice, His righteousness, His holiness . . . and watch your faith grow!

QUESTIONS

1. What promises or personal experiences have taught you about God and have built up your faith?

2. Have you had any personal experiences that you feel have decreased your faith? What does God's Word have to say regarding those experiences?

3. What is something that you need faith for right now? How can you increase your knowledge of God in that area?

LOVE

God Is Love

"Love is not only something you feel,
it is something you do."
DAVID WILKERSON[1]

Definitions are important. They offer us a starting point. They direct and guide us, showing us how to view the world and live in it. Unfortunately, many definitions are getting blurry today because of sin. When is the unborn considered a child in the mother's womb? What is marriage? What is truth?

And the most important definition: What is love?

The word *love* is the most important word in the human language, yet it is hard for us to define. People say: I love my family. I love my wife. I love my job. I love my church. I love my dog. I love your hair. But how exactly would you define love? Remember, definitions guide and direct us. If our definition of love is incorrect, we will get further off course the longer we live by that flawed understanding. It will affect our relationships with people as well as with God.

I have tens of thousands of books in my library. I have read a lot, and although love is often talked about, nowhere does anyone seem to give an adequate definition of love.

So what is love? Let's see what the Bible says.

"God is love" (1 John 4:8). It is one of the greatest descriptions of God. And although it is completely true, some specifics would be helpful. Of course, the Bible does not disappoint. In fact, the Bible dedicates an entire chapter to defining love:

If I speak in the tongues of men or of angels, but do not have love, I am only a resounding gong or a clanging cymbal. If I have the gift of prophecy and can fathom all mysteries and all knowledge, and if I have a faith that can move mountains, but do not have love, I am nothing. If I give all I possess to the poor and give over my body to hardship that I may boast, but do not have love, I gain nothing.

Love is patient, love is kind. It does not envy, it does not boast, it is not proud. It does not dishonor others, it is not self-seeking, it is not easily angered, it keeps no record of wrongs. Love does not delight in evil but rejoices with the truth. It always protects, always trusts, always hopes, always perseveres.

Love never fails. But where there are prophecies, they will cease; where there are tongues, they will be stilled; where there is knowledge, it will pass away. For we know in part and we prophesy in part, but when completeness comes, what is in part disappears. When I was a child, I talked like a child, I thought like a child, I reasoned like a child. When I became a man, I put the ways of childhood behind me. For now we see only a reflection as in a mirror; then we shall see face to face. Now I know in part; then I shall know fully, even as I am fully known.

And now these three remain: faith, hope and love. But the greatest of these is love. (1 Corinthians 13:1–13 NIV)

Let's pause at the last part: "When I was a child . . ." It is important that Paul included this in the chapter. It is a call to put away childish views of love—a call to retire your high school letterman jacket and start acting like an adult in relationships, defining love in the correct, grown-up 1 Corinthians 13 way.

The problem is that we often confuse *love* with *like*. Like is emotion. Love is action. We want the feeling because we want to like what we love. But love is often a decision before it is a feeling. In 1 Corinthians 13 and throughout the New Testament, love is more of a verb than a noun. You can love what you do not like. God knew He could not command a feeling, but He can command us to act. Do something first, feel something second. The great fifteenth-century writer Thomas à Kempis said it best: "Whoever loves much does much."[2]

I was once doing a marital counseling session where the husband told me, "I don't love my wife anymore."

"The Bible tells us: 'Husbands, love your wives,'" I explained.

"I don't see her as my wife anymore," he objected. "I see her as nothing but a person I live with. We are just in the same house."

"Okay, but Jesus said, 'Love your neighbor.' So you still have to love her."

And then he thought he had me. "I hate her! We can't get along."

"Well, Jesus also said, 'Love your enemies!'"

It doesn't matter what category you put your spouse in—you must love him or her. If love is a command, then we have destroyed marriage by defining love as a feeling. You cannot leave a marriage simply because you do not feel love for someone. God wants to do something in your heart. Whether you want to call them your spouse, your neighbor, or your enemy, Jesus can help you to love if you make the choice. Biblical love starts with a decision that can turn into an emotion. Doing before feeling.

One of the most well-known verses in the Bible is John 3:16:

> For God so loved the world that He gave His only begotten Son, that whoever believes in Him should not perish but have everlasting life. (NKJV)

With that in mind, now look at what John said in his later epistle. Since God so loves us, this ought to be our response:

> This is how we know what love is: Jesus Christ laid down his life for us. And we ought to lay down our lives for our brothers and sisters. (1 John 3:16 NIV)

God's love to you must now come *through* you. If we have received God's love, we are not meant to be a pond. We are a river. God's love comes to us so that it can flow through us. We have been saved to do something—to love God and love people.

Look at Jesus' response to a man who asked Him what the greatest commandment is:

> Jesus said to him, "'You shall love the LORD your God with all your heart, with all your soul, and with all your mind.' This is the first

and great commandment. And the second is like it: 'You shall love your neighbor as yourself.'" (Matthew 22:37–39 NKJV)

In my studies of other religions, I know of no other religion in the world besides Christianity and Judaism that exhorts its people to *love* God. Obey God, yes. But never to love God with all your heart, mind, and soul. That was Jesus' challenge to His people. If we believe God loves us, our response is that we love God. First John 4:19 says, "We love, because He first loved us."

The Bible also says that whoever believes in the Son has eternal life:

If you confess with your mouth Jesus as Lord, and believe in your heart that God raised Him from the dead, you will be saved. (Romans 10:9)

It does not specify that you must believe with all your heart. It just says to believe in your heart, and you will have eternal life. Could it be that God leaves room for doubt in the beginning of coming to faith? On the other hand, when it comes to loving God, the command is to love with all your heart, all your soul, and all your mind! He cannot let anything get in the way.

The grave danger lies in the church being full of *believers* in God but not *lovers* of God. Believing and knowing all the rules yet lacking passion and extravagant love for the beauty of Jesus is what causes legalism and religion. I cannot think of anything more harmful to me than to live with my wife but not be in love with her. One can do all the husband things but have it all just be a form. When you are not in love, the conversation is shallow and limited. But when you are in love, there is talk and there is praise. When we are not lovers of God, the church eventually becomes like a gathering of twenty-first-century teenagers—we only come out of our rooms when we want something.

Notice that Paul began the love chapter by explaining that without love, your effectiveness as a church is not diminished; rather, it is eliminated (see 1 Corinthians 13:1–3). Tongues is not a sign of love; neither is prophecy. You can have heaven on the tongue but hell in the heart. You can even give all your money to charities or be burned as a martyr but still gain nothing.

The Bible also warns us that in the last days, "because of the increase of wickedness, the love of most will grow cold" (Matthew 24:12 NIV). But the contrast in the last days will be Christians who do love.

By this everyone will know that you are my disciples, if you love
one another. (John 13:35 NIV)

Though the love of many will grow cold, I want to be among the few whose
love is on fire. If that is your desire as well, let's first take a little test. Since God
is love, when you read 1 Corinthians 13, you can insert God's name in place of
love. God is patient, God is kind, God does not envy . . . But the challenge is:
Can you substitute *your* name in there?

I heard Adrian Rogers once say: "When you teach people their rights, you
have a revolution. When you teach people their responsibilities, you have a revival."[3] We have responsibilities clearly laid out for us in 1 Corinthians 13.

Now as we go through God's definition of love in this chapter, notice that it
does not involve anything physical, sensual, emotional, or the feeling of butter-
flies in your stomach. It is about obedience. These are all decisions before they
become emotive. When we make the choice to act the way God wants us to, we
will find His divine help. This is especially critical in a world that is growing
cold in love.

So let's take a more detailed look at 1 Corinthians 13 to discover our responsibilities as Spirit-filled believers.

1. Love Is Patient

Patience waits. Patience defers. Patience puts others first. When you have
patience, you do not rush people with tapping feet and annoyed exhales.
Instead, you are willing to wait until they get it. My natural instinct is to believe you should be where I am right now. But patience says, "I will wait for you
to get there."

Because God is love, God is patient. Look at Peter's description of God:

The Lord is not slow about His promise, as some count slowness,
but is patient toward you, not willing for any to perish, but for all
to come to repentance. (2 Peter 3:9)

God is giving everyone space and time to change. We tend to want everyone on a schedule, but God is willing to give us grace to be patient in our marriage, with our children, and with others' spiritual growth.

I was reading the story of one of the most prominent and outspoken atheists over the centuries named Robert Ingersoll. At the end of all his lectures, he would open his pocket watch and put it on the lectern for his audience to see, declaring, "I will give God five minutes to strike me dead for all the things I said to disprove Him." Uncomfortable silence would ensue as he would count off each minute. When the five minutes were over, he would shut the watch and say, "God did not retaliate because God does not exist."

One day, sitting in one of those lectures was an evangelist named Theodore Parker. When Parker was asked about this antic of Ingersoll, his response was classic: "And did the gentleman think he could exhaust the patience of the eternal God in five minutes?"[4]

God is bigger than our threats and our foolishness. Thank God for His patience!

2. Love Is Kind

Kindness is a powerful tool. Kindness is love's response to somebody who is weak or disadvantaged. For example, weakness might be needing to ask for financial assistance—whether from a relative or a bank. When someone is weak, they can either be manipulated and exploited, or they can be shown kindness.

Something as simple as a uniform can present an opportunity for people to exploit or control others. You can be working as a TSA checkpoint agent, and suddenly you are given control over people's future—whether they will get on the plane or not.

Kindness is the decision to do for others what they cannot do for themselves in that moment. Someone said it like this: "When we are kind, we put our strength, abilities, and resources on loan to someone who lacks them." Now if there were anyone who could easily exploit or manipulate others, it would be God. After all, we humans are just made of dust! Thank God He is kind.

> Just as parents are kind
>   to their children,
> the Lord is kind
>   to all who worship him,

because he knows
  we are made of dust.
(Psalm 103:13–14 CEV)

Our LORD, everything you do
  is kind and thoughtful.
(Psalm 145:17 CEV)

Or do you think lightly of the riches of His kindness and restraint
and patience, not knowing that the kindness of God leads you to
repentance? (Romans 2:4)

When we are at a disadvantage, God intervenes with His kindness and
power. He does so in order to draw us to Himself, knowing that we cannot
and will not start moving on our own. Time and again, He extends kindness
to us—until we finally acknowledge that the One who got us through it all was
God Himself!

One Sunday in 1987, I experienced one of the most surreal things in
my life. I was living in Detroit, and I went to drop off a pastor friend at the
Detroit Metropolitan Airport. I wasn't even home yet when I heard on the
radio that Northwest Flight 255 crashed right on the I-94 in Detroit. My mind
immediately began to race—what was happening? Was that pastor on there?
Thankfully he wasn't. But tragically, the plane was not even 300 feet off the
ground when it plummeted—right onto the section of the I-94 that I drove by
on my way home.

One hundred fifty-four people on the flight were killed. What is incredible,
however, is that there were 155 people on that flight. One survivor remains
today. Her name is Cecilia; she was only four years old at the time. When
they found her, they could not believe she was alive. It was later learned that
Cecilia's mom—knowing that the plane was going down—grabbed Cecilia and
wrapped her arms around her. It was her mom's embrace that saved four-year-
old Cecilia's life.[5]

That is exactly what the kindness of God did for every one of us. He knew
what was happening; He knew where we would end up because of sin. But He
said, "You're mine. I've got you. I don't want you going down." He stepped in
and embraced us. It is because of His kindness that we are saved.

3. Love Does Not Envy, Boast, nor Is It Proud

Paul grouped these three together: envy, boasting, and pride. This trio is toxic in all relationships. They usually show up when someone does better or receives more than you. Pay close attention to your reaction to the success of those closest to you.

R. T. Kendall said to me a few months ago, "I am going to give you the definition of a friend." He proceeded to speak from Romans 12:15: "Rejoice with those who rejoice, and weep with those who weep."

It is much easier to weep with someone than to rejoice with someone. A friend is not merely someone who can feel bad when you feel bad. It is someone who can rejoice with you when you are blessed and successful. That is the true test.

Think about it—can you rejoice with someone else? When they tell you about their success, do you try to trump them with a story of your own? Or do you remain quiet and simply be happy for them? Pride is what keeps us from celebrating what others have accomplished.

If God is love, then God does not boast, He does not envy, and He is not proud. God doesn't need to. Unfortunately, I can remember a horrible boasting moment in my life. When we lived in Detroit, my son was playing Little League, and I was coaching. I was doing batting practice with the kids, and one of the dads offered to help. But I had been a very good high school baseball player—I batted 400; I knew what I was doing. So I told him to go stand against the fence, and I would send kids to him later (after I imparted my great knowledge to them, of course).

So he did. He went and stood against the fence. I would work my expertise with the kids, and then I would send them over to him. Later as we were leaving, I overheard his son telling my son, "My dad played for the San Francisco Giants and Cincinnati Reds. He's been playing in Major League Baseball for twelve years!" It turns out that he was a two-sport all-American at Stanford! He took over John Elway's position as starting quarterback and was later drafted as a catcher by the Yankees . . . and I told him to stand against the fence because I got this?!

He never told me who he was. Someone else did.

God will stay on the fence until you acknowledge who He is. Perhaps you may think you are something else with your high school batting average. But you have a superstar God waiting for you to call Him off the fence! And He is so humble that He waits for you.

C. S. Lewis called it "Divine Humility" and said this: "It is a poor thing to strike our colors to God when the ship is going down under us; a poor thing to come to Him as a last resort, to offer up 'our own' when it is no longer worth keeping. If God were proud He would hardly have us on such terms: but He is not proud . . . He will have us even though we have shown that we prefer everything else to Him."[6]

4. Love Honors

To understand this, let me pose a question. The closest I have been to a house fire was when I was in Detroit and the house next to us burned down. Our house was evacuated, but I was still sleeping. They had to send the firemen to get me. I finally ran out into the street with my pajamas on.

Now here is the question: You are awakened to your house on fire; what do you save first? (What item, not person.) A ring? An heirloom? Now think about how you would feel if someone mishandled that very item, treating it casually.

Protection is central to honor. We protect things we value. In fact, Paul used that word later when he said in verse 7: "It always protects." (NIV). Honor is expressed through protection. If I honor you, I protect your character and your reputation. I guard your purity and virginity if we are dating. Honor always handles the person as valuable.

When we got married, Cindy and I had a table painted with a picture of us. That thing was a prized possession done by our friend, Jeanette. We would not put anything on it. But after a while, we started putting our laundry basket and coffee cups on it. And now I am not even sure where it is.

When there is dishonor, we have lost sight of value. The work in relationships is to not allow something valuable to become the place you dump your trash and junk on!

5. Love Is Not Self-Seeking

When I am counseling a couple in a crisis, this is one of the first questions I ask: "Do you love Jesus, and are you willing to love what He loves and hate what He hates? He hates divorce. Are you willing to do whatever it takes to do it God's way with your marriage?"

If they are willing, no matter the issue, it always works out. It is hard work, but it is worth it. If it does not work out, then someone has his or her own agenda.

Love is not self-seeking. It does not have its own agenda. Love says, "You go before me. I want you to be first." It means that I prefer you over me. What you need comes before what I need. It is not, "Why don't you support my dream?" but rather, "What can I do to make your dream come to pass?"

A person's disobedience does not have to make me be disobedient. If they don't do their part, that does not relieve me of doing my part. "You speak well to me, then I will speak well back to you" is not love. Love says, "It does not matter what your response is. I want you to receive the compliment and the encouragement first." Love does not wait until the other person gives before they give. Many do not realize that marriage is not 50/50, give and take. Marriage is 100/100, give and give!

6. Love Is Not Easily Angered

Love does not have a short fuse. Love does not react; love responds.

In today's society, it does not take much to have a conversation blow up. Talk police, politics, racism, abortion, religion, and you are at risk. If there is a topic that brings heat to the talk in your house, do not avoid the topic. Search your heart. The person who is easily angered blames others but fails to look within his or her own heart. Blame is lame.

Love is not easily angered. Anger is a selfish response. When you are yelling, you are revealing that you have a love issue. You love yourself more than the other person. Blowing off steam is only for your benefit, and everyone else gets the brunt of it. So if you are angry and yelling, stop and apologize. Then ask God to deal with your love issue.

7. Love Does Not Keep Records of Wrongs

I was once at a funeral and watched a woman pull out a forty-three-year-old letter from a preacher that she was still angry about. People who keep records of what others have done to them never seem to keep records of the wrongs *they* have done! It is always one-sided.

Someone once suggested that love does not forgive and forget, but rather remembers and still forgives. "I forgive you" is harder to say than "I am sorry." To say "I forgive you" means that you have shut the chapter on the issue and it is never reopened. It becomes off limits.

> Whoever would foster love covers over an offense,
>> but whoever repeats the matter separates close friends.
> (Proverbs 17:9 NIV)

If you do bring something back up again, you did not actually forgive; you just filed it away for later. A big lie is that "time heals all wounds." Time does not heal wounds. Apologies and forgiveness do!

8. Love Does Not Rejoice in Unrighteousness but Rejoices in Truth

I vividly remember almost forty-five years ago reading the Bible as a young man and coming across this verse in Isaiah: "Woe to those who call evil good, and good evil; who substitute darkness for light and light for darkness; who substitute bitter for sweet and sweet for bitter!" (Isaiah 5:20). I was stunned because it seemed so unrealistic. How could people call evil good and good evil? There is no way men would substitute darkness for light and light for darkness. Fast-forward to the present, and it's here—we are living in that time that Isaiah prophesied about almost 2,700 years ago.

We have substituted "my truth" for *the* truth. We live in a culture that celebrates anyone's and everyone's truth. There is no moral compass anymore; we have entered the time that the book of Judges described as "everyone did what was right in his own eyes" (Judges 21:25). What is interesting about the writer's description of the times he lived in was that he attached a phrase prior to the description: "In those days there was no king in Israel" (verse 25). When there is no king, there is no truth. Men establish their own truth. We did not realize that when we removed God, we removed truth, leaving people to come up with their own standards of right and wrong. The great Russian author Dostoevsky summed it up when he said: "If there is no God, everything is permitted."[7] That was the book of Judges, and that is the world we live in today.

In contrast, Paul said that love does not rejoice in unrighteousness but rejoices in truth. Somehow love finds truth in the midst of the malaise of unrighteousness. So how does love keep from falling into despondency when it seems there is more unrighteousness than truth? Thankfully, God has purposed to always have a remnant of truth in uncertain times. There will be Daniels in Babylon. There will be Esthers and Mordecais in Persia. There will be Pauls in Rome. There will be Moseses in Egypt. Darkness can never overcome the light but must flee at even the single candle of a righteous life. There is a great deal of unrighteousness in today's music, government, entertainment, politics, and schools—but truth can always rise to the top in those environments, for truth is a flame burning in the darkness. That makes me rejoice.

9. Love Bears All Things, Believes All Things, Hopes All Things, and Endures All Things

Paul finished his epic definition of love with a battery of optimistic declarations. He reminded us that in a depressed and despondent world, love can dominate by bearing all things, believing all things, hoping all things, and enduring all things. In essence, love is left standing while everyone else gives up. I believe that is why Paul summed up bears, believes, hopes, and endures with "love never fails" (1 Corinthians 13:8).

Love finds a way to cling to Romans 8:28: "And we know that God causes all things to work together for good to those who love God, to those who are called according to His purpose." Love can bear, believe, and endure because love sees God working all things together for good. First Corinthians 13:7–8 holds true because Romans 8:28 is written for us. First Corinthians 13 is my attitude in "all things" as God is working out the "all things" of Romans 8.

When I read about God working out all things for good, it brings me back to my days of being single and having to cook for myself. When I was trying to do for myself what my mom used to do for me, it just didn't make sense. I remember taking a store-bought cake mix, following the directions, and feeling puzzled. How did I eat my mom's cake with the ingredients I am being asked to put into the mix? Eggs are not sweet. Flour is not sweet. Oil is not sweet. Yet they are all part of the recipe. Then comes the 350-degree oven, which is definitely not comfortable but an essential part of these things working together. Yes, love can bear. Love can believe. Love can hope. Love can endure. It is all because God is the master chef who takes every sweet and bitter experience of our lives—perhaps adding some heat and a furnace occasionally—mixes it all together, and brings out good. Love never fails!

QUESTIONS

1. Think of how you defined love before you became a believer. How does that definition differ from the biblical definition of love?

2. What are some ways 1 Corinthians 13 love has been shown to you?

3. Is there someone in your life whom you are struggling to forgive? How can you show them love today?

MONEY

When The Windows of Heaven Are Opened, the Blessings of God Are Poured Out

"Tell me what you think about money, and I will tell you what you think about God, for these two are closely related. A man's heart is closer to his wallet than anything else . . . If a person gets his attitude toward money straight, it will help straighten out almost every other area in his life."

BILLY GRAHAM[1]

What is the fear of Lord? I do not believe the fear of the Lord has anything to do with being afraid or scared. Rather, the fear of the Lord is the awareness of God's constant presence in my life as well as an awareness of eternity. When you fear the Lord, you will fear nothing else. Let's look at some of the rewards for those who fear the Lord:

And by the fear of the LORD one keeps away from evil. (Proverbs 16:6)

The fear of the LORD prolongs life. (Proverbs 10:27)

In the fear of the LORD there is strong confidence, and his children will have refuge. (Proverbs 14:26)

The LORD confides in those who fear him; he makes his covenant known to them. (Psalm 25:14 NIV)

The angel of the LORD encamps around those who fear him,
    and he delivers them.
(Psalm 34:7 NIV)

The fear of the LORD is a fountain of life,
    turning a person from the snares of death.
(Proverbs 14:27 NIV)

But from everlasting to everlasting
    the LORD's love is with those who fear him,
    and his righteousness with their children's children.
(Psalm 103:17 NIV)

Fear the LORD, you his godly people,
    for those who fear him will have all they need." (
Psalm 34:9 NLT)

The fear of the LORD is the beginning of wisdom;
    all who follow his precepts have good understanding.
(Psalm 111:10 NIV)

By humility and the fear of the LORD
Are riches and honor and life.
(Proverbs 22:4 NKJV)

The fear of the LORD leads to life,
So that one may sleep satisfied, untouched by evil.
(Proverbs 19:23)

You get to sleep at night, meaning the fear of the Lord is better than a pill or essential oils! None of us can deny that since the rewards are massive, we ought to be a people who fear the Lord. I began to ask: How can I learn to fear the Lord? Perhaps you may consider it a strange way to discover the fear of the Lord, but this is what I found in the book of Deuteronomy:

You shall surely tithe all the produce from what you sow, which comes from the field every year. You shall eat in the presence of the LORD your God, at the place where He chooses to establish His name, the tithe of your grain, your new wine, your oil, and the first-born of your herd and your flock, so that you may learn to fear the LORD your God always. (Deuteronomy 14:22–23)

Do you want the fear of the Lord in your life? Then do not simply ask for it, do something for it! Tithing answers the prayer for learning the fear of the Lord. But how do these two go together? It is helpful to know that another word for tithing is *stewardship*. Stewardship is not about raising money; it is about raising Christians who willingly trust God and fear the Lord.

There is an amazing song in Revelation that is sung around the throne. Look at its lyrics:

Worthy is the Lamb that was slaughtered to receive , wealth, wisdom, might, honor, glory and blessing. (Revelation 5:12)

I know of many songs that have the big three in its lyrics: blessing, glory, and honor—but zero songs with wealth! So many have skipped that word and taken it out of heaven's song. But God is saying, "Before you dance and lift up your hands in worship, you owe Me something."

Did you realize that there are two things that reveal a lot about you? Your calendar and your bank account. They reveal how we spend two of our precious resources: time and money. In this chapter, we are going to deal with finances. It is imperative that we get a biblical worldview, not a corporate viewpoint.

There is nothing wrong with men possessing riches. The problem arises when riches possess men. So what is the best way to fight money's control? By being a giver! Understand that God never directs you to go anywhere because of money. If you make decisions based on salary alone, you are not walking in the fear of the Lord. Look at the Apostle Paul's warning:

For the love of money is the root of all kinds of evil. And some people, craving money, have wandered from the true faith and pierced themselves with many sorrows. (1 Timothy 6:10 NLT)

I read something astounding in Billy Graham's biography. In the 1960s, as he was reaching the apex of his career and influence as "America's pastor," he was offered $6 million by a Dallas billionaire to run against Lyndon B. Johnson for president. It took Dr. Graham a mere six seconds to answer: "Absolutely not."[2] He knew God was not calling him to politics. He was not led by finances; he was led by faith.

Paul went on to tell Timothy to teach like this:

> Teach those who are rich in this world not to be proud and not to trust in their money, which is so unreliable. Their trust should be in God, who richly gives us all we need for our enjoyment. Tell them to use their money to do good. They should be rich in good works and generous to those in need, always being ready to share with others. By doing this they will be storing up their treasure as a good foundation for the future so that they may experience true life. (1 Timothy 6:17–19 NLT)

It is said that money can buy: a bed but not sleep, a house but not a home, medicine but not health, amusement but not happiness, a crucifix but not a Savior, a safe haven but not forever heaven. We must make sure we are not putting our trust in something that cannot deliver.

Of course, there are many people who get angry when the church speaks about money. But it reminds me of when I went to the doctor a few years ago because of an issue with my knee. He began to poke, prod, and press various places, all the while asking, "Does this hurt? How about this?"

"Yes, right there!" I would exclaim.

"Then we better do more tests because it's not supposed to hurt there," he explained. The same happens when pastors talk about finances. If what you read in this chapter hurts or makes you upset, that means there is something wrong . . . but we can get it right!

Now over the years, I have found that most of the people who have a problem with tithing . . .

1. Don't tithe regularly or have never done it. After thirty years of dealing with people like this, I cannot think of one exception. No one has ever said to me, "I tithed, and it ruined us."
2. Hate people telling them what to do with their money, so they launch into the Old Covenant and New Covenant talk. (Unaware of the fact that New Testament giving is actually more intense, with higher percentages

than the Old Testament. The widow: 100 percent, Barnabas: 100 percent, Zacchaeus: 50 percent. People should be happy we don't say to do it like all the givers of the New Testament!)

3. Don't have the financial blessing of God to prove that what they are doing is right.

4. Are afraid to show their records to prove me wrong.

If reading that made you uncomfortable, strap in! I am going to be doing some more pushing and prodding. The Bible does not shy away from the topic of money, and neither should we. You may cry out in pain, but remember, just like at the doctor's office, it is ultimately for your own good.

Consider these New Testament facts: sixteen of the thirty-eight parables that Jesus spoke were concerned with how to handle money and possessions. In the Gospels, one out of ten verses (288 in all) deals directly with the subject of money. The Bible offers 500 verses on prayer, less than 500 verses on faith, but more than 2,000 verses on money and possessions. Jesus Himself was quoted in Acts 20:35, "It is more blessed to give than to receive."

My father was the son of an immigrant from Italy; he went through the Depression as a kid. He taught me a lot about finances. Here is what he said to do with every paycheck:

Pay God: Tithing

Pay yourself: Savings

Pay your bills: Integrity

I watched him faithfully take out his checkbook every Sunday to pay his tithe.

So let's start off with the basics: What is tithing?

Tithing is consistent, joyful, and thoughtful giving to God's church—the one you attend. You don't eat at Pizza Hut and pay the bill at Olive Garden! God defines the tithe as 10 percent (see Leviticus 27:30–33; Deuteronomy 14:22). That means if you make $100, then $10 belongs to God. If you receive a $1,000 check, you write your $100 thank you note to God. God is careful to say, "Bring the *whole* tithe" (Malachi 3:10, emphasis added). Most people tip God; few tithe. Many take more care with a restaurant bill than with their tithe.

The tithe is not just 10 percent but the *first* 10 percent. God's Word shows us that He considers the 10 percent His property. Perhaps you might insist: That is my money. I worked hard, I built this business, I got that degree. I earned it. But let me ask you this: Who gave you the legs to walk? The eyes to see? The brain to think? The air to breathe?

The tithe is a reminder to us that God owns everything—100 percent of every resource! Think of it like this:

> The earth is the LORD's, and everything in it. (Psalm 24:1 NIV)

> The wicked borrows and does not pay back. (Psalm 37:21 NASB)

If the planet belongs to God, that makes us borrowers, not owners. However, we often treat everything as if we own it all. It is like when I would take my kids out to eat, and if I reached for one of their fries, they would protest, "Hey!" But the real question is: "Who owns the fries?" The tithe is both a payback and a reminder of who is the source of all our wealth and blessings.

Now I confess that in the past, I tried to find loopholes in tithing—even as a pastor. When I started in the ministry making $47 a week, I thought perhaps my donations to the poor was my tithe. Or my low pay and full hours at church was my tithe. But let me be clear: serving is not a tithe; giving to charitable causes is not a tithe; volunteering and singing is not a tithe. The tithe is tangible. Every year, Cindy and I can look at our annual income, measure it against our church giving statement, and know exactly how much tithe we gave. There is no "I tithed in the spirit."

In the end, tithing is not a financial issue. It is a lordship issue. Remember, tithing is a command. Until we have tithed, we cannot call anything we give an offering. Tithing is not the finish line; it is the starting line. Generosity begins where tithing ends.

As we delve in further, let's now take a moment to look at the purpose in giving, the power in giving, and the practicalities of giving.

1. THE PURPOSE IN GIVING

Many people were shocked recently as First Congregational Church in Spencer, Massachusetts, went up in flames. It was struck by lightning and burned to the ground—one week after the pastor said that the Bible has contradictions, the Bible is not dictated by God, and that God is a woman. Everyone has his opinion as to whether or not the lightning strike was an act of God. But all I know is: You cannot mock God. And what is even larger than that is what Malachi said: You cannot rob God. In the book of Malachi, God equates refusing to give with robbery.

> Would anyone rob God? Yet you are robbing Me! But you say, "How have we robbed You?" In tithes and offerings. (Malachi 3:8)

I have had my home, my car, and our church robbed. Someone once broke into my car and stole preaching CDs and my Bible I loved. At least perhaps it was a Christian criminal. Nevertheless, the feeling of being violated is unlike any other feeling. If you do not tithe, you rob God. What is God feeling when He is robbed?

> "You are cursed with a curse, for you are robbing Me, the entire nation of you! Bring the whole tithe into the storehouse, so that there may be food in My house, and put Me to the test now in this," says the LORD of armies, "if I do not open for you the windows of heaven and pour out for you a blessing until it overflows. Then I will rebuke the devourer for you, so that it will not destroy the fruits of your ground; nor will the vine in the field prove fruitless to you," says the LORD of armies. (Malachi 3:9–11)

After the warning of robbing God, Malachi continued to describe the incredible blessings of obedience. Tithing gets God involved with spiritual warfare. God promises that tithing will open the windows of heaven to pour out a blessing on our lives. He even says, "Put Me to the test now in this." Cindy and I tested God, and I can personally testify that His Word is true. We both came into our marriage with no debt yet in the first year racked up many thousands of dollars in debt. We did not make enough to fix it. But we did the test. Cindy and I gave our way out of debt. We upped our percentage of giving and saw the principle of giving change our lives. It is truly more blessed to give than to receive. Many of us love receiving but have not experienced the blessing of giving.

Just as Malachi equated failure to give with robbery, Solomon equated tithing with honor.

Honor the LORD from your wealth,

And from the first of all your produce.

(Proverbs 3:9)

Tithing is honoring the Lord. What is honor? Honor is defined as tangibly and joyfully valuing a person's character—who they are and what they do. If the Bible says we are to honor God with our wealth, the first fruits of what we receive, what are we doing when we refuse to tithe? We are dishonoring God. When you keep the tithe, you honor yourself. When a long time Christian acts like tithing is something new, it means it has been a long time since he or she put God first!

Remember, tithing is not a matter of accounting. It is a matter of whether we believe God. Do we really believe what He said about our finances? Clearly, God does not need or even want your money. He wants *you*. Until you give Him the tithe, He doesn't have you.

2. THE POWER IN GIVING

Now as we look at this next passage of Scripture, keep in mind that when the Bible was written, it was not broken up into chapters and verses. You and I read the Bible and often assume that the end of a chapter is the end of a period of time. However, let's look at this passage without any breaks:

> Behold, I am telling you a [a]mystery; we will not all sleep, but we will all be changed, in a moment, in the twinkling of an eye, at the last trumpet; for the trumpet will sound, and the dead will be raisedimperishable, and we will be changed. For this [c]perishable must put on [d]the imperishable, and this mortal must put on immortality. But when this perishable puts on the imperishable, and this mortal puts on immortality, then will come about the saying that is written: "Death has been swallowed up in victory. Where, O Death, is your victory? Where, O Death, is your sting?" The sting of death is sin, and the power of sin is the Law; but thanks be to God, who gives us the victory through our Lord Jesus Christ.

Therefore, my beloved brothers and sisters, be firm, immovable, always excelling in the work of the Lord, knowing that your labor is not in vain in the Lord.

Now concerning the collection for the saints, as I directed the churches of Galatia, so you are to do as well. On the first day of every week, each of you is to put aside and save as he may prosper, so that no collections need to be made when I come. (1 Corinthians 15:51–16:2)

Did you see what happened? Paul went from talking about the Rapture right into "now concerning the collection." He was essentially saying, "Giving is just as important as the Second Coming!" In preparation for Jesus' return, Paul exhorted us to be steadfast, to continue in the work of the Lord, and to tithe. We see once again that tithing is not an act of generosity; it is an act of obedience . . . and there is power when we do it!

3. The Practicals of Giving

In his letters to the Corinthians, Paul told us four ways we should give:

1. Consistently

On the first day of every week, each one of you should set aside a sum of money in keeping with your income, saving it up, so that when I come no collections will have to be made. (1 Corinthians 16:2 NIV)

Here Paul said, "the first day of every week"—referring to payday. We are to tithe every time we get paid.

2. Thoughtfully

He also said in that verse to "set aside money in keeping with your income." This means you must think it out; do not just throw some money in the basket. You should give according to your income, lest God make your income according to your giving!

When it comes to thoughtful giving, people always ask: Do you tithe on net or gross? Malachi said you give more to your governor than you do to God (see Malachi 1:8). What does your government take from—net or gross?

3. Generously

> But remember this—if you give little, you will get little. A farmer who plants just a few seeds will get only a small crop, but if he plants much, he will reap much. Everyone must make up his own mind as to how much he should give. (2 Corinthians 9:6–7 TLB)

If you give a little, you get a little. People are always wondering: How do I get money? You do not get it by dropping hints of your financial need to others. That is covert manipulation. You also do not really get financial assistance by simply praying. I know that is shocking and makes people angry. Jesus told us exactly how it is done:

> Give generously and generous gifts will be given back to you, shaken down to make room for more. Abundant gifts will pour out upon you with such an overflowing measure that it will run over the top! The measurement of your generosity becomes the measurement of your return. (Luke 6:38 TPT)

Jesus put the return amount you get back in your own hands! Every time I get a new Bible, I write the same thing in each one—I put it right on the flyleaf. It is a 500-year-old poem that a prison convict wrote: "There was a man, and they called him mad; the more he gave, the more he had." That prison convict was John Bunyan, the author of *Pilgrim's Progress*. The more he gave, the more he had.[3] It seems like a contradiction, but it is the biblical way!

4. Joyfully

The verse in 2 Corinthians 9 continues:

> Don't force anyone to give more than he really wants to, for cheerful givers are the ones God prizes. God is able to make it up to you by giving you everything you need and more so that there will not only be enough for your own needs but plenty left over to give joyfully to others. (2 Corinthians 9:7–8 TLB)

God loves a *cheerful* giver. It is the only time this word is used in the Bible, and it means "to be hilarious." In our day, everything but joy gets associated with giving. Perhaps you may insist, "Well, I'm not happy about it, so do I still have to give?" Yes, the church still accepts angry money.

In the end, remember that our ultimate goal is to be like God. The Bible tells us: "Be imitators of God in everything you do" (Ephesians 5:1 TPT). God is a giver.

> For God so loved the world, that He gave His only Son, so that everyone who believes in Him will not perish, but have eternal life. (John 3:16)

Thank God that He did not just tithe from heaven. Thankfully when Jesus went to the cross, He did not merely tithe His blood but gave His entire life! The Lord gave generously and sacrificially out of His great love for each of us. How can we do anything less?

QUESTIONS

1. From where or from whom did you learn your approach to finances? Is it biblical?

2. What do you think compelled believers in the New Testament to give generously—far beyond the 10 percent tithe (see Mark 12:42–44; Luke 19:8; Acts 4:32–36)?

3. How have you personally experienced that it is "more blessed to give than to receive" (Acts 20:35)?

NEW BIRTH

The New Birth and Starting New Birth Conversations

*"I have won more people to Christ by holy
conversations than all my meetings."*
D. L. Moody[1]

Gaylord Kambarami, the general secretary of the Bible Society in Zimbabwe, tried to give a New Testament to a very belligerent man one day. The man said he would only accept it if allowed to use the pages for smoking purposes. In rural areas, people would use newspaper and whatever else they could find to roll their cigarettes.

Mr. Kambarami said, "Fine, on one condition: Read each page before you smoke."

The man agreed, and the two went their separate ways. Two years later, the two met at a convention in Zimbabwe. The Scripture-smoking pagan had been saved. He told the audience that he had smoked Matthew, he had smoked Mark, and he had smoked Luke.

But he said that when he got to John 3, "A light shone in my face. And now I am a churchgoing person. I saw the light!"[2]

In this chapter, we are going to look at this life-changing passage in John 3. It is here that an unexpected conversation occurred, resulting in an amazing exposition and explanation on eternity and what it means to be born again.

I, too, recently had an unexpected conversation with a young man named Bashir, who was our waiter at breakfast. I was chatting with Bashir and learned that he was a Muslim from West Africa. By the end of our conversation, I asked him, "If I give you a good tip, would you come to church?" When I talked with Bashir, it was a Friday. You see, every day is a day of salvation. The Bible says, "Today is the day of salvation" (2 Corinthians 6:2 NLT). Not just Sundays.

I have one purpose in life before God calls me home: I want to see God win a billion souls to Christ. But that cannot happen on Sundays alone. Simply relying on Sunday services will not suffice. We must discover what it looks like to be a lover of Jesus—one who is excited to share about who He is—the other six days of the week!

You see, you cannot secretly be in love. When I fell in love with Cindy, it was back in the mid-'90s when there were no cell phones. That meant no selfies to show my friends who I was in love with, though I was certainly excited for everyone to know. (I was thirty years old at the time; people had already given up hope for me.) So what did I do? Well, Cindy was working as vice president in the loan department of a bank, and I ended up finding her picture in a business magazine. I cut her picture out, folded it up, and put it in my wallet. Whenever I would talk to people about Cindy, I would proudly pull out her picture and say, "Right there, that's the girl!" When you are in love, you cannot help but tell people. And when you fall in love with Christ, all you want to do is share about who He is and what He has done in your life!

Can you think of someone you want to see come to Jesus? Do you know people who need to be born again? Remember, eternity is too long to be wrong. That's why I want to take some time to look at not only the new birth but how to start new birth conversations.

There is a special section of ten chapters in the Bible that I love, found in the middle of the Gospel of Luke. Where these chapters occur is important because they deal with the "Monday through Saturday." Most of the biblical accounts of Jesus speaking were actually Him in informal settings. In other words, it was not Sunday sermon talk. Jesus was eating meals, being asked questions, and responding to various interruptions. Luke 9:51 through Luke 19:44 is important for us because it is another one of Jesus' non-sermon talks. This section of Scripture is known as "the travel narrative."

At this point, Jesus was leaving Galilee, which was predominately Jewish.

That means they understood Jewish talk. He was on His way to Jerusalem, where people definitely understood all the Old Testament talk. However, Jesus ended up spending ten chapters in Samaria, located between Galilee and Jerusalem. It is almost as if Jesus was in between Sunday services. I want you to notice two things about the travel narrative:

1. Samaria is not home field advantage.

Samaria was enemy territory or at least unfriendly territory. The Samaritans did not understand church talk; they were distant from the synagogue and the temple. They had little in common with the Jewish people.

This is like the Christian in between Sundays—which is where most of our life is lived. Samaria is where we spend most of our time, making it imperative that we know how to communicate effectively with non-church people. Samaria talk is non-church talk. It is how Jesus spoke outside of the temple and synagogue.

2. These are unscheduled conversations about things that really matter.

These are the conversations you did not prepare for. Jesus had plenty of them—answering questions, having discussions around a supper table. I have noticed that many of the questions I get outside of the church are tests, not inquiries. Beware of answering tests like an inquiry. It is often the case that people are not looking for answers; they are looking to see which side you are on. They are waiting for you to say the wrong thing.

How did Jesus respond to questions? Jesus questioned the questioner! Many people ask questions but never have been questioned themselves.

So how do you question the questioner? I have been asked questions about everything, including all types of transgender issues. Here would be my line of questioning the questioner:

Do you believe in God? (Or you can add to that: Are you a Christian?)

If yes, then: Do you believe that the Bible is God's Word?

If yes, then: What if the Bible says something that contradicts your lifestyle or opinion? Who wins the argument?

Why did Jesus ask questions? The Bible says that "out of the abundance of the heart his mouth speaks" (Luke 6:45 NKJV). When you hear people talk, you hear their heart. The problem is that we talk too much and never take the time to hear people's hearts.

Starting New Birth Conversations

How do we start these new birth conversations? Remember, these are the "Monday through Saturday services"—the ones we forget to prepare for. We prepare for sermons but not for encounters. We are trained to speak to many people but forget how to speak to one.

The grid that I often use for these conversations is what I call the "Joseph way" to minister. At one point in his life, Joseph was wrongfully imprisoned, which is where he met two men from Pharaoh's court—the chief cupbearer and chief baker. When he was in that prison cell, Joseph was essentially on "Samaritan soil," just like Jesus was. Let's see how Joseph witnessed in prison:

> When Joseph came to them in the morning and saw them, behold, they were dejected. So he asked Pharaoh's officials who were with him in confinement in his master's house, "Why are your faces so sad today?" And they said to him, "We have had a dream, and there is no one to interpret it." Then Joseph said to them, "Do interpretations not belong to God? Tell it to me, please." (Genesis 40:6–8)

In this passage we find three key things to help us from Monday through Saturday:

1. Observe people.

Joseph came to them in the morning and "saw them." We, too, must take time to notice people and moods. Jesus said to His disciples after speaking to the Samaritan woman at the well, "Lift up your eyes, and see that the fields are white for harvest" (John 4:35 ESV). He was basically saying, "Look around and see people!"

I knew a young lady named Linda who was gifted in the prophetic. One day at the supermarket, she felt the Lord tell her that the lady at the checkout who was scanning her items was going through a divorce. So Linda asked, "Hey, what is your name?" to which the lady replied, "Sally."

Then Linda explained, "It's been impressed upon my heart that you are in the middle of a divorce and that your heart is broken." Immediately, Sally's eyes filled with tears, and Linda offered to pray for her right then and there.

If you have a gift from the Holy Spirit, it is not just for use inside a church building. Let the Lord use it wherever you go!

2. Ask questions.

Joseph then asked the cupbearer and the baker why their faces were so sad. We ought to ask questions to people wherever we go! They can just be simple questions. *How is your day going? How long have you been doing this? Why are you sad?*

Ask a lot of questions before you make any statements. Questions do a few things: They show that you care and that you are interested in them. When people speak, you get to hear their heart. You never know what doors the Lord will open up. That is how I started speaking with Bashir on Friday. *Where are you from? Do you go to church?* Christianity today is more conversational than declaratory.

3. Add the God part.

It was not until after Joseph observed and heard them out that he began to speak about God. Before interpreting their dreams, Joseph asked this question: "Do interpretations not belong to God?" We might ask: *Do you think God has something to speak to you? Has anyone ever prayed for you? Can I pray for you today?*

I have been doing this for more than four decades, and I remember fewer than five people who refused when I offered to pray for them. So make it your goal: Just one person today. Pray for one, talk to one, evangelize to one, be kind to one, give money to one, smile at one, compliment one. Without the one-on-one talks that Jesus had, we would be missing most of the Gospels!

THE NEW BIRTH

In order to engage in these new birth conversations, obviously we must be familiar with what the new birth is. I don't know of any better way to define it than by taking you to a private conversation between Jesus and a man named

Nicodemus.

Jesus spoke His greatest words not in a prepared sermon but to this Jewish fellow who showed up at night. Nicodemus was *the* religious guy of his day. Religion is working hard to impress God, and this man was the best at it. Nicodemus had three credentials. He was:

1. A man of the Pharisees

There were never more than 6,000 Pharisees in Palestine at one time. They were noted for their external dos and don'ts. The Pharisees made up their own laws, which they added to the Old Testament laws. For instance, God gave them the Sabbath and commanded them to keep it holy, but the Pharisees added more to it. Their manual, the Mishnah, included twenty-four chapters on what it meant to work and not work on the Sabbath. Tying certain knots was considered work while tying others was not. People were instructed to walk on the dirt because it would be considered work to break a blade of grass while walking.

2. A ruler of the Jews

Nicodemus was one of the best of the 6,000 and was even part of the seventy on their supreme court.

3. The teacher of Israel

Furthermore, Nicodemus was the spokesman of the Jews. Jesus never encountered a more prestigious Jew than Nicodemus in all His ministry on earth. That is why Nicodemus came at night; he did not want to be recognized. He was unaware that the conversation would move from religion to regeneration. It is the most important conversation in the entire Bible; our forever depends on our response to this conversation:

> Now there was a man of the Pharisees, named Nicodemus, a ruler of the Jews; this man came to Jesus by night and said to Him, "Rabbi, we know that You have come from God as a teacher; for no one can do these signs that You do unless God is with him." Jesus responded and said to him, "Truly, truly, I say to you, unless someone is born again he cannot see the kingdom of God."

Nicodemus said to Him, 'How can a person be born when he is old? He cannot enter his mother's womb a second time and be born, can he?" Jesus answered, "Truly, truly, I say to you, unless someone is born of water and the Spirit, he cannot enter the kingdom of God. That which has been born of the flesh is flesh, and that which has been born of the Spirit is spirit. Do not be amazed that I said to you, 'You must be born again.'" (John 3:1–7)

Jesus said that real life begins with the new birth. We received physical life from the first birth. But what we need is spiritual life from the second birth. So let's look at three eternity essentials from this one-on-one conversation between Jesus and Nicodemus.

1. Don't Create Another Way When *the* Way Is Given

In June 2023, every day the world followed intently what was thought to be a race against time with the *Titan* submersible. On Sunday, June 18 at 8 a.m., the twenty-two foot capsule launched its journey 2.4 miles underwater off the coast of Newfoundland to see the *Titanic* wreckage, at a price of $250k per seat. Seventeen bolts locked them in from the outside, leaving no way of escape unless someone unbolted the door. A billionaire and a millionaire and his son joined the team to venture where very few have been. One hour and forty-five minutes into their eight-hour excursion, all communication was lost. That left five people with ninety-six hours of oxygen. Every day, the news would remind us that they were running out of time.

Canada, France, and the United States all sent their best to rescue these five, sending robots and sonar buoys into the ocean to search out an area the size of Connecticut. The world soon found out that a catastrophic implosion occurred less than two hours into the journey. Apparently, there was a breach in the *Titan* that had compromised the vessel.[3]

Here is what made me an engaged bystander for those ninety-six hours: I knew that at some point ninety-six hours would be up, and life would be lost. I remember Thursday morning when the news announced that the deadline had been crossed.

But a deadline was not just in place for five people in a submersible; it is a reality *for all of us.* The moment you are born, the clock starts ticking, and you start dying. However, there is a rescue plan for you to live forever. It is called the new birth. It is all part of the gospel. Gospel means "good news."

So how do we respond to a world that views the good news as bad news? When the world criticizes Christianity for endorsing only one way to heaven, we might ask, "Yes, but aren't you glad there is at least *one* way?" Shouldn't we all be grateful that God has made it possible for there to be a way at all? Who are we to demand that one way is not good enough? If you were in a burning building, would you refuse to flee because there was only one exit?

This is what Jesus told Nicodemus:

> Truly, truly, I say to you, unless someone is born again he cannot see the kingdom of God. (John 3:3)

Because "born again" is so significant, we often miss the significance of another word: "cannot." You and I *cannot* enter heaven in the sinful condition of our first birth.

> Jesus said to him, "I am the way, and the truth, and the life; no one comes to the Father except through Me." (John 14:6)

> Salvation is found in no one else, for there is no other name under heaven given to mankind by which we must be saved. (Acts 4:12 NIV)

If there were 1,000 ways to God, we would want 1,001. The issue is not how many ways lead to God; the issue is our autonomy before God. We want to make our own way. God made it simple, but men do not want simplicity; they want autonomy.

2. Don't Make Optional What Jesus Says Is Mandatory

> Do not be surprised because I tell you that you must all be born again. (John 3:7 GNT)

You must all be born again. *All* means "no one is excluded." Therefore, each of us must seriously consider our response to the question: Have you been born again?

If your answer is: "I think," "I hope," or "I'm not sure," please read carefully what it means to be born again.

When you were born the first time, you received natural life. When you are born a second time, you receive spiritual life. Only someone with spiritual life can exist and survive in heaven. To enjoy, commune with, and understand God, you *must* have the kind of life that He has.

Being born again means that every sin is forgiven. It means Jesus lives in you through the Holy Spirit to give you peace, power, and purpose. It means you are not afraid of death because you know you are going home to heaven when you die.

So what happens if you sin after being born again? Jesus is a Savior, not a probation officer. If we must depend on our behavior to keep us born again, then we are in trouble! Thankfully, there is mercy to forgive. And as you continue to walk with Jesus, you will also find grace to empower you to live a holy life.

3. Don't Complicate What Jesus Says Is Simple

Years ago, when the Betty Crocker company first began selling their cake mixes, they offered a product that only required water. All you had to do was add water to the box mix, and you would get a perfect, delicious cake every time. It bombed. No one bought it.

The company could not understand why, so they commissioned a study, which brought back a surprising answer. It seemed that people were not buying the cake mix because it was too easy. They did not want to be totally excluded from the work of preparing a cake; they wanted to feel that they were contributing something to it. So Betty Crocker changed the formula and required the customer to add an egg and oil in addition to water. Immediately, the new cake mix was a huge success.

Being born again has a simplicity to it. Let me explain. This one conversation gives us the greatest twenty-six words ever penned in human history. It is God's heart; it is our rescue; it is Jesus' mission and our future. Here is the climax of the conversation:

> For God so loved the world, that He gave His only Son so, that everyone who believes in Him will not perish, but have eternal life. (John 3:16)

"Believes in Him." Belief is crucial because it is the hinge upon which the door to heaven turns. Notice how important this word *believe* is in the verses before and after John 3:16:

> So that everyone who believes will have eternal life in Him. For God so loved the world, that He gave His only Son, so that everyone who believes in Him will not perish, but have eternal life. For God did not send the Son into the world to judge the world, but so that the world might be saved through Him. The one who believes in Him is not judged; the one who does not believe has been judged already, because he has not believed in the name of the only Son of God. (John 3:15–18)

Jesus used variations of *believe* five times in four verses! If you were to speak three sentences, and you included one verb five times, I would get the feeling you were stressing a highly critical point. For example, if I were to say to my children: "Dinner is great, but now it is time to clean up. When you clean up, Mom and Dad are happy because cleaning up means that you respect our words. You are doing your part when you clean up, but when you don't clean up, you're going to get in trouble." I am sure you can find the key word!

That is what Jesus did with the word *believe*. He said *believe* five times. He made it simple. So why are you going to add oil and an egg? John 3:16 begins with God and His love, and it ends in heaven. But the one variable in the equation is the word *believe*. *Believe* is the fork in the road of perish and eternal life. Believe, not baptize. Believe, not communion. Believe, not join a group or a denomination. Believe!

Robert Bennett said this about the thief on the cross: "How does the thief on the cross fit into your Christian belief system? No baptism, no communion, no confirmation, no missions trip, no volunteerism, and no church clothes. He didn't even bend his knees to pray, and he didn't say the sinner's prayer. And among other things, he was a thief."[4]

A thief walked into heaven the same hour as Jesus simply by believing. There was no spin from a brilliant preacher. There was no ego, no arrogance, no shiny lights, no crafty words. There was no coffee or donuts at the entrance. It was just a naked man on a cross, unable even to fold his hands to pray. He had nothing more to offer than his belief that Jesus was who He said He was.

Now I have had people tell me that they tried Jesus and it just didn't work. I usually tell them, "Wait one second. You may have tried church or Sundays or religion or a denomination. But you did not try Jesus." It is impossible to try Jesus and find that it just didn't work. Why? The Bible tells us that "no one who believes in Christ will ever be disappointed" (Romans 10:11 TLB). Can you name one true follower of Jesus who ended up on his deathbed, saying, "Jesus is a liar, and I regret ever following Him"?

Recently, we saw a resurgence of interest in the *Titanic* because of the *Titan* tragedy. On April 14, 1912, word came over telegraph to New York City that the giant vessel—the ship that men boasted not even God Himself could sink—had indeed sunk. More than 1,500 people perished in the waters off Newfoundland. Yet despite all the rich and famous on the ship, a list came back with only two columns of names: those who were lost and those who were saved. Those two columns still exist today. It does not matter whether you work on Wall Street, whether you are an ambassador or an actor, or whether you just signed a multimillion-dollar contract for a sports team. When it comes to the end, there are only two columns: lost and saved. You had no choice about your first birth, but you do have a choice in your second birth.

Believe. It's that simple.

QUESTIONS

1. Have you been born again? If not, or if you are unsure, please see the addendum at the back of this book titled "How Do You Get to Heaven?"

2. In a world full of distractions, what are some ways you can remember to stay observant of the people around you?

3. Who is at the top of your list of people you want to see born again? Would you make a commitment to pray every day that God would provide an opportunity to have that crucial conversation with them?

OBEDIENCE

The Worshiping Backslider

"Disobeying God is the same as telling Him to hold back all of the blessings that come with obedience. That is not only stupidity, it's insanity."

JOY DAWSON[1]

When E. Stanley, a missionary to India and a Christian statesman in the twentieth century, was about to board a plane, he heard God speak to him, "Do not get on that airplane." He later learned that the plane crashed, leaving no survivors. He shared his experience with another missionary, who remarked, "You mean to say that you were the only one God told not to get on that plane?"

Jones said, "By no means. But it is possible that I was the only one listening."[2]

I believe God is always speaking. God speaks through His Word, His servants, His providence, His acts, His Holy Spirit. I do not want to just be listening, I want to listen and obey. My spiritual father, Leonard Ravenhill, would say: "Maturity comes from obedience, not necessarily from age." I have seen many old, immature Christians and many young, mature Christians. The determining factor is always obedience. One decision of obedience is more powerful and produces more growth than listening to a hundred sermons. Truth without obedience is hypocrisy.

Of course, it is not always easy to obey God. Obedience can be inconvenient, lonely, and difficult. But obedience gets the attention of God. Obedience could be praying over a meal in public, speaking up on a biblical issue among coworkers or fellow athletes, or choosing not to lie about numbers on the job.

The word *obedience* comes from the Latin word *ob-audire,* which means "to listen with great attentiveness." Without listening, we become deaf to the voice of love. The Latin word for "deaf" is *surdus.* To be completely deaf is to be *ab-surdus*—which is where we get the word *absurd.* When we no longer listen, it can be absurd for us!

The greatest gift I can give my family is to live a life of obedience to God. Did you know that your obedience has a generational effect? It lives far beyond you.

> Be careful and listen to all these words which I am commanding
> you, so that it may go well for you and your sons after you forever,
> for you will be doing what is good and right in the sight of the LORD
> your God. (Deuteronomy 12:28)

When I obey God, it goes well not only with me but with my son and daughters, my grandchildren to come—extending far into the future. Obedience to God has long-lasting effects. But on the flip side, disobedience also has long-lasting effects. In fact, people's lives may even be at stake when you are disobedient.

Early Sunday mornings are always a special time for me. That is when I pray for our church services, inviting the presence of God to come. During that time, I also have my phone with me, and as the Lord puts people on my heart, I text them. I send a simple text telling them that God put him or her on my heart and what I am praying for them.

A couple of weeks ago, I was speaking with a pastor who told me, "I have to thank you for listening to the Holy Spirit." He went on to explain that two months prior, he woke up on a Sunday morning and was getting ready to go to church. However, his body had been failing him, and he was in a lot of pain. He even felt his mind was under attack. Faced with the fact that he had to preach and lead that day, he suddenly felt as if he could not go on. He cried out to the Lord, "I am finished. I can't do this anymore. Take my life!"

He told me that just as those words came out of his mouth, his phone dinged, and there was a text from me that said: "Praying for you. Praying that God would give you strength to go on. May you preach today with a new anointing and new strength."

He looked at me with tears in his eyes and said, "Thank you for being obedient. Thank you for listening to the Lord!" Now to me, it had just seemed like a simple text. But God knew what that pastor needed at that moment! You have no idea what your obedience could mean for someone else!

Now let me ask you an important question: How do you know if you love Jesus?

The Bible tells us plainly: "If you love me, obey my commandments" (John 14:15 NLT). Love for Jesus means obedience. Obedience is doing God's will, God's way, in God's timing. Or in other words, obedience means that you do what God says, when He says it, and how He says it. The danger comes when we know His commands yet we edit them to our liking, our taste, and even to our culture. According to the Scriptures, various forms of "obedience" are actually disobedience:

Delayed obedience is disobedience.

> I hurried and did not delay
> To keep Your commandments.
> (Psalm 119:60)

Obedience with murmuring is still disobedience.

> So all these curses shall come upon you and pursue you and overtake you until you are destroyed, because you would not obey the LORD your God by keeping His commandments and His statutes which He commanded you. And they will become a sign and a wonder against you and your descendants forever. Since you did not serve the LORD your God with joy and a cheerful heart." (Deuteronomy 28:45–47)

Partial obedience is disobedience.

> But a man named Ananias, with his wife Sapphira, sold a piece of property, and kept back some of the proceeds for himself, with his wife's full knowledge, and bringing a portion of it, he laid it at the apostles' feet. But Peter said, "Ananias, why has Satan filled your

heart to lie to the Holy Spirit and to keep back some of the proceeds of the land? . . . You have not lied to men, but to God." And as he heard these words, Ananias collapsed and died; and great fear came over all who heard about it. . . .

Now an interval of about three hours elapsed, and his wife came in, not knowing what had happened. And Peter responded to her, "Tell me whether you sold the land for this price?" And she said, "Yes, for that price." Then Peter said to her, "Why is it that you have agreed together to put the Spirit of the Lord to the test? Behold, the feet of those who have buried your husband are at the door, and they will carry you out as well." And immediately she collapsed at his feet and died . . . And great fear came over the whole church." (Acts 5:1–5, 7–11)

There is another story found in 1 Samuel 15 that involves partial obedience—or in other words, disobedience. God clearly spoke to Saul, the first king of Israel, and instructed him to *utterly destroy* the Amalekites.

Then Samuel said to Saul, "The LORD sent me to anoint you as king over His people, over Israel; now therefore, listen to the words of the LORD. This is what the LORD of armies says: "I will punish Amalek for what he did to Israel, in that he obstructed him on the way while he was coming up from Egypt. Now go and strike Amalek and completely destroy everything that he has, and do not spare him; but put to death both man and woman, child and infant, ox and sheep, camel and donkey." (1 Samuel 15:1–3)

However, Saul decided to edit God's command.

But Saul and the people spared Agag and the best of the sheep, the oxen, the more valuable animals, the lambs, and everything that was good, and were unwilling to destroy them completely; but everything despicable and weak, that they completely destroyed. (1 Samuel 15:9)

He ended up bringing home the enemy king and the best of the animals. In other words, Saul got rid of what he wanted to get rid of, and he kept what he wanted to keep. It was a defeat within a victory. Saul won but lost. He won the battle he was told to win, but he lost the future. Interestingly, he forfeited his future and anointing through this act of disobedience, yet he kept his position. God is the only employer who will fire you and let you keep your job! Saul kept his job *unanointed* for twenty years.

It is a lot easier to do what God tells us to do, no matter how hard it is, than to face the consequences of not doing it. The rest of the story is what frightens me because it is the evolving of "the worshiping backslider." Look at how Saul even greeted Samuel with religious talk:

> So Samuel came to Saul, and Saul said to him, "Blessed are you of the Lord! I have carried out the command of the Lord." But Samuel said, "What then is this bleating of the sheep in my ears, and the bellowing of the oxen which I hear?" (1 Samuel 15:13–14)

Sin will always give you away! If you are disobedient, it will come out. Someone once told me that when a person is living in disobedience, before you even know what the specific sin is, you will see it in their attitude. That is the bleating of the sheep. Something will just not sound right.

> Saul said, "They have brought them from the Amalekites, for the people spared the best of the sheep and oxen to sacrifice to the Lord your God; but the rest we have completely destroyed." (1 Samuel 15:15)

Saul was now trying to cover his disobedience with religious activity! Samuel then rebuked him with these words:

> "The Lord anointed you as king over Israel. And the Lord sent you on a mission, and said, 'Go and completely destroy the sinners, the Amalekites, and fight against them until they are eliminated.' Why then did you not obey the voice of the Lord? Instead, you loudly rushed upon the spoils and did what was evil in the sight of the Lord!"
>
> Then Saul said to Samuel, "I did obey the voice of the Lord, for I went on the mission on which the Lord sent me; and I have brought Agag the king of Amalek, and have completely destroyed

the Amalekites. But the people took some of the spoils, sheep and oxen, the choicest of the things designated for destruction, to sacrifice to the LORD your God at Gilgal." Samuel said,

> "Does the LORD have as much delight in burnt offerings
> and sacrifices
> As in obeying the voice of the LORD?
> Behold, to obey is better than a sacrifice,
> And to pay attention is better than the fat of rams.
> For rebellion is as reprehensible as the sin of divination,
> And insubordination is as reprehensible as false
> religion and idolatry.
> Since you have rejected the word of the LORD,
> He has also rejected you from being king."
> (1 Samuel 15:17–23 NASB)

God was saying, "I would rather you obey Me than do religious stuff with enormous passion." Notice how Samuel described the opposite of obedience. It is not just disobedience but also rebellion, witchcraft, stubbornness, false religion, and idolatry! It is extremely dangerous to know what God is saying yet still refuse to do it.

Samuel told Saul that God had rejected him from being king. This must have frightened Saul, for look at the next words out of his mouth:

> Then Saul said to Samuel, "I have sinned I have violated the command of the LORD and your words, because I feared the people and listened to their voice." (1 Samuel 15:24)

This must mean that Saul was lying earlier; he knew he had not obeyed God. It was upon hearing the words "you cannot be king anymore" that he finally responded, "I have sinned." Oftentimes it is not until one hears words such as "I want a divorce" that the response "I messed up" finally comes out. We suddenly become humble when we hear the consequences.

Saul continued:

> "Now then, please pardon my sin and return with me, so that I may worship the LORD." But Samuel said to Saul, "I will not return with

you; for you have rejected the word of the LORD, and the LORD has rejected you from being king over Israel." Then Samuel turned to go but Saul grasped the edge of his robe, and it tore off. So Samuel said to him, "The LORD has torn the kingdom of Israel from you today and has given it to your neighbor, who is better than you. Also the Glory of Israel will not lie or change His mind; for He is not a man, that He would change His mind." Then Saul said, "I have sinned; but please honor me now before the elders of my people and before Israel [In other words, "Don't make me look foolish!" It was an image issue.], and go back with me, so that I may worship the LORD your God." So Samuel went back following Saul, and Saul worshiped the LORD. (1 Samuel 15:25–31)

Saul left to worship. Here we see the origin of a dangerous practice in Christianity. The worshiping backslider is the Christian who worships with intensity while living in blatant disobedience. It is happening today with preachers, leaders, and other believers. This is the false theology that they embrace: "My worship is my repentance. If I am living in disobedience, I can cover it by doing something passionate." However, the truth is that the *only* thing that covers sin is the blood of Jesus!

Let's pause for a moment: What is backsliding? Backsliding is the easiest thing to do—you do nothing! People seldom lose their fire for God by a blowout. It is typically a slow leak.

Jerry Vines defined it best: "Are you backslidden now? I'm going to help you answer that question. A backslidden Christian is any Christian who is not as close to Jesus as he used to be. Was there ever a time in your life when you were more consecrated to the Lord than you are now? Was there ever a period in your life when you felt the presence of God more than you feel it now? Was there a moment in your life when your love for Jesus Christ was more real than it is this minute? If so, you need a revival!"[3]

We must protect the fire within us. When was the last time you lifted your hands in worship and suddenly had the thought, "Wait, I need to make this right first"? Jesus said this will happen to His disciples.

Therefore, if you are offering your gift at the altar and there remember that your brother or sister has something against you, leave your gift there in front of the altar. First go and be reconciled to them; then come and offer your gift. (Matthew 5:23–24 NIV)

The Lord was essentially saying that the worst thing you can do is get into the habit of thinking you can worship through disobedience. In today's language, it would read something like this: While you are singing "All my life You have been faithful . . ." the Holy Spirit convicts you and says, "I am faithful, but you have not been faithful. You are lifting your hands but sleeping with your girlfriend. You are lifting your hands but speaking evil of this person. You are singing loud and kneeling on the floor, but you are robbing Me in tithes and offering." At that point, you must put your hands down and make things right. That is what disciples do.

Once while I was leading a communion service—even before I could get the little cup of juice open—the Holy Spirit told me not take to communion until I apologized to a staff member to whom I had spoken sharply. So I had the worship team continue singing until I could reconcile it. This is serious to me. Before I honor the blood, I need to make sure my heart is right. I do not want to get in the habit of preaching when I know something is not right between my wife and me, or if there is sin in my life. The danger is leaning on a gift or talent when inside the fire is being quenched.

Saul said, "I have sinned; let me worship." But he never did what God asked him to do. Saul wanted to worship, but he did not want to obey. The story ends with two unbelievable things: While Saul was lifting his hands in worship, it was Samuel who walked in to deal with Agag and carry out the act of obedience.

Then Samuel said, "Bring me Agag, the king of the Amalekites." And Agag came to him cheerfully. And Agag said, "Surely the bitterness of death is gone!" But Samuel said, "As your sword has made women childless, so shall your mother be childless among women." And Samuel cut Agag to pieces before the Lord at Gilgal. (1 Samuel 15:32–33)

If I was told that I had just lost the throne, I would have immediately gone to the source of my issues and started hacking it up. But not Saul. And not others. Saul lifted his hands when he should have had a sword in his hand.

Swordless hands are those that insist on holding onto things that God is asking for. Perhaps it is holding onto friends, emails, phone numbers, text messages, acquaintances, an offense. But humility says, "Let's hack it up."

Now that is not the end of the story. I would like to give you an addendum to the 1 Samuel 15 story. It really ends almost twenty years later. First Samuel 15 takes place in 1028 BC. Second Samuel 1 takes place in 1010 BC. It is in this chapter that we learn something devastating about Saul's death, just before David is about to take the throne.

> Then David said to the young man who told him, "How do you know that Saul and his son Jonathan are dead?" The young man who told him said, "By chance I happened to be on Mount Gilboa, and behold, Saul was leaning on his spear. And behold, the chariots and the horsemen had overtaken him. When he looked behind himself, he saw me, and called to me. And I said, 'Here I am.' Then he said to me, 'Who are you?' And I answered him, 'I am an Amalekite.' And he said to me, 'Please stand next to me and finish me off, for agony has seized me because my life still lingers in me." So I stood next to him and finished him off." (2 Samuel 1:5–10 NASB)

Saul was killed by the very thing he was supposed to kill! Remember Saul had edited God's command and kept what he called "the best." In his eyes, it was best for him. Yet he ended up being killed by what he considered the best. We often choose to keep what we think is best for ourselves. But editing what God says ultimately ends up killing you.

Therefore, when God speaks . . . obey! Whatever He says to you, do it. That was the only commandment the Virgin Mary ever gave (see John 2:5). Decide obedience before the command. We often get it backward. We say, "Speak, Lord. I will listen, and then I will decide." Yet it ought to be: We set our hearts to obey. God speaks, and then He explains (maybe). Actually, a youth pastor from Alabama taught me a prayer that encapsulates it well. I cannot tell you how many times I have whispered this prayer: "God, the answer is YES even before You ask!"

I was reading the biography of Peter Marshall, who was pastor of New York Avenue Presbyterian Church in Washington, D.C., and was also considered one of the great chaplains of the U.S. Senate. He tells the story about how he attempted to avoid a call to ministry and instead join the navy. However, he failed the test and was not able to enlist. Feeling despondent, he decided to take a shortcut home across a desolate area on a rainy, foggy day. Suddenly he heard his name being called. "Peter!"

He stopped and asked, "Who is that?" Then he kept walking.

He heard it again. "Peter!"

"Who is calling me?" he asked. But he continued walking. By the third time, he knew it was God calling him. He finally stopped and fell on his knees in the fog. God called him to be a pastor and to bring revival to Congress, and he surrendered his future to God. In the end, while he was trying to get up off his knees, he pushed his hand down, but nothing was there. It turned out that he was on the precipice of a cliff to a stone quarry that was hundreds of feet down! If he had taken one more step instead of yielding to the voice of God, he would have plummeted to his death. When he said yes to God, God rescued him and his future![4]

May that prayer always be on our lips: *God, the answer is YES even before You ask!*

QUESTIONS

1. Is there anything you are holding onto that God has told you to "completely destroy"?

2. What is often the biggest obstacle between you and obedience to God?

3. Can you think of an example of when obeying God was difficult, yet you saw the fruit of your obedience in the end?

PRAYER

My Favorite
Name for God

*"The greatest tragedy in life is not
unanswered prayer but un-offered prayer."*
F. B. Meyer[1]

One Saturday night while on a prayer walk through my city, I was curious about something. I wanted our church to sing a song on prayer during service the next morning, so I stopped on a park bench and googled songs about prayer. A popular Christian website listed the top fifteen songs about prayer.

I was surprised to discover that twelve of the fifteen songs were written fifty years ago! The other three contemporary songs were only marginally about prayer or contained a line about prayer. Sadly, it seems that no one is writing songs about prayer anymore—the very key that opens heaven! It is as if we are trying to find an alternative way to bring heaven down. However, the only way for heaven to come down is for the church to begin to pray. Look at the prayer of the prophet Isaiah:

Oh, that You would rend the heavens!
That You would come down!
That the mountains might shake at Your presence—
As fire burns brushwood,
As fire causes water to boil—

To make Your name known to Your adversaries,
That the nations may tremble at Your presence!
When You did awesome things for which we did not look."
(Isaiah 64:1–3 NKJV)

Isaiah asked God to tear apart the heavens and come down. But then he went on to lament:

There is no one who calls on Your name,
Who stirs himself up to take hold of You.
(Isaiah 64:7 NKJV)

May we be a people who stir ourselves up to call on His name! In order to see revival in our land and get a nation back on its feet, the church must get on its knees. This is God's charge to us today.

A prayerless church finds substitutes and alternatives. But when you lose prayer, you lose the power of the Holy Spirit.

But you will receive power when the Holy Spirit comes on you; and you will be my witnesses. (Acts 1:8 NIV)

When you lose prayer, you lose praise.

Those who seek the LORD will praise him. (Psalm 22:26 NIV)

When you lose prayer, you lose wisdom.

But if any of you lacks wisdom, let him ask of God.
(James 1:5 NASB)

Power, praise, and wisdom are lost in prayerlessness! Lose prayer, you become a plagiarist. Lose prayer, you need Google. Lose prayer, you need podcasts to preach. When prayer is lost, praise needs props. The need for deliverance becomes a need for therapy; preachers become communicators; and anointing is replaced with antics.

What we actually need is heaven opened. "Thy kingdom come, Thy will be done in earth, as it is in heaven" (Matthew 6:10 KJV). All that we need is in heaven, and the key that unlocks heaven is prayer.

Jesus said, "MY HOUSE WILL BE CALLED A HOUSE OF PRAYER" (Matthew

21:13). Not a house of praise and worship, not even a house of preaching, but a house of *prayer*. The Bible also instructs us to "pray without ceasing" (1 Thessalonians 5:17). Not read without ceasing. You cannot read down revival. You cannot read people into salvation. We must therefore fight to bring the prayer meeting back into the church.

It starts by remembering to Whom we are praying. Max Lucado once said: "The power of prayer is not in the one who prays but in the One who hears it."[2] It reminds me of the story of when the professional golfer, Arnold Palmer, played a series of exhibition matches in Saudi Arabia years ago. When he had finished, the king of Saudi Arabia was so impressed with Palmer's expertise that he desired to give Palmer a gift. Palmer, a multimillionaire in his own right, insisted, "It isn't necessary. I just enjoyed meeting your people and playing in your country."

The king indicated his extreme displeasure at being unable to give the golf pro a gift. Palmer wisely reconsidered and said, "Well, how about just a golf club? A golf club would be a wonderful memento of my visit here." The king was pleased. The following day, a messenger delivered to Palmer's hotel room the title to "a golf club"—a country club with thirty-six holes, trees, lakes, and buildings![3]

The moral of this story? Every time I pray, I must remember that I am in the presence of a King. And in the presence of the King of Kings, do not be foolish and merely ask for small things . . . go big!

There are two passages I want us to look at as we go deeper into prayer. Psalm 65 is the reason we pray; 1 Kings 20 is the challenge to pray. There is a charge and then a challenge, the hallelujah and then the hurdle.

Let's begin by looking at my favorite name for God. In Psalm 65, David was praising God, unaware that in his praise, we would hear something revolutionary about prayer:

> Praise awaits you, our God, in Zion . . .
> You who answer prayer.
> (Psalm 65:1–2 NIV)

You who answer prayer. That is my favorite name for God! "Who answer prayer" is the adjectival phrase for "You," and it describes an attribute of God. David is talking about the King who is waiting for a request.

Don't miss the first part of verse 1—our praise is in pause right now. That means if we pray to the One who answers prayer, who needs a preacher or music? There is going to be enough praise in us because God answers prayer! If you have never prayed and then experienced answered prayer, you are missing something in praise and worship. There is praise that is birthed within when we see that God answered—He healed me, He protected me, He guided me!

Now I would do this verse a disservice to be profound without being practical. We must recognize that the problem isn't God not answering; it is God's people not praying! How sad it is to have a God who answers yet a people who do not ask—people who find other things to do each day instead. In fact, we have received a terrible indictment in James 4:2: "Ye have not, because *ye ask not*" (KJV, emphasis added). This tells me that there are people in the body of Christ who are literally self-impoverished—improvished of miracles, impoverished of blessings, impoverished of revival. Isn't it amazing that prayer is our biggest struggle of consistency in our Christian walk? If I were to give an altar call for those who have inconsistent prayer lives, probably 99 percent of the church would come forward. The other 1 percent would be lying. Why is there always a fight for consistency in prayer? It is because we have a God who answers prayer. That scares the enemy and is why he makes it a constant battle.

Over the years, I have learned that when you have four kids, you love two things: Costco and rebates. Whenever we were in the market for a big purchase such as a new appliance, we would look for rebates. Buy it for $300 but send in a form for a $150 rebate. Of course, these companies are not offering rebates because they are generous; they are doing it because they know people never send it in! In fact, studies show that between 40 percent to 60 percent of rebates ae ever redeemed![4]

How many people do you think cash in on the most wonderful name of God, "You who answer prayer"?!

Look at the instructions Jesus Himself gave us regarding prayer—right in the middle of His Sermon on the Mount:

> But you, when you pray, go into your room, and when you have shut your door, pray to your Father who is in the secret place; and your Father who sees in secret will reward you openly.
> (Matthew 6:6 NKJV)

The word *reward* is a payment term—a salary for a task or job you performed. It is like clocking in for work. In other words, God is saying, "When you pray, I see it, and it always pays off!"

I want you to notice that Jesus also did something interesting here in Matthew 6:6 that is connected to prayer. It is the only verse in the Bible that has the singular personal pronoun in it eight times: you, you, your, you, your, your, your, you. Jesus was saying that the challenge to pray is on *you!*

I remember personally being faced with the challenge to pray at age nineteen. It was my first year in Detroit, and every day my team and I would be out on the streets evangelizing and handing out tracts—Monday to Friday from 12 to 5 p.m.; twenty-five hours a week. I remember almost two months went by and not a single person got saved. We had no success whatsoever. Now during that season, I was also busy doing all these other things. I will never forget when I got so dissatisfied over our lack of power. I said to the Lord, "God, I'm doing everything else but probably not the thing I need to be doing." I made a commitment to Him right then and there. "I am going to get up every morning at 7 a.m. and pray for one hour for You to come move on the streets of this city."

And so I did. I got up at 7 a.m. each morning. I may have offered up some hallelujahs for the first few minutes, but then I would proceed to just sit there for the remaining fifty-seven minutes. All I could say was, "Well, I'm here." As I sat there, God was not upset with me, saying, "Well, say something!" Every morning I came and just sat before the Lord, and then it seemed like heaven began to crack open. God was doing something in my heart. That following week, the breakthroughs started to happen. God was moving, and people were getting saved! It was as if God was saying, "Just ask!" Ask for people to be saved! Ask for your spouse, your family members, your neighbors . . . just ask! Don't leave any prayer unoffered.

Now since we know He is the God who answers prayer, why is it such a challenge for us to pray? What is at the heart of this battle for a consistent prayer life?

Francis Chan summed it up well when he said this: "Our greatest fear should not be of failure but of succeeding at things in life that don't really matter."[5] In other words, we ought to fear becoming an expert in the temporal—in the things that do not translate into eternity. If we are going to succeed in anything, we ought to succeed in prayer, for we have a God who answers prayer!

There is a two-verse story in the Old Testament that gives a good illustration of the hurdle—the danger of succeeding at things that really don't matter. This short story occurs in the middle of a larger story. But remember, nothing is in the Bible without reason, including this conversation. At this point, Israel is in the middle of a war with the Arameans. While the king is passing by, this compelling two-verse dialogue takes place:

> As the king passed by, he cried to the king and said, "Your servant went out into the midst of the battle; and behold, a man turned aside and brought a man to me and said, 'Guard this man; if for any reason he goes missing, then your life shall be forfeited in place of his life, or else you shall pay a talent of silver.' Now while your servant was busy here and there, he disappeared." And the king of Israel said to him, "So shall your judgment be; you yourself have determined it.'" (1 Kings 20:39–40)

While the servant was busy "here and there," the prisoner disappeared! This servant could not even name what his time was given over to! But whatever it was, his busyness lost him his prisoner. Likewise, how much of what we are supposed to be doing gets neglected for the sake of things we cannot even remember? We confuse motion with progress, busyness with productivity. The great Christian psychologist Dr. James Dobson explained it this way: "If Satan can't make you sin, he'll make you busy, and that's just about the same thing."[6]

What is the fix for this trap? How do we avoid getting caught up in busyness and losing what we were supposed to hold on to? For the 1 Kings man, it was his prisoner that was lost. For some of us, it is a marriage, our children, a job, a relationship with God. And for every Christian, it is also prayer.

The Apostle Paul said, "See then that you walk circumspectly, not as fools but as wise, redeeming the time, because the days are evil" (Ephesians 5:15–16 NKJV). We must recognize that our goal is not to be busy but rather to unclutter our life by redeeming the time. We become best at what we are supposed to be best at when we redeem the time. Isn't it interesting that Paul would use such a monumental word when referring to time? *Redeemed* by the blood, *redeemed* by the cross. Why would he associate *redeem* with *time*? It is because time is costly and valuable; there is a price to be paid for it. The Apostle Paul was reminding us to be intentional with how we spend these few precious years God has given us to live on earth.

How do we redeem the time and avoid becoming experts in things that do not really matter? Let's look at three ways.

1. Make God First, Not Part

The "God thing" does not work just one day a week. That is religion. That is why the Bible likens our relationship with Jesus to a marriage relationship. Try talking to your spouse only on Sundays. Try making decisions without him or her involved.

I was talking on my phone the other day, and it suddenly began to beep because the battery was running low. After a few minutes, it shut off. The battery died because I forgot to charge it the night before—yet I still wanted to use it normally without having done so. However, my phone lost its ability to operate at the level it was designed for because it was away from the power source for too long. Every day it needs to be plugged in. So it is for the Christian—we cannot merely pray and worship on Sunday and then expect that to sustain us for the rest of the week. We need a fresh charge every day! The problem with us is that we are more serious about our cell phone being charged up than our own spirit.

The disciples saw Jesus plugging into God constantly. In fact, the only time the disciples asked for a curriculum and study course was after seeing what prayer accomplished for Jesus.

> It happened that while Jesus was praying in a certain place, when He had finished, one of His disciples said to Him, "Lord, teach us to pray." (Luke 11:1)

How we need God to teach us to do this each day! We need a fresh touch every single morning. I learned that meeting with the Lord every morning was something I had to do because of who I want to be. You see, your calendar is more than an organizer for what needs to get done each day. It is the primary tool for helping you to become who you want to be. It plays a critical role in determining who you will become as a Christ follower, a family member, a leader, a friend.

There was a season in my life when individuals were asking to meet with me before work or at a certain time early in the morning. I would simply tell people, "No." If they would ask why, I would tell them I had an appointment. One guy asked me three times to meet in the morning, and I kept explaining that I had an appointment. He finally asked, "Who are you meeting with every single morning?"

The One who answers prayer! I told this man that he would not want to meet with me anyway, unless I first met with *Him*. You see, in the end, prayerlessness is pride. It is declaring that I can make it without inviting God into my day.

If you do not schedule your life, people will schedule it for you. So start with a non negotiable on your schedule. This is the time God gets priority.

2. See the End of Things, Not the Beginning

So many people rush into something because in the beginning, it is shiny and exciting, and everybody else is doing it. However, we must try to see things five or ten years down the road: Will it really matter then? Is it going to matter that I am really good at being the commissioner of fantasy football? Will I still care that I am an expert at pickleball? None of those things are bad, but do not become an expert at things while neglecting what really matters.

Solomon, the richest man who ever lived on the planet—who had every resource available to him—used a famous word at the end of his life: "vanity." In the Hebrew language, the word for vanity was a word picture of a bucket put in a well and brought up with nothing in it. You go through all the toil and strain, yet when it is finally pulled up, it is empty! If you are going to give yourself over to hours of doing something, see the end from the beginning. Will it turn out to be a bucket without water? At least you know that every time you get up in the morning and cry out to God, your bucket will come up full.

3. Invite God into Every Area

George Müller, the orphanage director known for his prayer life and great faith, said this in his autobiography: "Four hours of work after an hour of prayer will accomplish more than five hours of work without prayer."[7] Let me tell you what happens when Jesus is invited into your life each day. *He* redeems the time.

> Now when evening came, His disciples went down to the sea, and after getting into a boat, they started to cross the sea to Capernaum. It had already become dark, and Jesus had not yet come to them. In addition, the sea began getting rough, because a strong wind was blowing. Then, when they had rowed about twenty-five or thirty stadia, they saw Jesus walking on the sea and coming near the boat; and they were frightened. But He said to them, "It is I; do not be afraid." So they were willing to take Him into the boat, and immediately the boat was at the land to which they were going. (John 6:16–21)

Did you see that? The disciples were rowing and rowing, yet once Jesus came into their boat, they immediately arrived at the land to which they were headed! If they had not invited Him in, they would still be rowing. It is just like when we try to do life without Jesus . . . we end up rowing and rowing but never reaching our destination. How does He do it? I don't know, I can just tell you what the Bible says! He redeems the time.

I read somewhere that many people who would visit Mother Teresa and her Missionaries of Charity in Kolkata, India, were surprised that at every lunchtime, the sisters would all leave their life-sustaining work with people who were dying and disappear for a couple of hours. Some would question them, "With so much need, why do you leave?"

The sisters replied, "We go to pray. We learned that to work without prayer is to achieve only what is humanly possible. Our desire is to be involved in divine possibilities!"

Remember, if we do not pray, it will be up to us to row the entire time—often with the wind against us. I therefore encourage you to invite Jesus into every area of your life. It is your great honor and privilege to call on that famous name: *You who answer prayer!*

QUESTIONS

1. Is there an area of your life where you have been rowing endlessly instead of inviting Jesus to come in?

2. How have you experienced God as the One who answers prayer?

3. What are you investing in today that may not really matter in ten years?

4. What commitment are you willing to make to God regarding your prayer life?

QUARRELS, CONFLICTS, AND DIVISIONS

Fixing the Fights Fixes the Future

"Because of quarreling, the Father is dishonored, the Son is disgraced, His people are demoralized and discredited, and the world is turned off and confirmed in unbelief. Fractured fellowship robs Christians of joy and effectiveness, robs God of glory, and robs the world of the true testimony of the gospel. A high price for an ego trip!"

JOHN MACARTHUR[1]

The first New Testament church in Acts 1 started fifty days after Jesus' resurrection. Its growth even within its first year was staggering. The Scriptures tell us that the church grew from 120 members to 3,120 on the day of Pentecost, and then to 5,000 by the beginning of Acts 4—which is accounting for just the men, not the women and children (see Acts 2:41; 4:4).

The low estimate of Jerusalem's population at that time was 25,000.[2] That means the church literally made up about 20 percent of the population. God was clearly building that first church to be a force and a foundation in Jerusalem. However, an enemy was about to rise up against the church—one that could have derailed it all. The church was on the verge of becoming neutralized and irrelevant. And this underestimated enemy is not only still present in the church today but also in our homes and in our society.

Quarrels, conflicts, and divisions—an insidious enemy that can sabotage the future of a church, a family, a country!

A key phrase that launched the day of Pentecost in the upper room was "one accord," a phrase that appears in the book of Acts eleven times, highlighting the fact that it was critical to a move of God (see Acts 1:14; 2:1; 2:46; 4:24, 5:12; 7:57; 8:6; 12:20; 15:25; 18:12; 19:29). Let's look at what happened in the upper room:

> When the Day of Pentecost had fully come, they were all with one accord in one place. And suddenly there came a sound from heaven, as of a rushing mighty wind, and it filled the whole house where they were sitting. (Acts 2:1–2 NKJV)

When you lose "one accord," you lose being one voice. The church only wins the fight against external enemies when in one accord and with one voice. That means in order for the church to be an influence today, we must find our "middle C" again. It is the standard that every piano is tuned to. In his book *The Pursuit of God*, A. W. Tozer explained it this way:

> If you have one hundred concert pianos and you tune the second piano to the first, and the third to the second, and the fourth to the third, until you have tuned all one hundred of them, you will have discord and disharmony. But if you tuned each piano to the same tuning fork, you would have harmony and unity. So too, in the body of Christ; when we each tune ourselves and our lives to Christ, we will have unity.[3]

We do not tune to people's notes or preferences, cultures or denominations. We tune to Christ and His Word. Failing to do so results in quarrels, conflicts, and divisions. Suddenly there are a thousand middle Cs, meaning we are trying to cater to everyone's preferences and tastes. In the church, this might include anything from the opinion that not enough hymns are being sung to why don't we serve coffee, we need new songs, where are the flags, or we want church to be like it used to be! All of these are personal middle Cs.

If we cannot resolve these quarrels, conflicts, and divisions, then someone is using the wrong tuning fork. Some years ago, a certain Dallas church decided to split, with each faction filing a lawsuit to claim the church property. A judge finally referred the matter to the higher authorities in the denomination. A church court assembled to hear both sides of the case and awarded the church property to one of the two factions. The losers withdrew and formed another church in the area. During the hearing, the church courts learned that the conflict had all begun at a church dinner when an elder received a smaller slice of ham than a child seated next to him, and he felt dishonored. Sadly, this was reported in the newspapers for everyone to read.[4] I can only imagine how the people of Dallas must have laughed at that situation!

Did you know that food fights are not new? The beginning of Acts 5 tells the story of Ananias and Sapphira. Most of us read that story but forget the rest of the chapter. If you continue reading Acts 5:17–42, you see that the first church goes through three waves of persecution, yet they bounce back each time. In the first wave, the authorities take all twelve apostles to jail, but they end up being released by an angel (see verses 17–25).

In the second wave, the authorities bring the apostles before the Sanhedrin. They command them not to preach, but the apostles say, "We ought to obey God rather than men" (see verses 26–33).

In the third wave, the authorities flogged all the apostles (see verses 34–40). Yet after all this, look at the apostles' astounding response:

> So they went on their way from the presence of the Council, rejoicing that they had been considered worthy to suffer shame for His name. And every day, in the temple and from house to house, they did not stop teaching and preaching the good news of Jesus as the Christ. (Acts 5:41–42)

What a victorious testimony throughout all the persecution! Now what is both insightful and insidious is that the next attack was not from outside but the *inside*. This resilient New Testament church ended up fighting over food!

> During this time, as the disciples were increasing in numbers by leaps and bounds, hard feelings developed among the Greek-speaking believers—"Hellenists"—toward the Hebrew-speaking believers because their widows were being discriminated against in the daily food lines. (Acts 6:1 MSG)

Time and again a church has warded off a frontal attack, only to be subverted from within. In Acts 6, we see Satan trying to disrupt the inward peace of the early church. Unhappy with the new church growing by leaps and bounds, he sowed a spirit of murmuring and gossip among God's people, hoping to set believer against believer. Countless works for God have been destroyed in this way.

We might think everybody would have been so occupied with each day's new blessings that there was no room for murmuring. Not so! Here we see the Grecian Jews among them complaining against the Hebraic Jews because their widows were being overlooked in the daily distribution of food.

To give you a bit of history, Jerusalem had a large minority of Hellenistic (Greek-speaking) Jews. These Jews, though they spoke no Hebrew after having lived abroad for centuries, returned to Jerusalem because it was their holy city. Many of them had returned so they could spend their final days in Jerusalem, much like modern-day Zionists. As a result, there was an abundance of Greek-speaking women who had outlived their husbands. Resentful, the native Aramaic-speaking Jews discriminated against the Hellenistic Jews, whom the Pharisees held in utter contempt and deemed second-class Israelites. Then came Pentecost, and thousands of Aramaic-speaking Jews plus hundreds of Hellenistic Jews became one in Christ. Yet conversion, as wonderful as it was, did not erase all their prejudices.

Verse 2 implies something epic:

> So the twelve summoned the congregation of the disciples and said, "It is not desirable for us to neglect the word of God in order to serve tables." (Acts 6:2)

Evidently, some had suggested that the way to dispel hard feelings between the foreign Jews and the hometown crowd was to have Peter, John, and the others divvy up the widows' goods. They wanted the apostles to fix the situation and run the food program.

By the time we get to Acts 6, the church had withstood jail, persecution, and accusation. Now the church would face internal fighting. Quarrels and infighting were not unique to the Jerusalem church; the Apostle Paul later addressed it with the Corinthian church as well:

> When you come together as a church, I hear that divisions exist among you; and in part I believe it. For there also have to be factions

among you, so that those who are approved may become evident among you. (1 Corinthians 11:18–19)

Quarrels and divisions prove people and expose people. How you deal with the fight can determine the future of your ministry. In the case of the first church, I love what the apostles ended up doing here: They don't just solve the problem by automatically catering to the complaints; they change the culture of the church. We have deacons today because of the decision they made.

Let's look at three things that happened because of the way the apostles dealt with the fight:

- The apostles got focused.
- New leaders rose up.
- More people were reached.

The apostles knew what only they could do, so they got laser focused in order to be effective. Prayer and the Word became their job, and they delegated others to handle the food. In other words, they became specialists, not generalists. When there is focus, there is multiplied effectiveness.

> The announcement found approval with the whole congregation; and they chose Stephen, a man full of faith and of the Holy Spirit, and Philip, Prochorus, Nicanor, Timon, Parmenas, and Nicolas, a proselyte from Antioch. And they brought these men before the apostles; and after praying, they laid their hands on them. (Acts 6:5–6)

What strategic placement and delegation—all those chosen had Greek names. Though Hebraic Jews comprised most of the congregation, they chose Hellenistic Jews to administer the program! They got the right people in their places. The result? More people reached!

> The word of God kept on spreading; and the number of the disciples continued to increase greatly in Jerusalem, and a great many of the priests were becoming obedient to the faith. (Acts 6:7)

And as a result, new leaders rose up. Two all-stars emerged out of the food ministry—Stephen and Philip.

Stephen preached the second longest sermon in the New Testament and became the first martyr of the church. Stephen's death gives us incredible insight as to what happens when a believer leaves this earth. The Bible says that Jesus sat down at the right hand of the Father (see Hebrews 10:12), yet Stephen looked up into heaven and saw Jesus standing at the right hand of the Father (see Acts 7:55). I have a sense whenever a believer is about to enter eternity, he or she gets a vision of heaven. I believe Stephen did not feel one of those stones because of the overwhelming realization that he was about to be with Jesus! Not only that, but also a young man named Saul was there to witness it all. Saul would go on to become the Apostle Paul—one of the greatest Christians in all church history and author of thirteen New Testament epistles!

The other all-star who rose up was Philip—whom the Holy Spirit instructed to run alongside a chariot with an Ethiopian eunuch (see Acts 8:29). Philip shared with him the gospel from Isaiah 53, and it is said that this marked the entrance of the gospel to the continent of Africa—where today there exists over half a billion believers!

We see that it is critical that quarrels are dealt with and resolved. Notice that until Acts 6, everything was right in Jerusalem. Acts 6 was the food fight; Acts 7 was Stephen's speech; and Acts 8 was when the gospel started going out. It is evident that God would not allow the church to expand until it dealt with the internal fighting, for He did not want them exporting their own bondage and divisions.

Not only was the quarrel dealt with, but they fixed the fight in the right way! They did not know it then, but an entire continent and much of our New Testament hung in the balance. The apostles could have simply decided to order more food and serve it themselves to appease the crowd. But instead, they decided to figure out what God was asking them to do.

Similarly, when you are faced with a ministry problem, ask yourself: I know I can fix it, but *should* I fix it? Or can I refine the culture? When we personally fix food problems, we often fix the short-term and forfeit the future. We exalt ourselves instead of discovering the other gifts in the church. In the end, the effectiveness of the church is at stake.

How should we deal with the quarrels and conflicts we all face today? Have you ever wondered about certain situations: "Why is everything always an argument with them?" or "Why can't we simply discuss this like adults?" Though it typically seems to be someone else's fault, it is important that we get to the root of all conflict.

This reminds me of when we were in Detroit, and Cindy and I bought an old house near the XXX theater that we turned into a church. We began working in the house's basement to fix it up and make a play area for the kids. The walls had paint that had bubbled up, so we scraped and repainted it all. Within a month, the paint bubbled up again. So we did the quick fix and repainted it again—only to have it bubble up once again. We finally hired a professional who said there was a drainage issue, and he would have to dig deep into the wall. You see, when there is a leak, you can dress it up all you want, but the problem will remain. Likewise, in many of our conflicts, "paint" is not our problem. Bubbling paint is just a product of a deeper issue.

Take a moment to ponder this question: "What causes fights and quarrels among you?"

This is actually a biblical question posed in the book of James. James essentially said, "I am about to tell you the source of all your conflicts and quarrels: marriage fights, roommate fights, child/parent fights, even the fight with your most important relationship—you and God." James went right for the jugular; he minced no words as he revealed the source:

> What is the source of quarrels and conflicts among you? Is the source not your pleasures that wage war in your body's parts? You lust and do not have, so you commit murder. And you are envious and cannot obtain, so you fight and quarrel. You do not have because you do not ask. You ask and do not receive, because you ask with wrong motives, so that you may spend what you request on your pleasures. (James 4:1–3)

I have had the opportunity to do a lot of marital counseling over the years. I have sat with couples on the verge of divorce. Every time, I would give the first thirty to forty minutes to the couple to allow them to tell me their story. It typically boils down to a barrage of complaints about their spouse. I let them get it all out, and when they are finished, I ask each of them this question: "What are *you* doing wrong?"

Most never considered that. I even had a woman claim she could not think of a single thing she was doing wrong! I then say, "Meeting's over. You are going to go home and, for one week, take a notebook and sit before the Lord for thirty minutes every day, saying, 'Search me, Lord. Show me my heart.'"

That woman who had been so conditioned to assuming the problem was her spouse came back with thirteen pages! Some of you are always in counseling because you never look at yourself. When you fail to look at yourself, you are missing the source, and the problem will never be resolved. You might put a new coat of paint on, only to have it eventually bubble up again.

I find it interesting that we only have two accounts in the Bible of Jesus using the word *church*. One deals with conflict outside the church (in Matthew 16:18, where Jesus said the gates of hell will not prevail against the church); the other deals with conflict inside (in Matthew 18:17, where Jesus discussed the church's role in the reconciliation of brothers and sisters). In other words, fighting with Satan and fighting with believers. Thankfully, James offered us revelation regarding this second type of conflict. Let's look at three big thoughts from his book.

1. IF YOU ARE IN A FIGHT WITH SOMEONE, THERE IS A FIGHT INSIDE OF YOU

Is the source, your pleasures that wage war in your body's parts? You lust and do not have, so you commit murder. And you are envious and cannot obtain, so you fight and quarrel. (James 4:1–2)

We have the tendency to minimize conflicts, simply concluding, "We just don't get along." But James said, "Hold on! Nothing is further from the truth." Conflicts reveal an internal struggle, which James called a "war within you" (NLT). That means the struggle is not between people but *within* people.

What exactly is this internal fight? You cannot get what you want. How eye-opening to realize that it's not them, it's me! So here is the question: What do I want from someone that he or she is not giving me? Let me explain with this example: The Bible lays out specific challenges and responsibilities for both husbands and wives. It says, "Husbands, here is your job in the marriage: Love your wives , just as Christ also loved the church and gave Himself up for her. Wives: Subject yourselves to your own husbands, as to the Lord" (see Ephesians 5:22, 25). Another version says ,"Wives, respect your husbands."

What Paul was saying is that each of you has a need, and the other is called to keep an eye on that need. When you are not having these needs met, the quarrels begin. This is what I hear across the board in marital counseling, probably 90 percent of the time:

Husband: "She doesn't respect me."

Wife: "He doesn't love me."

As a husband, I must realize that everything I do for Cindy is saying "I love you" to her, and what I don't do is not saying "I love you" to her. So when I am not being respected, instead of complaining, "She doesn't respect me!" I need to ask myself: "Why am I not giving her something to respond to?" If she knows she is loved, she will respect me. And if I know I am respected, I am going to love her.

Yet when needs go unmet, James said the war is so intense that people are willing to kill to get what they want. They will kill a marriage, a ministry, a relationship, a friendship. They will kill it while blaming others, never examining themselves. That is because people often see what has been done to them but never bother to look at what is going on within them.

James said, "Start with *you*, not simply the issue." *Source* is more important than issue. Remember, conflict is a revelation of you; conflict is a revelation of what is in you. In fact, James said three times that the source is *you*: "Your pleasures that wage war," "You lust and do not have," "You are envious and cannot obtain" (James 4:1–2). And then James followed up with something even more intense as he made this statement:

You do not have because you do not ask. (James 4:2)

Which leads to our next point . . .

2. Prayerlessness and Conflict Are Connected

Am I trying to get from someone else what I can only get from God?

When we do not pray and allow God to meet our needs, we end up trying to make people meet our needs. In that case, we will always be left short. Marriage and children do not meet the core need; that is why you can have them yet still be fighting. The problem is that we are trying to get our value and significance from people. This puts God-sized expectations on marriage, friends, children. It is God alone who gives you your value and significance.

3. You Cannot Fix What You Do Not See

There is something that each of us does before leaving the house (hopefully)—we look into a mirror. James told us that there is a mirror to see ourselves in:

> Those who listen to the word but do not do what it says are like people who look at their faces in a mirror and, after looking at themselves, go away and immediately forget what they look like. (James 1:23–24 TNIV)

You cannot fix what you do not see. When you neglect spending time with God, it is actually a very selfish thing to do. The people who are closest to you are now tasked with pointing out your issues. However, when you spend time in the presence of God, He will show you what is out of place. It is so much better to confess than to be told by someone else what is wrong.

Consider the following scenario: "Honey, you spoke very harshly to me," the wife says. At that point, things can go either way. It could get volatile.

Now consider a second scenario: "The Holy Spirit convicted me about the way I spoke to you," the husband says. What do you think happens to his wife in this case? She feels protected.

When was the last time you apologized because you were convicted by the Holy Spirit? When you are in God's presence, you see yourself, and there is great strength to a relationship when you let God identify issues before others have to. But when you leave off prayer and the Word from your life, you lose your mirror. Instead of the conflict being dealt with in prayer, it happens with people.

Now of all the conflicts that arise, the biggest one in some people's lives is between them and God. They are mad at God and refuse to serve Him because He has not done what they think He should have. It goes like this:

"I asked God to heal my mother, but He didn't."

"I asked God to give us a child, but He didn't."

"I asked God for that job, but He didn't give it to me."

"I asked God to let me get married, but I haven't even been asked out on a date."

Now they are in conflict with God. They have pointed out all that is wrong, yet they never dealt with themselves. Some even cover up their anger with God by calling themselves an atheist or agnostic. But that is not the problem. The problem is that they did not get what they wanted.

As a result, it is just as Thomas Merton said: "We cannot be at peace with others because we are not at peace with ourselves, and we cannot be at peace with ourselves because we are not at peace with God."[5] A bad relationship with God means a bad relationship with people. The Bible shows us the way to true fellowship with one another:

> But if we are living in the light, as God is in the light, then we have fellowship with each other, and the blood of Jesus, his Son, cleanses us from all sin. (1 John 1:7 NLT)

Walk in the light! What does that mean? It means to live with nothing hidden, nothing undealt with. Everything in your heart is out in the open before God. I love David's prayer:

> Search me, God, and know my heart;
> Put me to the test and know my anxious thoughts;
> And see if there is any hurtful way in me,
> And lead me in the everlasting way.
> (Psalm 139:23–24)

Notice he does not say, "Search *them*, try *them*." It is not him, her, them, that pastor. It is *my* heart, try *me*, *my* anxious thoughts, in *me*, lead *me*.

Let's not simply repaint the wall. It is time to scrape and dig, allowing God to deal with the battle in our soul. May we allow the Lord to search us daily, and may we find in Him everything that we need. Then we will truly experience "how good and how pleasant it is for brothers to live together in unity!" (Psalm 133:1).

QUESTIONS

1. Think of a recent or recurrent conflict in your life. Spend some time before God and allow Him to search your heart. What is He speaking to you about your next steps?

2. Read 1 Corinthians 6:7. What does this tell you about the values of God's kingdom?

3. Can you think of an example of when you have seen a quarrel or conflict dealt with wisely?

REPENTANCE

The Missing Piece to Victory

"Repentance is not an emotion. It is not feeling sorry for your sins. It is a decision. It is deciding that you have been wrong in supposing that you could manage your own life and be your own god."
EUGENE PETERSON[1]

Before Jesus went to celebrate communion in the upper room, before Gethsemane and the cross, He made His triumphal entry into Jerusalem—riding upon a donkey as the crowds shouted, "Hosanna!" The Scriptures tell us that Jesus then entered the temple and overturned the tables of the money changers, declaring, "MY HOUSE WILL BE CALLED A HOUSE OF PRAYER" (Matthew 21:13). This cleansing of the temple was Jesus coming to remove and to restore. Men had taken prayer out of God's house and instead set up tables to buy and sell. However, removing prayer meant they now had to depend on what money could buy instead of what God could do. It sounds much like the predicament of the church today.

The cleansing of the temple happened toward the end of Jesus' life in the Synoptic Gospels (see Matthew 21; Mark 11; Luke 19). Yet what often gets overlooked is the fact that in the book of John, the cleansing of the temple occurred not at the end but at the beginning of Jesus' ministry (see John 2:13–17). That means there were two temple cleansings, three years apart.

Why was there a cleansing of the temple at the beginning *and* at the end of Jesus' ministry?

Simply put, it is because junk always tries to come back into the temple. The things that Jesus kicked out somehow made their way back in three years and set up shop again. What is sobering about this is that you and I, being the temple of the Holy Spirit (see 1 Corinthians 6:19), are constantly faced with the same challenge. When you become born again, God does a renovation work—throwing out the old furniture, restoring and redecorating. However, the things that God removed from the living temple are always trying to make their way back into our souls.

Fortunately, He has given us a weapon to counter all that is constantly trying to overthrow what God has established in our hearts. It is the most forgotten word for freedom: *repentance*. Jesus showed us two cleansings of the temple to remind us that our temple needs cleaning every day.

Tragically, we have created a delusional church that mistakenly assumes freedom comes from attendance of a service or seminar. Without repentance, churches will begin to support unbiblical lifestyles, for all we are doing is adding Christ to a life that needs reformation while never subtracting sin. The goal of the gospel is not to add Jesus to our sinful life; it is to invite Jesus to be Lord and take over every part of our life!

Confession of sin without repentance of sin results in a 360-degree Christian life. So many Christians today are experiencing 360s in their life instead of 180s. Making a 180 means you were heading one way, but a profound change occurred, causing you to head in a different direction. On the other hand, doing a 360 means something caused you to temporarily stop engaging in a sinful practice. However, it is not long before you find yourself involved once again.

Did you know that repentance was Jesus' first sermon as well as His last sermon? Here are His first recorded words in the Gospels:

> From that time Jesus began to preach and say, "Repent, for the kingdom of heaven is at hand." (Matthew 4:17)

The last thing Jesus ever said is not found in the Gospels but in the book of Revelation:

> Those whom I love, I reprove and discipline; therefore be zealous and repent. (Revelation 3:19)

It would therefore do us well to examine what repentance is and why it is important for the church today!

Several years ago, the *Peanuts* comic strip had Lucy and Charlie Brown practicing football. Lucy would hold the ball for Charlie's placekicking, and he would approach to kick with all his might. But at the point of no return, Lucy would remove the ball. Charlie's momentum, unchecked by the ball that was no longer there, would cause him to fall flat on his back.

One particular comic strip opened with Lucy holding the ball, but Charlie Brown finally wising up and refusing to kick. "Every time I try to kick the ball, you pick it up, and I fall on my back."

Lucy kept insisting he kick while Charlie Brown continued to refuse, until finally Lucy broke down in tears and admitted, "Charlie Brown, I have been so terrible to you over the years, picking up the football like I have. I have played so many cruel tricks on you, but I've seen the error of my ways! I've seen the hurt look in your eyes when I've deceived you. I've been wrong, so wrong. Won't you give a poor penitent girl another chance?"

Charlie Brown was moved by her display of grief and responded, "Of course I'll give you another chance." He stepped back as she held the ball, and then he ran. At the last moment, Lucy picked up the ball and Charlie Brown fell flat on his back.

Lucy's last words were, "Recognizing your faults and actually changing your ways are two different things, Charlie Brown!"[2]

Lucy understood! The emotion of feeling sorry for what you have done is remorse. Repentance takes it a step further and makes the change.

When I was a young pastor with just a small church, we had a food ministry that fed a couple thousand people a month on the streets of Detroit. A dear friend and fellow pastor gave us money to help with that food ministry. At the time, we were a struggling church. Bills were mounting. We ended up taking that financial gift, specifically intended for the food ministry, and using it to pay the electric and heating bills. After all, you cannot have a food kitchen if you don't have lights and heat, I reasoned. However, that money had been earmarked to feed the poor. I remember going to the Lord in prayer one day, asking for provision. His response caught me by surprise: "You took money and used it for something you were not supposed to use it for. Call that pastor and repent."

People think that just because you feel bad about something, change is coming. But I knew I needed to pick up the phone and come clean with this pastor. It was not an easy phone call. I hoped he would say, "Go ahead, do what you need to do. I'll send another check." To his credit, he did not let me off the hook—for which I am ever grateful. I felt his words pierce my soul: "Tim, you need to learn now that if somebody gives you money for something specific, you cannot use it for something else. That's lying and that's cheating." It stung, but the message came across clearly. Though I felt God speak to me in prayer, that was just the remorse. To repent, I needed to change what I was doing.

The word *repentance* means "to change your mind." When you repent, you change your mind and recognize that God's mind is better than yours. God was telling me I should not have used those finances in that way, and I agreed that His mind was better than my mind.

Repentance changes our minds about four things:

- **Self:** We no longer live with an inflated self-importance. We finally realize it is not all about our happiness, recognition, opinions, or comfort. It is about Jesus.
- **Sin:** We see sin as seriously as God sees it. Sin is no longer simply a vice or dysfunction; it is a crime against God.
- **Savior:** We see Jesus as our Savior—the only way to heaven, healing, and freedom.
- **Salvation:** We understand we are saved not because we earned or deserved it, but by grace.

In a world without moral absolutes—where everyone now has their own "truth"—repentance is vital. You cannot serve God with your own truth; you cannot walk with Jesus without being of the same mind. It says in Amos 3:3, "Can two walk together, unless they are agreed?" (NKJV). Without repentance, you may have changed your mind about Jesus, but you have not changed your mind about your sin.

John described what true forgiveness looks like:

> If we confess our sins, He is faithful and just to forgive us our sins
> and to cleanse us from all unrighteousness. (1 John 1:9)

When you get forgiven, you also get cleansed. We often want forgiveness, but we do not want the cleansing work of God in our lives. The word *confess* means "to say the same thing." Confession means you agree with God. When you repent, you are saying, "God, I agree with You. I see my destructive behavior that is becoming toxic to my soul. I need not only Your forgiveness but also Your cleansing to be free!"

When I first started in ministry, our church was located right by the projects in Detroit. One day, the secretary told me someone was there to see me. She didn't know who he was, only that he was from the projects. Moments later, a young man entered. He laid a loaded gun on my desk and said, "I shot someone last night. I need to get right with God."

"Is that the gun you shot someone with?" I asked, quickly taking the gun and unloading the bullets. He acknowledged that it was but had no idea if the victim was injured or killed.

I led this young man to the Lord, and God visibly touched him. The next thing I said was, "God has forgiven you, and now He has to cleanse your soul. In order to do this, we are going to take the gun down to the police station, and you are going to confess what you did last night."

He looked at me and said, "Absolutely."

When it is true forgiveness, cleansing is what comes next. This young man was not merely adding Jesus, he was subtracting the sin. That is why repentance and remorse are not the same. Remorse comes more easily. It is a feeling of sorrow, a reaction to wrong in my life. Repentance is a deliberate action to right my wrong living. Repentance says, "I want forgiveness, and I also want cleansing." The reason we pull so many 360s is because we have been forgiven but never cleansed.

The Scriptures give us a picture of the difference between remorse and repentance. As we look at seven people in the Bible who said the phrase "I have sinned," the difference will become evident.

The Seven "I Have Sinned" Statements of the Bible

1. Pharaoh

> Then Pharaoh sent for Moses and Aaron, and said to them, "I have sinned this time; the Lord is the righteous one, and I and my people are the wicked ones". . . . But when Pharaoh saw that the rain and the hail and the thunder had stopped, he sinned again and hardened his heart, he and his servants. (Exodus 9:27, 34)

Timed repentance: sorrow that lasts until the sky clears up—until you know you are out of danger. When the clouds are gloomy and the skies are dark, we want desperately for God to intervene. But once everything clears up, it is easy to return to an old lifestyle.

2. Balaam

> Balaam said to the angel of the Lord, "I have sinned, for I did not know that you were standing in the way against me. Now then, if it is displeasing to you, I will turn back." (Numbers 22:34)

Death repentance: confession of sin out of the fear of facing eternity. An angel was about to kill Balaam; he was a step away from perishing. Today such a reaction might be prompted by a doctor's report or other life-threatening situation. Balaam ultimately ended up getting killed for his bad decisions.

3. Achan

> Achan, son of Carmi, son of Zabdi, son of Zerah, from the tribe of Judah, was selected. Then Joshua said to Achan, "My son, I implore you, give glory to the Lord . . . and tell me now what you have done. Do not hide it from me." So Achan answered Joshua and said, "Truly, I have sinned against the Lord, the God of Israel, and this is what I did." (Joshua 7:18–20)

Exposed repentance: admission of sin only when found out. Achan had stolen silver and gold in the battle at Ai, even though God had prohibited the Israelites from taking the spoils. When Joshua questioned the Lord as to why they had lost the battle, God told him there was sin in the camp and exposed who had done it. It was at that point that Achan finally confessed.

When counseling someone, I ask this question: "Did you confess, or did you get exposed?" If they were exposed, then their sorrow is often suspect.

4. Shimei

This is the guy who threw rocks at David before he was king. Later, when David becomes king, Shimei comes into the throne room with repentance in hopes that his life might be spared.

> He said to the king, "May my lord not consider me guilty, nor call to mind what your servant did wrong on the day when my lord the king went out from Jerusalem, so that the king would take it to heart. For your servant knows that I have sinned; so behold, I have come today, the first of all the house of Joseph to go down to meet my lord the king." (2 Samuel 19:19–20)

Reward repentance: admission of sin without the mind change. Shimei was no longer talking to David the refugee; he now stood before David the king. He was essentially saying, "Can we just forget about when I threw rocks at you?"

Today it might sound like: "I repented, don't divorce me. I don't want to pay child support," or "Don't fire me, I need health insurance." In other words, "I don't want you to mess up what I have going here." Though David showed him mercy, Shimei walked in rebellion and eventually got killed.

5. Saul

We discussed Saul, the worshiping backslider, in the chapter on obedience. Saul pleaded with Samuel:

> I have sinned; but please honor me now before the elders of my people and before all Israel, and go back with me, that I may worship the Lord your God. (1 Samuel 15:30)

"Let's move on" repentance or *"I don't want to lose my position" repentance*: admission out of embarrassment. Saul wanted to look right more than be right. "I did it, I get it, can we just pick up where we left off? I'm the king, so let's just rewind and keep going."

Now the last two "I have sinned" statements exhibit a stark contrast, and I am going to tackle them together.

6. and 7. David and the Prodigal Son

Here is David's response to Nathan when confronted about his sin with Bathsheba:

> I have sinned against the LORD. (2 Samuel 12:13)

The prodigal son, after coming to his senses, said to himself:

> I will set out and go back to my father and say to him: Father, I have sinned against heaven and against you. (Luke 15:18 NIV)

What sets these two apart from the others? Both David and the prodigal son recognized they had sinned against God. They were not repenting in order to get something or to save their reputation. Their relationship with God was of utmost importance. David said in his psalm:

> Against You, You only, I have sinned
> And done what is evil in Your sight.
> (Psalm 51:4)

Why did the first five of the "I have sinned" men become 360-men? Almost all of them ended up back in sin. It was because their confession of sin had to do with their own benefits. They never realized they were affecting their relationship with God. When you fail to realize it is against God that you have sinned, you set yourself up for a repeat.

Saul was a 360-man. He tried to kill David four times (see 1 Samuel 18:10–11; 19:10; 24:2; 26:2). The first two times he hurled a spear at him, then he hired 3,000 men to kill him. By the third time, Saul was weeping over what he had done. The fourth time, he said to David:

> I have sinned. Return, my son David, for I will not harm you again since my life was precious in your sight this day. Behold, I have played the fool and have made a very great mistake. (1 Samuel 26:21)

Saul said the right words, but there was no lifestyle to back it up. He never changed!

The first time it happened, it was a sin he should have repented over. Instead, he flirted with the envy and jealousy in his heart. Some people today are flirting with bitterness, pornography, or some other sin, oblivious to the bondage it brings them into. They may think they have a handle on it, just as Saul thought—yet he ended up with a murderous spirit. Something dangerous happens when you flirt with sin and the 360s are continuous: You develop a hard heart; you lose sensitivity to the Spirit. There must be a repentant heart that does not just say, "God forgive me" but "God cleanse me—I want this thing to die once and for all!"

When I first started in ministry, there was a time when there were imaginations and fantasies in my mind that God was convicting me of. Nothing was acted upon; they were just imaginations. Nevertheless, I remember leaving a prayer meeting and pulling into my garage, when I heard the Holy Spirit say, "You need to kill this thing once and for all. You are flirting with thoughts that can manifest." I knew I had to deal with it then and there. That is why David said: "Let the words of my mouth and the meditation of my heart be acceptable in Your sight, O Lord" (Psalm 19:14, NKJV). It is not just our words or actions that need cleansing. We need to deal with things when they are in our heart. If you find that anger is coming out in your words, it is because there is anger in your heart. Before it even makes it to your mouth or hands, cry out for God to make you pure!

The Bible tells us there must be fruit of our repentance:

> Prove by the way you live that you have repented of your sins and turned to God. (Matthew 3:8 NLT)

How do we prove our repentance? Look at how the Apostle Paul described true repentance. It starts with godly sorrow, then true repentance, and then the fruit of repentance follows:

> For godly sorrow worketh repentance to salvation not to be repented of: but the sorrow of the world worketh death. For behold this selfsame thing, that ye sorrowed after a godly sort, what carefulness it wrought in you, yea, what clearing of yourselves, yea, what indignation, yea, what fear, yea, what vehement desire, yea, what zeal, yea, what revenge! In all things ye have approved yourselves

to be clear in this matter. (2 Corinthians 7:10–11 KJV)

We do not prove our repentance by weeping or even from confession. When a heart is truly repentant, this will be the evidence:

1. *Diligence*: You stay away from anything that could bring you back into that sin.
2. *Clearing of yourselves*: You make things right. Restitution may be financial, a phone call, etc.
3. *Indignation*: You have a sense of anger toward what sin took from you.
4. *Fear*: You have a renewed fear of the Lord. You are alarmed at what could have happened—perhaps the loss of your marriage, kids, trust, etc.
5. *Vehement desire*: You long to maintain your freedom. You begin adding godly disciplines that were not previously present in order to avoid that sin.
6. *Zeal*: You have a renewed fire and passion for the Lord, a new devotion of consistency.
7. *Vindication*: You want to inflict revenge upon the enemy for all those he has deceived in that area. You become God's ambassador against hellish schemes.

Allow me to draw from my youth an example of when the breaking of the 360 pattern was distinct and definitive. Although I was born and raised in the church, I had a problem with stealing when I was young. My dad had a big collection of silver dimes, quarters, and half-dollars that he kept in his dresser—which I would help myself to (in order to fund my baseball card collection). I remember one time when I was about twelve years old, I snuck into his room to grab a handful of money while he was napping. As I walked out of the room with a bunch of coins jingling in my pocket, I ran into my mother who asked, "What's that?"

"It's money," I replied, matter-of-fact.

"Where did you get that?"

"The Lord provided."

This is what she told me next, which I still remember to this day: "If you don't tell me where you got that, I am going to ask the Holy Spirit, and He's gonna tell me!"

It didn't take more than a second for me to cry out, "I'm a thief! I'll never do it again!"

She woke my father up, who said to me, "If I ever catch you stealing again, I'm going to burn your hand off!"

Now he was a Christian, and I was not too worried, figuring I could always sue. I went on stealing from other family members. About a year later, I got caught again. My dad said to me, "Wait right here." He proceeded to go to our tool room and came back with a propane torch. He struck the flint to ignite it, and I thought he had lost his mind! At the sight of the flame, I started weeping. Suddenly my dad said, "I told you this would be the consequence. But God is a God of mercy."

Even my father's extreme scare tactic did not do the job of ridding me from stealing. Amazingly, it was not long before I was back at it again. It was the 360. Getting caught brought remorse. "I have sinned, don't ask the Holy Spirit. I have sinned, don't burn my hand off!" But I never got to "I have sinned against the Lord" until I was at church camp one year. I was in the church camp's bookstore and picked up a comic book based on *The Late Great Planet Earth*—about the rapture and second coming of Christ. I read it and was determined, "I'm not going to hell!" In there was the verse in 1 Corinthians 6:10 that says no thieves will have their part in the kingdom of God. I realized I was a thief. The fire did not bring true repentance; it was this comic book that showed me I had sinned against God. I went straight to the camp counselor and said, "I am a thief. I've stolen from everybody. I'm not going to hell, I'm going to heaven. I need to get this right . . . right now!"

When God speaks, you must respond! Otherwise, you risk developing a hard heart. A hard heart is one that ignores, refuses, and even dislikes the "inconvenient" convictions of the Holy Spirit. Immediate obedience is the greatest guarantee of maintaining a soft and pliable heart.

In the book of Hebrews, God warned the Christians about hard hearts four times within two chapters:

Therefore, just as the Holy Spirit says,

> "TODAY IF YOU HEAR HIS VOICE,
> DO NOT HARDEN YOUR HEARTS AS WHEN THEY PROVOKED ME,
> AS ON THE DAY OF TRIAL IN THE WILDERNESS."
> (Hebrews 3:7–8)

But encourage one another every day, as long as it is still called "today," so that none of you will be hardened by the deceitfulness of sin. (Hebrews 3:13)

While it is said,

> "TODAY IF YOU HEAR HIS VOICE,
> DO NOT HARDEN YOUR HEARTS, AS WHEN THEY PROVOKED ME."
> (Hebrews 3:15)

He again sets a certain day, "Today," saying through David after so long a time just as has been said before,

> "TODAY IF YOU HEAR HIS VOICE,
> DO NOT HARDEN YOUR HEARTS."
> (Hebrews 4:7)

The key word is *today! Today* is God's word. *Tomorrow* is the enemy's word. Today if you hear His voice or feel His conviction, thank God! That means the Holy Spirit is speaking to you, and you don't have a hard heart. It also means *today* is when you must respond and repent. The road of tomorrow leads to the town of nowhere and never.

Within the 150 psalms, there are special psalms called penitential or repentance psalms. The greatest is Psalm 51:

> Wash me thoroughly from my guilt
> And cleanse me from my sin.
> For I know my wrongdoings,
> And my sin is constantly before me.
> Against You, You only, I have sinned
> And done what is evil in Your sight.

Create in me a clean heart, God,
And renew a steadfast spirit within me.
Do not cast me away from Your presence,
And do not take Your Holy Spirit from me.
Restore to me the joy of Your salvation,
And sustain me with a willing spirit.
Then I will teach wrongdoers Your ways,
And sinners will be converted to You.
(Psalm 51:2–4, 10–13)

Today is when we stop doing 360s and walk in true freedom. I encourage you to invite God to cleanse the temple every day. If you are at a loss for words, pray Psalm 51. Notice the amazing thing that also results: "Then I will teach wrongdoers Your ways, and sinners will be converted to You." True repentance brings God's cleansing, freedom, and joy to your life—and salvation to others!

QUESTIONS

1. Have you been experiencing a 360 in an area of your life? Where do you need to move from remorse to *repentance*?

2. This chapter reminds us that thought patterns can be sinful and equally offensive to God as their eventual actions. Do you have any thought patterns that need to be brought before the Lord?

3. When a genuine desire for freedom from sin *does* follow remorse, there may be another pitfall. What are some ways we try to cleanse ourselves rather than relying on God's cleansing?

4. Of the five examples of people who confessed they had sinned but did not truly repent, which might have been you at different times in your life? What would true repentance have looked like in that situation?

SIN

The Cost of Sin

"Sin is the most expensive thing in the universe. If it is forgiven sin, it cost God his only Son. If it is unforgiven sin, it cost the sinner his soul and an eternity in hell."
CHARLES FINNEY[1]

I always like to tell a story to make a point, and I'm going to make a point about sin. I don't remember where I heard this story, probably on the news or social media. But it's good. A few years ago in a Midwest city, an unusual attempted robbery took place. From what I remember, the thief was never pursued, so he remains nameless. However, his crime was remembered for a long time. This young man had devised a plan to rob a convenience store. He would hand the clerk $20, and when she opened the cash register drawer, he would grab all the money in there. When the moment came, it all seemed to be unfolding according to plan . . . except for one small problem: As he grabbed the money from the register, there was only a total of $14 in the drawer—putting the crime at a net loss of $6!

That is sin, defined by a botched robbery. It will always leave you $6 short. You go through all that work only to be left empty and guilty. Sin never delivers what it promises. It always returns less than the sinner invests.

What is sin? Simply put, sin is the failure to do what is right. I also love how Ignatius of Loyola defined sin—as a refusal to believe God wants my best, my happiness, and my fulfillment. So I decide what's best for me.[2] Today we live in a world where we believe nobody is at fault, making it therefore hard for us to hear what the Bible says regarding sin: "For all have sinned and fall short of the glory of God" (Romans 3:23).

In reality, *everybody* is at fault today.

When you blame others, you give up your power to change. There is a world of difference between saying, "I have made a mistake" and "I have sinned." To say, "I have made a mistake," removes ownership and responsibility, rendering the rebellious act an accident or a mishap. Most of our preaching today does not allow people to see that they have sinned; they are merely part of a bad situation. When people see themselves as victims, then they are not part of a fall (see Genesis 3); they are involved in an accident of culture, education, community, society, government, and so on.

This puts us in a predicament, for when you do not know the severity of a disease, you cannot appreciate the cure. Sin is the disease; the cross is the cure. If we refuse to acknowledge sin as the foundational problem of humanity, we have no need for a Savior. Sin is not an act; it is a *condition*, and that condition can only be fixed by Someone outside of our sinful system. Yet we simply cannot understand the magnitude of forgiveness unless we understand the foulness and strength of sin.

Today this understanding eludes us as we continue to do our best to sanitize sin. People will call it "an affair" when the Bible calls it *adultery*. Some will call it a "woman's choice"; the Bible calls it *murder of an unborn child*. People will call it "just a white lie," but the Bible says it is *a lie*. Society will say you are "sticking it to the man"; the Bible calls it *stealing*. In the end, sin is still sin, no matter what euphemism we give it.

I have seen it said about sin:

- Man calls it an accident; God calls it an abomination.
- Man calls it a blunder; God calls it blindness.
- Man calls it a defect; God calls it a disease.
- Man calls it a chance; God calls it a choice.
- Man calls it an error; God calls it an enmity.

- Man calls it a fascination; God calls it a fatality.
- Man calls it an infirmity; God calls it an iniquity.
- Man calls it a luxury; God calls it a leprosy.
- Man calls it a liberty; God calls it lawlessness.
- Man calls it a trifle; God calls it a tragedy.
- Man calls it a mistake; God calls it a madness.
- Man calls it a weakness; God calls it willfulness.

When we do not call sin "sin," then every inner desire becomes legitimate and acceptable. Yet the Bible shows us that it is quite the contrary:

> From within, out of the hearts of people, come the evil thoughts, acts of sexual immorality, thefts, murders, acts of adultery, deeds of greed, wickedness, deceit, indecent behavior, envy, slander, pride, and foolishness. All these evil things come from within and defile the person. (Mark 7:21–23)

Someone once gave my sister a special treat for her dogs—expensive doggie biscuits from a bakery. They even came in a beautiful bakery box fastened with red and white twine. The box was left on the counter as my sister went out to run an errand, and she returned to find our mom sitting there with a cup of coffee, eating the dog biscuits! My mom told her, "Don't go to that bakery anymore! Those cookies were terrible. I had to dip them in coffee just to bite into them. No matter what I did, they were bad!" It is the same thing with sin. You can try to dip it in political correctness, a university, a woke society. Dip it in anything you want, but it is still sin!

The dangerous thing about sin is that it is never stagnant. Sin incubates in the dark. Irrespective of who you are—believer, unbeliever, society's highly esteemed, or society's disregarded—sin seeks to steal, kill, and destroy.

Undealt-with sin grows at an alarming rate. It always gets worse when left alone. Neglect feeds sin. If you plant apple seeds, you get apples. If you plant tomato seeds, you get tomatoes. If you plant nothing, you get weeds! That is sin. Do nothing about sin, and it comes in with a force! A. W. Tozer illustrated this idea in his book *The Root of the Righteous*. He called it "the rule of the wild."[3]

Every farmer knows the hunger of the wilderness. That hunger which no modern farm machinery, no improved agricultural methods, can ever quite destroy. No matter how well prepared the soil, how well kept the fences, how carefully painted the buildings, let the owner neglect for a while his prized and valued acres and they will revert again to the wild and be swallowed up by the jungle or wasteland. The bias of nature is toward the wilderness, never toward the fruitful field.[4]

When you have a garden, you never have to plant weed seeds. And what is true of the field is true also of the soul, if only we are wise enough to see it.

Furthermore, sin does not age people well. There are no good, happy, kind old sinners. Sin corrodes and corrupts. You do not grow wiser about what you are doing the longer you are in it. The longer you are in sin, the dumber you get. James Stewart described how sin dumbs us down in *The Strong Name*:

It might seem natural to suppose that every time a man sins, he would know a little more about sin, its nature and its methods. Actually, the exact reverse is true. Every time he sins, he is making himself less capable of realizing what sin is; less likely to recognize that he is a sinner; for the ugly thing (and this I feel sure has never been sufficiently grasped), the really diabolical thing about sin is that it perverts a man's judgment. It stops him from seeing straight.[5]

Because of sin's power to consume, there is no such thing as a small sin. The great nineteenth-century theologian C. F. W. Walther said, "Small sins become great when they are regarded as small."[6] Sin is septic—a catastrophic disease that has infected everyone. We experienced the destructive effects of COVID-19, but there has been in existence for thousands of years a far deadlier pandemic. This sin pandemic has left multitudes dying—not physically but spiritually.

There is no one who is rich enough, strong enough, or good enough to control sin. I remember ex-gang leader Nicky Cruz telling stories of the old days at Brooklyn Teen Challenge. There was a heroin addict who, wanting deliverance so badly, asked the director to handcuff him to the radiator. Since this was back in the late '50s, the director acquiesced. The next morning, the radiator was gone! Somewhere on the streets was a man dragging a radiator, buying heroin. That is the strength of sin!

A Description of Sin

In Romans 7, Paul showed us the ugly power of sin and why it must not be trifled with. Today if Paul were to tweet any of his statements about sin, he would be banned from social media. But he made no apologies. Right away, one of the biggest misconceptions regarding the goodness of man was annihilated by Paul.

> For I know that good does not dwell in me. (Romans 7:18)

Have you come to that conclusion about yourself? Sin deceives us by making us think that we are inherently good. It takes a man a long time to reach the conclusion that he is not good. It is from this misconception that we derive the age-old, faulty question: "Why do bad things happen to good people?" Here is the answer: Only once did a bad thing happen to a good person . . . they crucified Him!

The following verses in Romans give us Paul's personification of sin:

1. Sin is a resident.

> As it is, it is no longer I myself who do it, but it is sin living in me. (Romans 7:17 NIV)

Sin is a dweller, a resident living inside me. My life is a house, and sin comes in to run the house. It will not leave, no matter how many times I try in my own strength to evict it.

2. Sin is my prison warden.

> But I see another law at work in me, waging war against the law of my mind and making me a prisoner of the law of sin at work within me. (Romans 7:23 NIV)

I am a prisoner to sin. I am in chains; it holds me captive.

3. Sin is a retailer.

> We know that the law is spiritual; but I am unspiritual, sold as a
> slave to sin. (Romans 7:14 NIV)

I was sold into sin. According to sin and the enemy, I am just a piece of merchandise. Sin sold me to lust, anger, insanity, depression.

4. Sin is a tyrant.

> Therefore do not let sin reign in your mortal body so that you obey
> its evil desires. (Romans 6:12 NIV)

Reign means "to act like a dictator." Sin is not only my master but an ugly tyrant who abuses me. He is the Adolf Hitler of my soul who wants to come and enact his own personal will in my life.

5. Sin is a crushing weight.

> Jews and Gentiles alike are all under the power of sin.
> (Romans 3:9 NIV)

We are all under the power of sin; it is weighing us down, as if a boulder were on top of us. Under its crushing domination, we are left unable to breathe, move, or act as we desire.

6. Sin is a spreading disease.

> But where sin abounded, grace abounded much more. (Romans
> 5:20 NKJV)

The word *abound* means "to spread." Sin is a deadly disease that not only infects us but is passed on to our children at birth. Sin was an epidemic in Genesis with the beginning of the human race and later became a pandemic as the population grew and covered the globe.

THE ONLY ANSWER

Sin is all these things that want to come at us and control us. Clearly, sin is not some sweet sentimental word. It is a radical, violent, atrocious explosion in the soul. We are absolutely powerless to fix it ourselves. Paul understood the anguish of being a slave to sin. Look at the passage from Romans 7 again, this time in a paraphrase:

> But I need something *more*! For if I know the law but still can't keep it, and if the power of sin within me keeps sabotaging my best intentions, I obviously need help! I realize that I don't have what it takes. I can will it, but I can't *do* it. I decide to do good, but I don't *really* do it; I decide not to do bad, but then I do it anyway. My decisions, such as they are, don't result in actions. Something has gone wrong deep within me and gets the better of me every time. *It happens* so regularly that it's predictable. The moment I decide to do good, sin is there to trip me up. I truly delight in God's commands, but it's pretty obvious that not all of me joins in that delight. Parts of me covertly rebel, and just when I least expect it, they take charge. *I've tried* everything and nothing helps. I'm at the end of my rope. Is there no one who can do anything for me? Isn't that the real question? (Romans 7:17–24 MSG)

We need someone else! Thankfully, there *is* an answer—the *only* answer to sin:

> The answer, thank God, is that Jesus Christ can and does. He acted to set things right in this life of contradictions where I want to serve God with all my heart and mind, but am pulled by the influence of sin to do something totally different. (Romans 7:25 MSG)

When Jesus comes, He breaks the power of the dictator, HE bankrupts the merchant, He blows open the locks on prison doors, He gives me a clean bill of health for my disease, He unties this weight that was connected to me. To be forgiven is not just that I get to go to heaven. Forgiveness is a revolution—an overthrow of a dictator, a coup against sin.

I had a friend who would say, "How do you get rid of an old boyfriend who won't accept the breakup and leave you alone? Get a new and bigger boyfriend!" That is what happens when you become a Christian. Jesus moves in. He comes into your heart; He comes into your life. There is not room enough for sin the tyrant *and* Him! Someone is moving out, and it's not Jesus!

If you are a Christian and this tyrant is still squatting on land owned by Jesus, it is time for him to be evicted. Your wrists can be cut up; God loves you. You may have had an abortion; God loves you. Sin ravages people, but Jesus has come to crush sin.

> The reason the Son of God appeared was to destroy the devil's work. (1 John 3:8 TNIV)

I recently read an article about Sir Anthony Hopkins—one of Hollywood's most highly acclaimed actors who was even knighted by Queen Elizabeth II. Yet he said that in 1975, he could not get free from an alcohol addiction that was ruining his life. One day, "a woman asked him at an Alcoholics Anonymous meeting, 'Why don't you just trust in God?' Hopkins admits that he was at such a point of desperation that he thought, *Well, why not?* As he recalls his addiction and powerlessness to change on his own, he tells of a small inner voice that asked him to choose: life or death. After turning to God, his destructive desire for alcohol disappeared." It was as if the tyrant-killer, disease-healer, weight-crusher—Jesus—said, "Everybody out, this is My home now!"[7]

Near the end of Romans 7 Paul asked if there is any hope: "Wretched man that I am! Who will set me free from the body of this death?" (verse 24). Until you stop at Romans 7 and realize that you are a sinner, you have no need for Jesus. If you cannot acknowledge your helpless sin condition, you cannot step into Romans 8. You would be trespassing. You cannot grab Romans 8's promises—you cannot say "God causes all things to work together for good" (verse 28)—without a Romans 7 confession.

Here is the beauty of stepping into Romans 8:

> With the arrival of Jesus, the Messiah, that fateful dilemma is resolved. Those who enter into Christ's being–here–for–us no longer

have to live under a continuous, low-lying black cloud. A new power is in operation. The Spirit of life in Christ, like a strong wind, has magnificently cleared the air, freeing you from a fated lifetime of brutal tyranny at the hands of sin and death.

God went for the jugular when he sent his own Son. He didn't deal with the problem as something remote and unimportant. In his Son, Jesus, he personally took on the human condition, entered the disordered mess of struggling humanity in order to set it right once and for all. (Romans 8:1–3 MSG)

We are all part of the "disordered mess of struggling humanity"! Freedom starts by knowing who we are. In Genesis 32:27, when Jacob met God face-to-face, God asked him: "What is your name?" It is the strangest question ever from an omniscient mind. Why did God ask Jacob that question? The last time Jacob was asked that question, he lied. He said he was Esau so that he could steal his brother's birthright (see Genesis 27:18–19). God was now asking him that question because the Lord can only use honest and bankrupt people. This time he answered truthfully: "Jacob." *Jacob* means "supplanter." Upon that confession, God gave him the new name, Israel.

For us, it starts with being tired of always living $6 short—guilty, empty, and hopeless. We come before God and acknowledge, "I am a sinner; I am guilty before You. No good thing is in me." Brennan Manning said, "The Good News means we can stop lying to ourselves. The sweet sound of amazing grace saves us from the necessity of self-deception. . . . I can . . . admit I have failed. God not only loves me as I am, but also knows me as I am."[8] What comfort we can find in the following verses:

When you were stuck in your old sin-dead life, you were incapable of responding to God. God brought you alive—right along with Christ! Think of it! All sins forgiven. (Colossians 2:13–14 MSG)

All sins forgiven! Jesus moves in and moves sin out! This is the freedom that Jesus purchased for us at Calvary. It is the redeemed soul who is able to sing the lyrics of the old hymn "It Is Well with My Soul":

My sin, O the bliss of this glorious thought!

My sin, not in part, but the whole
Is nailed to the cross, and I bear it no more.
Praise the Lord, praise the Lord, O my soul!

QUESTIONS

1. Which part of Paul's personification of sin was particularly striking to you?

2. Read Mark 9:42–47. How does this challenge your current attitude toward sin?

3. How would you respond to someone who does not believe he or she is a sinner?

TEMPTATION

I Don't Want
to Be the
Devil's Next Meal

*"The power of all temptation is the
prospect that it will make me happier."*
ERWIN LUTZER[1]

I heard this story somewhere, and I don't even know if it's true, but it helps to illustrate temptation. So here it is. Shortly before leaving for California one day, a ship captain—who had a regular route from California to Colombia—received a message from drug dealers from the Colombian cartel. They were offering him $500k if he would allow a small shipment of illegal drugs through to the U.S. He quickly declined. On his next three trips, they raised the offer each time until they reached $2 million. The captain hesitated and finally responded, "Maybe." He then contacted the DEA. A sting operation was set up, and the drug dealers were arrested. One of the DEA agents asked the captain, "Why did you wait until they got to $2 million before contacting us?"

The captain replied, "They were getting too close to my price."

Temptation knows your price. Temptation knows where you are most defenseless and susceptible, and it will relentlessly make offers to your soul. J. Wilbur Chapman once said, "Temptation is the tempter looking through the keyhole into the room where you're living; sin is you drawing back the bolt and making it possible for him to enter."[2] You cannot avoid someone coming to your door or looking through the keyhole—but you do control the lock on the door. There is no stopping the devil from looking and knocking. In this chapter, I want to show you what the Bible says regarding how to keep the door shut and locked. Let's begin with a promise that offers hope in the midst of resisting temptation's relentless offers:

> No weapon formed against you shall prosper. (Isaiah 54:17 NKJV)

The word *formed* is a very personal word that means "tailor-made, custom-built." It is a word for someone purchasing pottery who wants it made to order. Isaiah is giving us a sobering warning that every battle we face is custom-built for us. There are demonically engineered weapons made specifically to go after your weakest areas. For some, it is intellect. For others, it is fear, greed, lust, pornography, a longing to be rich, or loneliness.

The bad news: Satan goes after your most vulnerable spot.

The good news: No weapon formed against you has to prosper!

Let's make sure we win the battle against temptation. Temptation is fighting the tailor-made offers and attractions. In order for temptation to be temptation, it has to attract me. It must have something that I want. Jesus' three temptations in the wilderness would not have been temptations if there was not something within them that tried to attract Him. That is hard to say, but it is the truth. If Jesus was tempted as we are, then this must be true.

> We have one who has been tempted in every way, just as we are—
> yet he did not sin. (Hebrews 4:15 NIV)

One old writer said it like this: "The devil had an apple for Eve, a grape for Noah, a change of raiment for Gehazi, and silver for Judas. He can dish out his meat for all palates." That is the tailor-made part of it all.

The good news gets better for us: The same presence and power of the Holy Spirit, who enabled Jesus to resist temptation, resides in every Christian!

Back when we were in Detroit, I had a deacon—let's call him Frank—who was a graduate of Teen Challenge and an overall amazing man. He was a hard worker and faithfully served as a key leader in our church. One day, Frank did not show up to church. He did not gradually fall off; he was suddenly gone. When I talked with his wife, she said that after ten years, Frank went back to the crack house in the neighborhood. So I gathered three of our biggest Christians, went straight to the crack house, and knocked on the door. A narrow opening in the door slid open. "What do you want?"

"I am Frank's pastor," I answered. "Send him out now!" The slot was shut, the door opened, and they literally pushed him out. I asked Frank what happened, and I will never forget his words. "Pastor Tim, every day I would leave my house and go to work. I would come to the main street where I would catch the bus. Every day I had a choice: turn right or turn left. If I turned left, it would take me to the crack house. If I turned right, it would take me to the bus stop and eventually to work. I don't know what happened. I chose left after ten years."

Those words always stuck with me. Frank chose left. What happened?

Puritan writer Thomas Brooks said: "If God were not my friend, Satan would not be so much my enemy."[3] The day Frank made God His friend was the day Satan became his enemy. The same holds true for you and me when we chose to follow Christ. Our enemy is given a description that makes me shudder:

> Be of sober spirit, be on the alert. Your adversary, the devil, prowls around like a roaring lion, seeking someone to devour. (1 Peter 5:8)

"Seeking someone to devour" means Satan is not only on a mission, but he is on a mission to devour God's children. I have determined: I am *not* going to be the devil's next meal!

I have learned some very interesting things about lions when they are on the hunt to devour. This helps shed light on some of Satan's tactics since Peter described the devil as a roaring lion.

WHAT MAKES A LION'S HUNT SUCCESSFUL?

1. A lion must first stalk undetected before it attacks.

"Surprise your prey" is how the lion feasts, for they are too slow to catch an animal who is alert to their presence. Lions' prey know that a visible lion is a safe lion. A herd of gazelle will allow a lion to walk past just a hundred feet away!

That means you will never see temptation and the devil coming. It is a surprise attack.

2. Lions catch whatever is easiest.

They often kill the young, the sick, the old, and the careless. Those four categories are in every church, and we must help warn them of impending danger.

3. When the fire goes out, the lions move in.

When the fire of a camp goes out at night, this is a lion's signal to move in and devour its prey. I was reading a story about a doctor and his wife traveling to the jungles of Kenya. After flying from America and enjoying a day of bird-watching and photography, they went to bed in their tent with a campfire outside. They had been warned to keep logs on the fire all night, lest the lions come in. The fire was blazing hot when they fell into such a deep sleep that the fire eventually became smoldering embers. When darkness settled in, a lioness stuck her head into the tent and killed the doctor's wife.[4]

When you lose your fire for God, you become a prime candidate for the devil's next meal. Don't let the fire go out! Some have lost the fire of God. The first warning that the fire is going out is when you are lukewarm. The best definition I have heard of lukewarm: "I still believe in God . . . I'm just not that excited about Him anymore."

The great missionary martyr Jim Elliot said: 'He makes his ministers a flame of fire.' Am I ignitable? God deliver me from the dread asbestos of 'other things.' Saturate me with the oil of the Spirit that I may be a flame. But flame is transient, often short-lived. Canst thou bear this, my soul, short life? . . . Make me Thy fuel, flame of God."[5]

4. Where stragglers roam, lions feed.

A lion knows his own strength, but he also knows the strength of numbers. When he looks at a herd of zebras, he knows if he attacks one and the herd stampedes, they will trample him. But when he sees a zebra rebelliously remove himself and independently feed away from the herd, that can be his next meal. When that zebra gets far enough away from the pack, the lion pounces, pulls it into the tall grass, goes for the jugular, and has begun eating the meat before the herd even knows what happened.

Stay in the strength of fellowship! Don't be a straggler and remove yourself from the family of God. The devil prowls around, looking for those operating by themselves—those who have distanced themselves from the people of God.

One of the most powerful books on how Satan attacks believers is called *The Screwtape Letters* by C. S. Lewis. I encourage every Christian to read it. It is an elaboration on the 1 Peter 5:8 passage. This book is unique in that C. S. Lewis wrote it from the standpoint of the devil.

There are three characters in the book: Screwtape is the senior demon training his young apprentice demon, Wormwood, on how to tempt a Christian. When Screwtape talks about "the Enemy," he is referring to God. Every chapter is a letter in the devilish art of devouring and causing Christians to fall and fail. The letters the demons exchange are haunting and accurate. Look at one of the letters the senior demon wrote:

> Dear Wormwood,
> Surely you know that if a man can't be cured of churchgoing, the next best thing is to send him all over the neighborhood looking for the church that "suits" his taste until he becomes a connoisseur of churches . . . The search for a "suitable" church makes the man a critic where the Enemy wants him to be a pupil.
>
> The safest road to hell is the gradual one—the gentle slope, soft underfoot, without sudden turnings, without milestones, without signposts . . . All extremes, except extreme devotion to the Enemy, are to be encouraged . . . A moderate religion is as good for us as no religion at all—and more amusing.[6]

Peter cautioned us to be sober, and these devil words certainly make me sober! Remember, we are in a constant battle, but with God, it is a battle we can win. I am going to issue you your battle orders—a call to duty that can be found in this powerful verse:

> No temptation has overtaken you except something common to mankind; and God is faithful, so He will not allow you to be tempted beyond what you are able, but with the temptation will provide the way of escape also, so that you will be able to endure it. (1 Corinthians 10:13)

Be aware that you are going to be tempted until you go to heaven. You can never be delivered from being tempted, but you *can* experience victory from giving in to temptation. Christ was tempted, so we will be tempted. But Christ overcame, so we can overcome. Read the passage again, this time from The Living Bible:

> But remember this—the wrong desires that come into your life aren't anything new and different. Many others have faced exactly the same problems before you. And no temptation is irresistible. You can trust God to keep the temptation from becoming so strong that you can't stand up against it, for he has promised this and will do what he says. He will show you how to escape temptation's power so that you can bear up patiently against it. (1 Corinthians 10:13 TLB)

No temptation is irresistible! British theologian Richard Sibbes wisely suggested: "Satan gives Adam an apple, and takes away Paradise. Therefore in all temptations, consider not what he offers, but what we shall lose."[7]

For twenty years, I pastored a church located in what was formerly a XXX theater. We bought the flagship pornographic theater and transformed it into a church, and right next to us was a prostitution hotel where they would post hourly rates for their rooms. For ten years, our church offices and soup kitchen were located directly above an adult bookstore. Every day, as I pulled my car into the parking lot, I was faced with temptation. There was a set of yellow stairs—the bottom had an entryway to the porn bookstore; the top of the stairs went to our offices. I had a choice to go up the stairs or to go forward. Each day, I would strap on my armor and think not about what was offered but about what could be lost!

Keep this in mind: Temptation is *not* sin. It is the offer. Temptation is a fork in the road. It is the presentation of a choice—the high road or the low road, the bus stop or the crack house, up the stairs or straight to the adult bookstore. Temptation feeds on curiosity. It tells us what we do not have and what we could have by just taking the next steps.

The word *temptation* simply means a test. It is a test to show God beyond a doubt that you love Him exclusively. Temptation's persuasion is that you will be happier if you follow it.

Look at the end of 1 Corinthians 10:13 once again: "But with the temptation [God] will provide the way of escape." Thankfully, God gave us tools to help in the fight. Here are three clear ways of escape:

THE ESCAPE ROUTE

1. The Word of God

Matthew 4 is the account of Jesus coming face-to-face with Satan in what is called "the three temptations in the wilderness." Jesus was setting a precedent. He was saying, "I am about to fight the main demon, Lucifer—not a junior devil or a thought but the main man of the underworld. I will show you very plainly how victory comes."

No amount of counseling, church attendance, or someone praying for you (though all these things are valuable) can ever replace the Word of God in your mouth and in your life. A wordless Christian is a powerless Christian. He cannot be a victorious Christian.

Three times Jesus said to the devil: "It is written . . ." He went back to the Word to fight every attack of Satan. If Jesus needed the Word of God to defeat the devil, what makes you think you can be victorious without it?

The very first question I ask every person who comes to my office who is in a battle or a struggle is: "Tell me about your time in prayer and in the Word." What is amazing is that in forty years of ministry, I have never had anyone say to me, "You know, I am reading the Word an hour a day and praying an hour a day, yet I can't stop looking at porn or hitting my wife or gambling." Never!

Many people think counseling will fix it. Ultimately, they do not need my word but God's Word. Give the Word of God prime time. I made a commitment that before I look at the news, ESPN, or the *Wall Street Journal*, I *must* be in the Word and in prayer. This has served me well.

Every book of the Bible is powerful and contains devil-defeating power. While He was being tempted, Jesus said, "It is written," three times, and each verse came from the same book: Deuteronomy!

It is written, "MAN SHALL NOT LIVE ON BREAD ALONE, BUT ON EVERY WORD THAT COMES OUT OF THE MOUTH OF GOD." (Matthew 4:4)

"It is written, "You shall not put the Lord your God to the test." (Matthew 4:7)

For it is written, "You shall worship the Lord your God, and serve Him only." (Matthew 4:10)

Jesus demonstrated the power of the Word using even an obscure book of the Bible. That means we are not limited to Psalms and Proverbs; we can use any book to beat Satan! Perhaps you are thinking, "I can't even spell Deuteronomy, let alone quote something from it." Or have you ever read the Bible and wondered what you just read? Have you questioned, "Is this really working?"

It is important to realize that even uninspired Bible reading is valuable. Let me explain it this way: As I was preparing to make a long drive from New York City to Canada, someone told me to try a drink called "5-hour Energy." As a coffee drinker, I initially figured I did not need it. But I ended up trying it, and it worked! Have you ever tried Red Bull or Monster? You feel it immediately.

Now answer this: Do you take vitamins? Do you feel it when you take vitamin E or vitamin C with rose hips? No, you don't! But just because you do not *feel* it does not mean it is not working. The same holds true with the Word of God. The Bible is not a 5-hour Energy drink; the Bible is vitamins. Even when you do not feel it, the Word is still working into your system.

2. Prayer

After the wilderness temptation, Jesus would have been at His most vulnerable in the Garden of Gethsemane. He was fighting the temptation to avoid drinking the cup of pain. Jesus said this to His sleeping disciples:

Keep watching and praying, so that you do not come into temptation; the spirit is willing, but the flesh is weak. (Matthew 26:41)

R. A. Torrey explained it this way: "The reason why many fail in battle is because they wait until the hour of battle. The reason why others succeed is because they have gained their victory on their knees long before the battle came. Anticipate your battles; fight them on your knees before temptation comes, and you will always have victory."[8]

Jesus added one more thing to His instructions to *pray*. He also said *watch*. In other words, do not put yourself in a compromising situation where you might be easily tempted. It is also imperative that you keep your eyes fixed on God. When I married Cindy, she brought a dog into our marriage. He was a very obedient dog—a product of obedience school. It was amazing. Cindy would put food on the ground and tell him, "Stay." When a dog is in that position, it does not look at the food. Dogs are taught to look at their master. If they look at the food, it will be gone in a second. So when Cindy said, "Stay," that dog knew, "I listen to that voice; I look at my master." The problem with us is that we are looking at everything else around us. Our eyes should be fixed on our Master, not the food the enemy is offering. Prayer keeps our eyes focused on God!

3. Submission

James 4 told us exactly how to put the devil on the run. I grew up in a church where binding Satan was a big deal and done very often. It was something you would pray and say, calling it "spiritual warfare." Saying the words, "I bind you, Satan!" was supposed to distance you from the devil. But when you read the words of James, it is a bit different. James taught us that binding is not done with the mouth but with the life—a life of *submission*.

> Submit therefore to God. But resist the devil, and he will flee from
> you. (James 4:7)

Submission is a hard but powerful word. Submission is a fighting word to the devil, yet its power is so easily missed by the Christian.

Submission starts with recognizing authority and then having a willingness to yield to that authority. When you recognize God as *the* authority in your life, you are saying, "Not only is God more powerful than me, but He is wiser than me. I yield, believing God knows better."

The best way to bind the devil is to submit to God. We have so many Christians "binding Satan" over themselves, people, churches, and cities, yet without a submissive spirit. Satan does not flee when there is no submissive spirit to God. It is impossible to resist the devil in any area without submission to God in every area.

For example, the Bible says, "Do not be unequally yoked together with unbelievers. For what fellowship has righteousness with lawlessness? And what communion has light with darkness?" (2 Corinthians 6:14 NKJV). Note that there is a difference between ministry and fellowship. You minister to everybody, but the Bible says light cannot have fellowship with darkness. "But he loves me," she might insist. The truth is that he loves her by *his* definition, not by 1 Corinthians 13 love. So when the Bible says, "Do not get entangled by committing your life to someone who is not a Christian," here is what submission says: "You are wiser than me, God. I trust that You know what You are doing."

Yes, the knocks will continue to come at the door. *You're not going to be lonely anymore. You are going to have a husband. You will finally be a mom!* But remember, do not merely consider what temptation offers. What is it going to *take* from you?

The greatest binding you can do is by always saying "yes" to God. Submission to God is the believer's way of binding Satan from his life. Of course, submission is not simply doing what someone said. Submission is obeying with the right attitude. That is what makes submission difficult. I want to live a life that says "yes" to God with a smile on my face, confident that He knows better!

THE RUNAWAY RAMP

Right before the 1 Corinthians 10 temptation verse comes a warning against arrogance:

> Therefore let the one who thinks he stands watch out that he does not fall. No temptation has overtaken you except something common to mankind; and God is faithful, so He will not allow you to be tempted beyond what you are able, but with the temptation will provide the way of escape also, so that you will be able to endure it. (1 Corinthians 10:12–13)

It is almost as if Paul were giving us a slap in the face to remind us that we all need God. The thinking man is in verse 12; the dependent man is in verse

13. It is a picture of a seemingly strong man and the faithful God. Many people keep unbolting the lock and letting the enemy come in. We have a choice between trusting our own betraying thoughts of personal strength or putting our trust in the faithful God who makes a way of escape.

Several years ago when I was speaking in Los Angeles, I saw something I had never seen before. The pastor picked me up from LAX, and as we were driving along the highway filled with hills, turns, and large drop-offs, there were these interesting exits called "runaway ramps." I had never seen anything like it. The pastor explained that we were driving on a highway that went over California hills with huge valleys below—which, for eighteen-wheeler trucks, can be very treacherous. Sometimes an eighteen-wheeler will lose air in its air brakes and come flying down the hill with no place to go but over the edge. The runaway ramp was about a 100-yard incline of total sand. When in trouble, an eighteen-wheeler could exit off the runaway ramp. Its wheels would sink into the sand, preventing it from flying off the mountain road. Basically, it was an exit for those who had no brakes.

Do you ever feel that way? Over and over, you are using your brakes as temptation keeps knocking. After a while, the exhaustion from continual resistance has set in, and it seems as if your brakes are no longer working. It gets harder to hit the brakes on the thoughts you used to quickly put a stop to. Suddenly you find you cannot stop what you are doing. The good news is that God always gives a way out.

It takes humility and transparency. It is coming before the Lord and saying, "I'm losing my brakes on this. I realize the potential losses. I am not going to trust in my own strength to stand but instead in Your faithfulness. I am taking the runaway ramp; I am not going over the cliff!" Let the Word of God take priority in your life. Watch and pray. Choose submission, acknowledging that God is wiser. No doubt the knocks will come again—perhaps through an email, a text, a wayward thought. But remember, you do not have to unbolt and open the door. In fact, you can say, "Jesus, this is *Your* house. You answer it!"

QUESTIONS

1. Is there an area of your life where you have been relying on your own strength to stand instead of our faithful God's way of escape?

2. Consider the quote by R. A. Torrey once again: *"The reason why many fail in battle is because they wait until the hour of battle. The reason why others succeed is because they have gained their victory on their knees long before the battle came. Anticipate your battles; fight them on your knees before temptation comes, and you will always have victory."*

   a. What are some personal battles you might anticipate?
   b. What are some things you deeply desire in life, and how can you be prepared to face any temptations to fulfill those desires in a non-godly way?

3. Why do you think God does not simply remove temptation from our lives?

THE UNSEEN PROVIDENCE OF GOD

Even When I Don't See It, He's Working

"God loves details! It is in the details that we discern His hand of providence—ruling, directing, providing, sustaining, preventing, surprising. What may look catastrophic from one point of view will appear from another angle to be the outworking of a plan in which God is in full control."

DEREK THOMAS[1]

If chance exists, then God does not exist. Why? Chance means there is something that God does not control. J. C. Ryle put it this way: "Nothing whatever, whether great or small, can happen to a believer without God's ordering and permission. There is no such thing as 'chance,' 'luck' or 'accident' in the Christian's journey through this world. All is arranged and appointed by God. And all things are 'working together' for the believer's good."[2]

That is the unseen hand of God. God is always present, and His day-to-day involvement in our lives is called His providence. God has left nothing to chance, accident, or coincidence. He is constantly working on our behalf, just as we sing in the song by Sinach, "Way Maker":

Even when I don't see it, You're working
Even when I don't feel it, You're working
You never stop, You never stop working.[3]

Though His work often goes unnoticed, God is always present and active. Daily things may look like happenstance or seem accidental, but the whole time, God was behind it all.

I spent some time in my early years studying the life of Abraham Lincoln. One of the most amazing stories of providence in his life was when he and his partner, Berry, ran a little country store in Illinois. One day as they were on the front porch of the store, Berry asked, "How much longer can we keep this going?"

Lincoln agreed with his partner's concern, saying, "It looks as if our business has just about winked out." Then he continued, "You know, I wouldn't mind so much if I could just do what I want to do. I want to study law. I wouldn't mind if we could sell everything we've got and pay all our bills and have just enough left over to buy one book: *Blackstone's Commentaries on the Laws of England*. But I guess I can't."

Suddenly they saw a strange-looking wagon coming up the road. The driver angled it up close to the store porch, looked at Lincoln, and said, "I'm trying to move my family out west, and I'm out of money. I've got a good barrel here that I could sell for 50 cents." Lincoln noticed the man's wife looking at him pleadingly, her face thin and emaciated. Lincoln ran his hand into his pocket and took out, according to him, "the last fifty cents I had." He said, "I reckon I could use a good barrel."

All day long, the barrel sat on the porch of that store. Berry kept chiding Lincoln about it. Late in the evening, Lincoln walked out and looked down into the barrel. He saw something at the bottom of it—papers he hadn't noticed before. His long arms reached down into the barrel and, as he fumbled around, hit something solid. He pulled out a book and stood dumbfounded. It was *Blackstone's Commentaries on the Laws of England*! Lincoln later wrote, "I stood there, holding the book and looking up toward the heavens. There came a deep impression on me that God had something for me to do, and He was showing me now that I had to get ready for it. Why this miracle otherwise?"[4]

That was no accident. It was God's providence. Providence reminds us that every detail is micromanaged by God, thereby disqualifying coincidence and chance. We honor God when we remove words like *luck, good fortune,* and *coincidence* out of our language and describe it as God's providential hand.

You do not happen to be in the right place at the right time. You are in Christ, which means you are in the right place. As the psalmist David said, "My times are in Your hand" (Psalm 31:15 NKJV).

We do not always understand what God is doing, nor do we have to. God often uses a string of seemingly unrelated events to accomplish His purposes. For instance, what does a great persecution and a great commission have in common? The providence of God!

> At that time a great persecution arose against the church which was at Jerusalem; and they were all scattered throughout the regions of Judea and Samaria, except the apostles. . . . As for Saul, he made havoc of the church, entering every house, and dragging off men and women, committing them to prison. Therefore those who were scattered went everywhere preaching the word. (Acts 8:1, 3–4 NKJV)

Does the tandem of Judea and Samaria sound familiar? Jesus mentioned these two places when He spoke to His disciples right before ascending to heaven.

> But you shall receive power when the Holy Spirit has come upon you; and you shall be witnesses to Me in Jerusalem, and in all Judea and Samaria, and to the end of the earth. (Acts 1:8 NKJV)

How would they get to Judea and Samaria? Through persecution! What seemed to be a problem was actually providence. Persecution caused scattering, but scattering caused preaching. We must not forget that what we think and what God thinks are two different things. As the Lord said through Isaiah: "So are My ways higher than your ways and My thoughts than your thoughts" (Isaiah 55:9). The word *higher* also means "greater." When God works on a higher level, He is writing a much greater story than we can conceive.

For example, how does God get the gospel to Africa? Philip *happened* to be on a desert road where nobody would be traveling, and there *happened* to be an Ethiopian eunuch reading Isaiah 53. The eunuch said, "I have no one to explain this passage to me," to Philip, who *happened* to be the first deacon of the church. Philip explained it to him and told him he should be baptized. Suddenly, there *happened* to be a body of water for him to be baptized in!

What about Joseph's life? He was falsely accused of rape and sent to prison, where he *happened* to meet Pharaoh's cupbearer and baker—both of whom *happened* to have dreams one night that Joseph *happened* to be able to interpret. Two years later, Pharaoh *happened* to have a dream, and his cupbearer who had been released from prison *happened* to remember Joseph. Joseph was brought from prison, interpreted Pharaoh's dream, and was appointed second in command!

When I think about Times Square Church, I see God's providence woven throughout its history. David Wilkerson originally came to New York City for the trial of members of the Dragons gang, who had killed a fifteen-year-old boy with polio in Central Park. When he attempted to get into the courtroom, they would not let him in. However, someone took a picture of him holding up a Bible outside the courtroom. His picture was published in the daily newspaper, which was seen by the Mau Maus—a New York City gang that Nicky Cruz was a part of. Later, while David Wilkerson was preaching on the streets of Brooklyn, Nicky Cruz was in the crowd listening. A cop was about to shut him down, but another cop—a Christian—who outranked him came by and said, "Why are you going to shut him down? Let the man preach!" That cop was my father!

There is no coincidence with God! David Wilkerson thought he was coming to New York City for one thing, but God brought him in order to meet Nicky Cruz, start Teen Challenge, and eventually Times Square Church.

Years later, while Times Square Church was growing, David Wilkerson knew he needed help. One day, he was cleaning out his glove compartment full of cassette tapes while stuck in traffic in the Lincoln Tunnel. He came across two tapes that Leonard Ravenhill had sent to him two years prior. He was about to throw them out when he felt he should listen to them. In May of 1994, God spoke to him to bring the man who was preaching on those tapes—Carter Conlon—to Times Square Church. Carter and Teresa Conlon ended up staying not just for one Tuesday night but for twenty-seven years!

When David Wilkerson started Times Square Church, he invited me to come and be the youth pastor. However, weeks before I was about to come, he called me up and said, "It's not the Lord." If I had come, I would not have started a church in Detroit; I would not have met Cindy, and we would not have our four children! God knew I was not supposed to come then. He was working in my life, taking me on a necessary journey before bringing me to Times Square Church thirty-eight years later!

> So we are convinced that every detail of our lives is continually woven together for good, for we are his lovers who have been called to fulfill his designed purpose. (Romans 8:28 TPT)

When you do not understand God's providence, you misinterpret who God is and what is happening in your life. Trusting God's providence means learning to see differently. What could seem like annoying traffic may be God slowing you down to avoid something dangerous. What might feel like a devastating breakup could be God rescuing you from the pain of a horrible marriage. What could be interpreted as unfortunate downsizing at your company may be God opening a door for you to go somewhere else because you did not have the faith to do it on your own!

I recently came across another incredible story illustrating God's providence, involving details that only He could have precisely orchestrated:

> When the plane leveled off at 14,500 feet, Joan Murray took a deep breath and jumped out the door. The bank executive from Charlotte, North Carolina, was enjoying her free fall through the air until she pulled the ripcord for her parachute and nothing happened. She had an extreme rush of adrenaline, but she didn't panic; she knew she had a backup parachute. She was falling 120 miles per hour when she released the reserve chute. It opened just fine, but she lost her bearings and, in her struggle to right herself, deflated the chute. While the chute briefly slowed her descent, she continued to fall at 80 miles per hour.
>
> She struck the earth with a violent blow that shattered her right side and jarred the fillings from her teeth. She was barely conscious; her heart was failing. Just when it seemed things could not get much worse, she realized she had fallen into a mound of fire ants

that didn't appreciate her disturbing their solitude. They stung her about 200 times before the paramedics arrived.

Amazingly, the doctors who treated Joan believe that the ants actually saved her life! They theorized that the stings of the ants shocked her heart enough to keep it beating![5]

In all of Charlotte, North Carolina, only God could find a mound of fire ants and say, "That's where you are going to land because I still need you around for longer!" God's unseen hand is behind the curtain, constantly co-ordinating circumstances, snatching us from death that we may not have known was lurking around the corner, turning the table on the devil, making all things work together for our good. Daniel summed it up well in two words that he spoke to the ruler of Babylon, the most powerful man in the world at the time: "Heaven rules" (Daniel 4:26 NIV). In other words, "Make no mistake about it, you may rule the most powerful nation in the world, but you are not in charge!"

Here is a key verse to keep in mind regarding the providence of God:

> So we fix our eyes not on what is seen, but on what is unseen.
> (2 Corinthians 4:18 NIV)

We do not focus on traffic or breakups but on God's providence, knowing that God is working things out even though we do not see or feel it. Paul followed up with these words in the next chapter: "We walk by faith, not by sight" (2 Corinthians 5:7). Faith often means walking blind. It is by faith that you fix your eyes on what is unseen.

Today there is a game available on Amazon called "The Holy Spirit Board," much like a Ouija board. Here is its product description: "The Holy Spirit Board is the only spirit board designed to directly contact our Lord and Savior Jesus Christ! Unlike other spirit boards that are often used to contact ghosts and demons, this is a one-way ticket straight to heaven. Try it today and discover a new way to pray!"

One reviewer wrote: "Got this as a last resort because I was in dire need to speak to Jesus and He seemed to be avoiding all my prayers. After setting it up, at 1 min and 16 seconds, I made contact!!!! It's been a while now and I feel that we are connecting so well."

Clearly this is counterfeit and demonic. Not only that, but now there is an app available with an AI Jesus that you can ask questions. Instead of just getting a daily Bible verse, now you get a chance through this app to chat with Jesus or anybody else in the Bible.

The AI Jesus people and the Holy Spirit Board people are losing, among many things, the providence of God. They cannot say, "Even when I don't see it, He's working. Even when I don't feel it, He's working. He never stops; He never stops working." Understanding an unseen God cannot be done through a spirit board or an AI Jesus. It means that we fix our eyes on the unseen.

> Oh, the depth of the riches of the wisdom and knowledge of God!
>   How unsearchable his judgments,
>   and his paths beyond tracing out!
>   (Romans 11:33 NIV)

How can any AI even come close to having "unsearchable judgments," or "paths beyond tracing out"? AI will never duplicate a God of unfathomable wisdom. An AI Jesus could never simulate the vastness of the true Jesus. It is impossible.

Amy Carmichael, a nineteenth-century missionary from Ireland who was a pioneer in the fight against sex trafficking, was taught early on by her mother that God answers prayer. When she was a little girl, each night before bed, Amy would ask God to change her eye color from brown to blue. Every morning, she would jump out of bed, run to the mirror, and check to see whether God had answered her prayer. To her dismay, every morning her eyes were still brown.

At age twenty, Amy sensed the Lord was calling her to serve as a missionary. After serving in various places, she moved to India. Amy went on to become one of the greatest missionaries to set foot in that land. In her time there, Amy founded an orphanage, a school, and a safe house for young girls. Amy played a major role in breaking the ancient practice of abandoning baby girls on the steps of pagan temples to be trained up as cult prostitutes. More than a thousand girls were saved from lives of prostitution and were instead taught to read. They were given back their dignity that society had taken away, and they were saved eternally through the gospel.

God's story is always bigger than ours. Amy learned that her unwanted brown eyes were a far more precious gift from God than the value she had once placed on blue eyes. Because of the risk involved in rescuing children, Amy had to do everything she could to blend into the Indian culture, even darkening her fair Irish skin with coffee. God had intentionally given her the features of dark brown hair and brown eyes—just like the thousands of young girls and women she would one day rescue. Amy soon understood that the "no" to a three-year-old's prayer was really a "yes" to a remarkable life designed specifically for her!

God's providence means that even the uncomfortable or painful moments in our lives are His designed paths. We just need eyes of faith to see His hand at work. Elizabeth Browning once wrote, "Earth's crammed with heaven, and every common bush is afire with God; but only he who sees, takes off his shoes, the rest sit round it and pluck blackberries."[7] I am sometimes a berry picker, but I am asking God for grace that I might see and take off my shoes! Consider the words of Solomon:

> I passed by the field of a lazy one,
> And by the vineyard of a person lacking sense,
> And behold, it was completely overgrown with weeds;
> Its surface was covered with weeds,
> And its stone wall was broken down.
> When I saw, I reflected upon it;
> I looked, and received instruction.
> (Proverbs 24:30–32)

Solomon was teaching us that fields, vineyards, weeds, and broken-down walls have an important message, but so many walk by, picking berries and missing what God is saying. Let's stop picking berries and see God's hand in a book of the Bible that, interestingly, does not once mention His name. As we go through it, I believe it will help you to see burning bushes every day in your life.

A Journey Through Esther Is a Journey of Providence

The book of Esther is the only book in the Bible where God's name is not mentioned. However, God's providence is clear in every chapter. It is about a woman who worked and lived in a an environment that was not God-fearing. It seems as if the biggest providence stories in the Bible involve believers working with powerful nonbelievers, such as the stories of Joseph and Daniel. It reminds us that we may not always hear His name, but He is always present.

Chapter 1

Many of the Jews who were taken by Nebuchadnezzar to Babylon eventually returned to Jerusalem to rebuild the wall and temple. However, some Jews remained in Babylon. A man named Mordecai and his cousin whom he is raising, Esther, are among those who stayed. Babylon became Persia when it was conquered. One day, the Persian ruler, King Ahasuerus, throws a great banquet and calls for His queen, Vashti, to attend.

> But Queen Vashti refused to come at the king's order . . . The king became very angry, and his wrath burned within him. (Esther 1:12)

Chapter 2

The king is incensed and searches for a new queen. Esther is taken to the king's palace to enter the queen contest, instructed by Mordecai not to reveal to anyone that she is Jewish. Esther finds favor and is made queen instead of Vashti. Now there is a Jew in the palace, and nobody knows about it except for Mordecai. Later, when Mordecai is sitting at the king's gate, he discovers an assassination plot against the king.

> Two of the king's officials from those who guarded the door, became angry and sought to attack King Ahasuerus. But the plot became known to Mordecai and he informed Queen Esther, and Esther told the king in Mordecai's name. Then when the plot was investigated and found to be so, they were both hanged on a wooden gallows; and it was written in the Book of the Chronicles in the king's presence. (Esther 2:21–23)

Chapter 3

After these events, the king promotes a man named Haman into authority. Whenever Haman comes to the gate, all bow to him except for Mordecai.
Mordecai refuses to bow to a man because the Word of God prohibits him
from performing such an act. Haman is infuriated to the point of wanting to
destroy not only Mordecai but all the Jews. The first genocide is being planned
against the Jews:

> Then Haman said to King Ahasuerus, "There is a certain people
> scattered and dispersed among the peoples in all the provinces of
> your kingdom; their laws are different from those of all other people
> and they do not comply with the king's laws, so it is not in the king's
> interest to let them remain. If it is pleasing to the king, let it be de-
> creed that they be eliminated, and I will pay ten thousand talents
> of silver into the hands of those who carry out the king's business,
> to put into the king's treasuries." Then the king took his signet ring
> from his hand and gave it to Haman, the son of Hammedatha the
> Agagite, the enemy of the Jews. (Esther 3:8–10 NASB)

Chapter 4

Although Esther almost loses sight of why she is in the palace, Mordecai
is well aware. It is important to remember that God is always thinking of the
greater story, not merely your comfort and prosperity. He may have blessed
you financially, but it is not just for you—that would be such a little story. In
this case, God put Esther in the palace not so she could proudly wear a crown
and enjoy people calling her Queen Esther. God was giving her resources for a
bigger story. A genocide was being planned to annihilate the Jewish race, and
God needed to stop it. He had to micromanage a thousand subplots to work
out the big plot.

Mordecai reminds Esther that if she becomes fearful and refuses to stand
up for her people, then she will perish, and God will raise up another deliverer.

> Who knows whether you have not attained royalty for such a time
> as this? (Esther 4:14)

Esther finds courage and instructs the Jews to fast and pray, as she and her
maidens will also.

> Then I will go in to the king, which is not in accordance with the
> law; and if I perish, I perish. (Esther 4:16)

Chapter 5

In those days, one could not simply walk in on the king without being summoned. He had to extend his scepter to show his acceptance. When Esther approaches him, King Ahasuerus does extend his scepter to her. He even says, "I will do whatever you want, up to half the kingdom!" It seems as if she becomes fearful, for Esther ends up inviting the king and Haman to a dinner party. At dinner, the king inquires once again about her request, and Esther implores him and Haman to return the next evening for another dinner party. Haman leaves the banquet feeling pleased with his exclusive invitation from the queen, but all his joy vanishes when he encounters Mordecai at the gate who once again does not honor him.

> Then Zeresh his wife and all his friends said to him, "Have a wooden
> gallows fifty cubits high made, and in the morning ask the king to
> have Mordecai hanged on it; then go joyfully with the king to the
> banquet." And the advice pleased Haman, so he had the wooden
> gallows made. (Esther 5:14)

All these subplots in the first five chapters of Esther culminate in chapter 6 to reveal what God had been doing behind the scenes for years.

Chapter 6

One night, the king has insomnia. He did not have NyQuil or lavender essential oil, so he basically says, "Bring me the most boring book you can find!" They bring the Book of the Chronicles and "just so happen" to read an account from five years prior.

> It was found written what Mordecai had reported about Bigthana
> and Teresh, two of the king's eunuchs who were doorkeepers, that
> they had sought to attack King Ahasuerus. Then king said, "What
> honor or dignity has been bestowed on Mordecai for this?" Have
> the king's servants who attended him said, "Nothing has been done
> for him." So the king said, Who is in the courtyard?" Now Haman
> had just entered the outer courtyard of the king's palace in order

to speak to the king about hanging Mordecai on the wooden gallows which he had prepared for him. So the king's servants said to
him, "Behold, Haman is standing in the courtyard." And the king
said, "Have him come in." (Esther 6:2–5)

If the subplot was all there was, then Mordecai would have received a com-
mendation, a medal, and a $50 gift card to Olive Garden for saving the king.
Instead, it seemed as though everyone forgot about him. Of course, God did
not forget! Some people are upset today because someone else got honored
or received the promotion, and they feel overlooked. God is saying, "I have a
much bigger story in mind than you getting a ceremony!"

Remember, wicked Haman was there to speak to the king about hanging
Mordecai on a fifty-cubit-high gallows. Little did he know that he was about to
get the surprise of his life!

Haman then came in and the king said to him, "What is to be done
for the man whom the king desires to honor?" And Haman said to
himself, "Whom would the king desire to honor more than me?"
Therefore Haman said to the king, "For the man whom the king
desires to honor, have them bring a royal robe which the king has
worn, and the horse on which the king has ridden, and on whose
head a royal turban has been placed; and then order them to hand
the robe and the horse over to one of the king's noble officials, and
have them dress the man whom the king desires to honor, and lead
him on horseback through the city square, and proclaim before him,
'So it shall be done for the man whom the king desires to honor.'"

Then the king said to Haman, "Quickly take the robes and the
horse just as you have said, and do so for Mordecai the Jew, who
is sitting at the king's gate; do not fail to do anything of all that you
have said." So Haman took the robe and the horse, and dressed
Mordecai, and led him on horseback through the city square, and
proclaimed before him, "So it shall be done for the man whom the
king desires to honor." (Esther 6:6–11)

How I wish I could have been there to see this! Haman runs home and cries, at which point the king's eunuchs arrive to bring him to Esther's banquet.

Chapter 7

At the banquet, the king once again asks Esther about her petition. She finally replies:

> "If I have found favor in your sight, O king, and if it pleases the king, let my life be given me as my request, and my people as my wish; for we have been sold, I and my people, to be destroyed, killed, and eliminated. Now if we had only been sold as slaves, men and women, I would have kept silent, because the distress would not be sufficient reason to burden the king." Then King Ahasuerus [a] asked Queen Esther, "Who is he, and where is he, who would presume to do such a thing?" And Esther said, "A foe and an enemy is this wicked Haman!" Then Haman became terrified before the king and queen.
>
> One of the eunuchs who stood before the king, said, "Indeed, behold, the wooden gallows standing at Haman's house fifty cubits high, which Haman made for Mordecai who spoke good in behalf of the king!" And the king said, "Hang him on it." So they hanged Haman on the wooden gallows which he had prepared for Mordecai, and the king's anger subsided. (Esther 7:3–6, 9–10)

Haman hangs on the very gallows that he had built for Mordecai!

Chapters 8–10

Mordecai is given the king's signet ring, which had been taken away from Haman. The Jews are issued an edict allowing them to defend themselves, and they defeat their enemies—including the ten sons of Haman (see Esther 9:5–9). To this day, the Jews celebrate Purim in remembrance of their victory. The book of Esther concludes:

> For Mordecai the Jew was second only to King Ahasuerus, and great among the Jews and in favor with his many kinsmen, one who

sought the good of his people and one who spoke for the welfare of his entire nation. (Esther 10:3)

Remember, God is not mentioned in this book at all, yet we see His providence throughout. Esther did not become queen by luck or good fortune. Mordecai did not stay back in Persia because he thought it was a good business decision. God was taking their subplots and forming a bigger plot. He had a plan all along to make Esther queen and Mordecai second in charge, and to rescue the nation of Israel from annihilation. Whatever their enemies designed for their harm, God was going to turn around to their benefit. Just as God put Esther and Mordecai exactly where they needed to be, God has put you where you are today. Even when you don't see it, He's working. Even when you don't feel it, He's working. He never stops working on your behalf!

QUESTIONS

1. Is there anything you have attributed to luck, chance, or unfortunate circumstances rather than the providence of God?

2. What is your favorite illustration of God's providence in the Bible?

3. In what ways have you been more concerned about your *subplot* than God's bigger plot?

VOLUNTEERING AND SERVING

This Is a Day of His Power; Now It's Your Move

"Everyone has some gift, therefore all should be encouraged. No one has all the gifts, therefore all should be humble. All the gifts are for one Body, therefore all should be cooperative. All the gifts are needful, therefore all should be faithful."

A. T. Pierson[1]

Let's take a journey for a moment back to the upper room and look at some of Jesus' last words to His disciples before being arrested and going to the cross. At the Passover meal, Jesus rescued the definition of *greatness*. He posed the question: "For who is greater, the one who reclines at the table or the one who serves?" (Luke 22:27). Keep those two words in mind—the recliner and the server. Jesus continued, "Is it not the one who reclines at the table?" In other words, "That is *society's* definition. But I am about to rescue the definition of *greatness*."

Jesus told the disciples which category He was part of in Luke 22:27: "But I am among you as the one who serves."

Just as it was for the disciples, it is critical for us to redefine *greatness* and *importance* according to Jesus' definition. Today there is an ongoing battle between recliners and servers. I have recently seen an increase of "keyboard warriors"—recliners who sit and critique others from their laptop. They have opinions, mindsets, and soapboxes. Because they do not actually serve or volunteer, they easily get critical and censor those who are out on the battlefield.

Meanwhile, I have noticed that those out in the battle, fighting the good fight on the front lines, do not have time to post their opinions or be critical of others. Instead, their time is spent making a difference. People who *do* stuff don't *post* much.

Some have criticized the way I lead people to Christ with the simplicity of the ABCs. My response is, "Please tell me how you are witnessing so I can learn." It is much easier to critique from the bleachers than it is from out on the field. Many people have an opinion from the bleachers but not, as they say in sports, blood on their uniform or grass stains on their pants to confirm, "This is a better way."

This chapter is a challenge to all of us to use the gifts we have been given by God. For those who are sleeping, it is an alarm clock. It is a sober challenge to a consumer-driven culture full of opinions but no battle scars. It is a call to anyone who may be on the sidelines—a call to get off the bench and back on the playing field.

I remember when David Wilkerson was asked by his grandson, "How could God exist and yet there be so much suffering all around?" He gave one of the greatest apologetic responses I have ever heard on this controversial topic: "First, the people who complain the most about this question do the least about it. And second, I don't concern myself with this question anymore. I have determined to spend the rest of my life helping everyone who is suffering."

Consider the challenge that the psalmist David issued in Psalm 110:

> Your people shall be volunteers
> In the day of Your power.
> (Psalm 110:3 NKJV)

When God is moving, it calls for a response from His people. I believe today is a day of His power, which means now it is our move. Will we volunteer? Will we be a part of that day?

The day of His power came in Acts 1–5. If you remember the story we discussed in the Q chapter on "Quarrels, Conflicts, and Divisions," God was moving mightily in the early church, adding to their numbers daily. By Acts 6, there was a call for volunteers.

But as the believers rapidly multiplied, there were rumblings of discontent. The Greek-speaking believers complained about the Hebrew-speaking believers, saying that their widows were being discriminated against in the daily distribution of food. So the Twelve called a meeting of all the believers. They said, "We apostles should spend our time teaching the word of God, not running a food program. And so, brothers, select seven men who are well respected and are full of the Spirit and wisdom. We will give them this responsibility." (Acts 6:1–3 NLT)

In the midst of rapid growth, the early church needed seven men—volunteers! When God is moving, He will always begin to inspire people and challenge them to be a part of His work.

Now back in the upper room where we started, Jesus told His disciples a parable on stewardship. We find this message in Matthew 25, which is followed by His arrest and trial in Matthew 26. Keep in mind that these disciples had received from Christ for three years. Now they were being challenged with what had been entrusted to them. Jesus was essentially saying, "You have been poured into; now it is time to be poured out. You have the jersey; now you need to get out on the field. You were not given this gift to sit; you were given this gift to get in the game!"

Someone once said that God's people can be divided into three categories: the flint, the sponge, and the honeycomb. Some are like a piece of flint: to get anything out of it, you must hammer it, and even then you only get chips and sparks. Others are like a sponge: to get anything out of a sponge, you must squeeze it. But others are like a honeycomb, overflowing with sweetness. Matthew 25 is a parable about two honeycombs and one flint, and at the end comes a last-days challenge about accountability.

For it [the kingdom of heaven] is just like a man about to go on a journey, who called his own slaves and entrusted his possessions to them. To one he gave five talents, to another, two, and to another, one, each according to his own ability; and he went on his journey. The one who had received the five talents immediately went and did business with them, and earned five more talents. In the same way the one who had received the two talents earned two more. But he who received the one talent went away and dug a hole in the ground, and hid his master's money. (Matthew 25:14–18)

While the term *talent* does not mean much to us, those hearing this story in the first century would have immediately known that it represented a tremendous sum of money. A talent was equivalent to twenty years' wages. So when the master gave five talents, two talents, and one talent to each of the three servants, he was putting them in charge of about 160 years' worth of wages. Today the talent represents all you have from God; He has made you a trustee of these things. The great writer on prayer from the twentieth century Andrew Murray once said, "The world asks, 'What does a man own?' Christ asks, 'How does he use it?'"[2] One day Jesus will ask each one of us: "What did you do with what I entrusted to you?" It is not about what you have but about how you use it. No church or ministry has a lack of gifts. Everything you need for your church to grow and make an impact is already on the premises, but every gift needs a good and faithful servant behind it for it to multiply.

The three men in the parable were given different amounts but the same assignment. The expectation was that they return something greater than what they were initially given. Notice that the master of the house also gave them sufficient time to do something with their talents.

Now after a long time the master of those slaves came and settled accounts with them. The one who had received the five talents came up and brought five more talents, saying, "Master, you entrusted five talents to me. See, I have earned five more talents." His master said to him, "Well done, good and faithful slave. You were faithful with a few things, I will put you in charge of many things; enter the joy of your master."

Also the one who had received the two talents came up and said, "Master, you entrusted two talents to me. See, I have earned two more talents." His master said to him, "Well done, good and faithful slave. You were faithful with a few things, I will put you in charge of many things; enter the joy of your master."

> Now the one who had received the one talent came up and
> said, "Master, I knew you to be a hard man, reaping where you did
> not sow, and gathering where you did not scatter seed. And I was
> afraid, so I went away and hid your talent in the ground. See, you
> still have what is yours." (Matthew 25:19–25)

Stewardship is not protecting what you are given; stewardship is *multiplying* what you are given. It is the challenge of moving from reclining to serving. The first two were entrusted with more and multiplied what they had been given, but the man entrusted with one talent did nothing with it! He buried it, reclined, and when the master returned, he gave him back exactly what had been entrusted to him. Nothing expanded, no lives changed. As a result, this man who sat in the bleachers received a scathing rebuke:

> The master was furious. "That's a terrible way to live! It's criminal
> to live cautiously like that! If you knew I was after the best, why did
> you do less than the least?" (Matthew 25:26 MSG).

Those who have been given a great gift from the Master yet choose to recline can expect a similar response. Starting with salvation, think of all that has been graciously given to us. Some have experienced healing, gifts of the Holy Spirit, provision, and wisdom. It's criminal to live cautiously with what God has entrusted to you! If God has given you a gift, then that gift must get bigger and better. We are all given "talents." It does not matter how many you are given. Even if you are given only one, God says, "I want you to use the one!"

This brings to mind the extraordinary work God is presently doing in the nation of China with revival sweeping through the underground church. A catalyst to this ongoing move was a missionary named Hudson Taylor, who brought the gospel to China in the nineteenth century. There is a story that on one occasion before moving to China, Taylor was speaking in Glasgow, Scotland. At the conclusion of the service, a man with a crutch came to the platform, hobbling on a wooden leg. He introduced himself to Taylor and said, "God has called me to China." Taylor glanced down at the wooden leg and then at the crutch and said, "Why, you can't go to China in this condition." The crippled man seemed terribly discouraged and shook his hand goodbye.

Some time later, Taylor was back in the city, and the man came to him again. "God has spoken to me," said the determined believer, "and told me I must be a missionary to China."

"Is that so?" replied Taylor with surprise. "Tell me, what did He say?"

The man quoted Isaiah 33:23 which says, "The lame take the prey." (KJV).

Taylor smiled and said, "You are lame, and there is plenty of prey in China; so you may go."

The man set sail for China, and on the ship someone asked him, "Why are you going to China as a missionary in that condition?"

"Well, I don't see many two-legged people going, so I am going with one leg."

When he reached his destination, the people were afraid to let him in the city. They described him as a funny-looking creature with bushy hair, a long nose, and three legs. Nevertheless, he started his work going door to door, telling people about Christ. When some would try to slam the door on him, he would stick his wooden leg in the door! All he had was one good leg, but God used him. The Lord simply asks us to use what is at our disposal.[3]

Young people often ask me, "How do I find my calling? How do I know what God wants me to do and be?" Here is the answer I give: "Serve, and you will discover it." Many times, the first things you do will not necessarily be what your calling is, but it is the entry ramp to get you closer. Say "yes" to serving opportunities—not just once in a lifetime, but seasonal "yeses" even when old chapters close and new ones are opening. This applies not only to young people but even those who believe their time of service is over. You may be retired, but consider the fact that God called Moses when he was eighty years old! He should have been working on his will and transitioning into assisted living. But God told him, "Now it's time for you to deliver My people out of Egypt!"

When I was nineteen years old, I said "yes" to going on a two-month missions trip to Detroit. At the time, I was in college studying to follow in the footsteps of my dad. My dad was part of the NYPD; he went to the FBI National Academy in Quantico, Virginia, and rose up through the department. I believed I was called to do likewise, for in our family you were either a fireman or a policeman. I had no idea that by simply saying "yes" to a missions trip, God would begin to open up doors and bring me closer to what He was calling me to do. On the missions trip, they needed someone to lead a Bible study in a prostitution hotel, so I said "yes." I don't know why. I was born and raised in the church. I had never been drunk, never been high. I was probably the worst candidate for running a Bible study in a prostitution hotel! Then they needed someone to run evangelism on the streets, and I said "yes" again. Someone was also needed to be the worship leader. "Yes!" I barely knew how to play the guitar, yet they had me do it for seven years! They had a wooden-leg worship leader who knew four chords. Why did I say "yes"? Because those who knew more about evangelism and worship were not stepping up. God chose the wooden-leg worship leader who didn't know very much but just kept saying "yes." It is what God has called us to do!

This is exactly what one of our Times Square Church "online host leaders" has personally discovered. She testified:

> During the COVID pandemic, I went through a season of asking God many 'why?' questions. Questions about my childhood and about current things I was going through and am still going through. God put in my heart the verse from Proverbs 3:5–6: "Trust in the LORD with all your heart and lean not on your own understanding; in all your ways acknowledge Him, and He shall direct your path." God told me something that I will never forget: "It's not your job to understand. It's your job to trust and obey."
>
> And so my journey with God began, and I decided to say 'yes' to God and His plans. A journey of letting go of trying to figure things out, not knowing where it would lead me.
>
> Well, a couple of months later, God put me to the test. My first 'yes' after God spoke to my heart was accepting an invitation to moderate for the Women Speaker Series, followed by being an online host on Church Online, and volunteering at Summit with other young adults.
>
> As an introvert, saying 'yes' wasn't always easy. I had feelings of uncertainty, fear, and of not being good enough. I also thought to myself, "With what time?" Around the same time, I joined the

Connect Group "419" where it challenged me to reach my fullest potential in Christ. This led me to start leading my very own connect group where I also had many doubts and insecurities. This then led me to raising another Connect Group leader, and eventually leading a team of my own.

This journey wasn't and isn't always easy, but I am always reminded of what God spoke to me on that day: to trust in the Lord with all my heart and not lean on my own understanding!

It all starts with giving God your "yes." After all, who would have thought that saying "yes" to delivering cheese would be the entry point for one of Israel's greatest kings? It is how David started on his journey to his destiny.

> Then Jesse said to his son David, "Take now for your brothers an ephah of this roasted grain and these ten loaves, and run to the camp to your brothers. Bring also these ten slices of cheese to the commander of their thousand, and look into the well-being of your brothers and bring back confirmation from them. For Saul and they and all the men of Israel are in the Valley of Elah, fighting the Philistines." So David got up early in the morning. (1 Samuel 17:17–20)

How did David get to the battle where Goliath was taunting the children of Israel? How would he eventually end up with a sling in his hand and a stone in a giant's skull—a moment that would forever define his life? Through Uber Eats! There was a need for cheese sandwiches to be delivered to the men and their commanders, and David said, "I'll do it!" David submitted, and he suddenly found himself face-to-face with his destiny. It started by saying "yes" to a mundane task that would yield an amazing result. Only God could do that!

I was reading a fascinating article about Navy SEALs. Some 200 men attempt to become the best of the best, going through twenty-four weeks of training called BUD/S. If you find that you can no longer go on and are ready to give up on the program, you have to walk up, ring a bell, and leave your helmet there on the ground. It is your testament that you quit and could not endure any longer. Ninety percent of those who go through BUD/S Navy SEAL training never make it.

A former Navy SEAL was asked about who makes it through BUD/S, and he offered amazing insight regarding the 10 percent who do make it through. He explained that it is not the big, muscle-bound, or tattooed tough guys, nor is it the college-educated stars. They may look impressive, but they do not have what it takes. In fact, the ones who make it through do not necessarily look impressive. There may even be times during the training when they are shivering in fear. But at some point during the grueling training—when they are physically exhausted and mentally spent, when it does not look as though they can go on—they dig deep and find a way to help the person next to them![4]

David was about to show the Navy SEAL mark. David was not thinking about himself; he was thinking about others. His brothers could use the cheese. The commanders needed it. But there was more that no one knew about except God: A nation needed his courage. What David thought was mere cheese was actually a door to his future. Serving is the door to calling.

If David assumed he was better than a cheese delivery man, he would have missed the door that God intended for getting him on the battlefield. If David were to wait for a more respectable assignment, he would still be watching after sheep. Entry ramps into your destiny start with humble little tasks that often do not match what you want to do. It is a humility test. It is often the case that the people who can defeat the giant are never selected because they hate cheese assignments. What you define as trivial may actually be massive. You do not kill Goliaths on Goliath missions but on cheese missions.

Now that you are familiar with the messages Jesus spoke in the upper room regarding recliners, servers, and then the parable of the talents, I want to highlight a remarkable story on how they found the upper room in the first place. It is one of the strangest sights in the New Testament:

> And He sent out two of His disciples and said to them, "Go into the city, and a man will meet you carrying a pitcher of water; follow him. Wherever he goes in, say to the master of the house, 'The Teacher says, "Where is the guest room in which I may eat the Passover with My disciples?"' Then he will show you a large upper room, furnished and prepared; there make ready for us." (Mark 14:13–15 NKJV)

The most famous meal *and* the most famous room—all started by a man doing what was, at the time, a job considered to be relegated to women. It was the women who carried water jugs in the first century in this part of the world. I don't know why he was carrying water that day. Was he voluntarily serving his wife? Whatever the reason, because he said "yes" to this humble task, he ended up being the leader to the upper room. He might have been simply thinking, "I'm serving my wife. She needed my help. I want to honor the one I love." Perhaps God was telling this man, "You have no idea that because you are serving your wife in doing this task, you are going to be part of the story of the most famous meal in the most famous room!" What he thought was a silly water jug on top of his head was actually an entry ramp into the Bible, to be talked about centuries later! This man was being the Navy SEAL of his day.

A cheese delivery or water jug on your head is doing something for others that will never get noticed, never receive praise. It may seem insignificant and beneath your skill set. Serving works on character and attitude. People fear that if they deliver cheese or work in the nursery, they will be forgotten. Yet as David and this man submitted, doors opened. Don't try to find your destiny; say "yes" to the little things. Hudson Taylor said, "A little thing is a little thing, but faithfulness in a little thing is a big thing." *Leader* is mentioned only six times in the Bible; *servant* is mentioned over 900 times!

FROM SERVING TO RECLINING

Although he only appears in the New Testament three times, there is a man named Demas whose story is worth mentioning. His name is unfamiliar to most but critical to understanding servanthood. The three verses that speak of Demas tell a very important story and progression of his life. It was a seven-year journey packed into three verses.

Here is Demas's first verse:

> Epaphras, my fellow prisoner in Christ Jesus, greets you, as do Mark, Aristarchus, Demas, Luke, my fellow workers. (Philemon 1:23–24)

This letter was written around AD 60. These men are not recliners: they are servers. Demas was called "my fellow worker" along with Luke and Mark. One version says "coworkers" and another "my companions in this ministry." Then something happened a couple years later.

Demas's second verse:

> Luke, the beloved physician, sends you his greetings, and Demas does also. (Colossians 4:14)

This letter was written two years later, in AD 62. Did you notice something was missing after Demas's name? He went from a fellow worker to just a name on the list.

Finally, Demas's third verse:

> Demas, having loved this present world, has deserted me.
> (2 Timothy 4:10)

This was Paul's last letter, written in AD 67. Now seven years later, Demas had deserted him, having loved this present world. I want you to notice a very scary progression: *Demas is helping. Demas is present. Demas has deserted.* In the beginning, he was helping Paul. But by Colossians, he was simply a name on the list. He was no longer a coworker or companion. He was just there—a name in the church. He had vacated his job of serving. It did not take long for Demas to exit when he was no longer invested. By his third mention, he had left Paul. He went from serving to reclining.

Erwin McManus explained it this way: "Your investment, not mine, is what keeps you stable."[5] What inevitably happens to recliners is that instead of loving to serve, they end up falling in love with the world. Eventually their gift is no longer used for the sake of the gospel and the benefit of others but solely for themselves.

From Serving to Destiny

In contrast, consider the ultimate servant, Jesus, and His progression from servanthood to destiny.

> Have this attitude in yourselves which was also in Christ Jesus, who, as He already existed in the form of God, did not consider equality with God something to be grasped, but emptied Himself by taking

the form of a bond-servant and being born in the likeness of men. And being found in appearance as a man, He humbled Himself by becoming obedient to the point of death: death on a cross. For this reason also God highly exalted Him, and bestowed on Him the name which is above every name, so that at the name of Jesus EVERY KNEE WILL BOW, of those who are in heaven and on earth and under the earth, and that every tongue will confess that Jesus Christ is Lord, to the glory of God the Father. (Philippians 2:5–11)

We can live forever because Jesus chose to become a servant. It says in Mark 10:45 that Jesus "did not come to be served, but to serve, and to give His life as a ransom for many." As Paul instructed us in the Philippians passage, we are to have that same attitude!

This is a day of God's power, and now it is your move. As educator and author Leo Buscaglia said, "Your talent is God's gift to you. What you do with it is your gift back to God."[6] You can take it and recline, or you can choose to have the heart of a servant—not living cautiously, but for the benefit of others!

QUESTIONS

1. Is the Lord highlighting an area of your life where you have been "living cautiously"? What obstacles, if any, are keeping you from serving?

2. Spend some time with the Lord. What would be your "dream" way of serving the Lord? What is one very menial way you can serve someone else today?

3. Jesus' parable of the talents described three servants: two of whom invested wisely and one who did not invest at all. Why do you think Jesus did not include a scenario in which a servant invests the talent but winds up losing money?

WORSHIP

The Power and Purpose of Worship

"Worship is the overflow of the heart that asks nothing of God."
CARL ARMERDING[1]

Some years ago, a group of missionaries spent twenty-five years translating the New Testament into the language of the Chol Indians—the Mayan Indians of northern Chiapas in southeastern Mexico. Today the Chol Church is thriving with more than 12,000 believers. What is amazing is that when the missionaries first arrived, the Chol Indians did not know how to sing. Yet when the gospel entered their lives, they became known as "the singers." They love singing because now they have a reason to sing![2]

How did that song end up in that tribe? The same way it ended up inside of you. The song you have today did not come from a studio, a stage, sheet music, or Spotify. The moment you were saved, God put a song within you, and you became a worshiper. Look at the words of the psalmist David:

> I waited patiently for the LORD;
> And He inclined to me,
> And heard my cry.
> He also brought me up out of a horrible pit,
> Out of the miry clay,
> And set my feet upon a rock,
> And established my steps.

He has put a new song in my mouth—
Praise to our God;
Many will see it and fear,
And will trust in the LORD.
(Psalm 40:1–3 NKJV)

The natural result of a supernatural work in the soul is worship and praise in the mouth. Because David was lifted out of the pit, set on solid ground, and free to walk, he could not help but sing and worship. Not only that, his song moved others to put their trust in God. Many who witness the worship of God's people today are left wondering, "Why are they so happy?"

As the song lyrics go, "This joy that I have, the world didn't give it to me, and the world can't take it away!"[3]

Have you been rescued by God? Then you must worship. Have you been set on solid ground? Then you must praise Him. Have you been walking with God, witnessing His faithfulness in your life? Lift your voice and thank Him!

There is a day coming when all preaching will cease and all sermons will be finished. Prayer meetings will no longer be necessary, and even evangelism will be useless. It is the day we enter into eternity to be with Jesus forever. However, there is something that we do right now that *will* continue throughout all eternity that includes everyone: worship and praise! We will join a service already in session:

Day and night they never stop saying: "'Holy, holy, holy is the Lord God Almighty,' who was, and is, and is to come."
(Revelation 4:8 NIV)

What is praise and worship? Here is the simplest way to distinguish between the two: We praise God for what He has done; we worship God for who He is. Allow me to use the two terms interchangeably in this chapter.

We as Christians are issued a challenge in Romans 6 that I call the "just as" and "so now" challenge:

I am using an example from everyday life because of your human limitations. Just as you used to offer yourselves as slaves to impurity and to ever-increasing wickedness, so now offer yourselves as slaves to righteousness leading to holiness. (Romans 6:19 NIV)

This was Paul's challenge to us: Just as you got crazy for the world, in the clubs, during college football or the World Series—now I need you to take that same exuberance and enthusiasm and go all out for God! And that applies not just to Sunday. If you are not worshiping God on Monday the way you did the day before, perhaps you are not worshiping Him at all. Worship does not happen when a choir, a band, or a guy gets on a stage with a guitar. It happens when we focus on Christ. I love what the early church theologian Augustine said: "A Christian should be a hallelujah from head to foot."[4] Head to foot—every day of the week, with Christ as the focus.

I believe praise and worship, in the simplest form, is vocalizing compliments to God. It is being so preoccupied with God that we are compelled to say something about who He is and what He has done.

I love Friday nights, which Cindy and I reserve for our date nights. We often go to a restaurant, and occasionally I will glance around at the other tables. What I find interesting is when I see a husband and a wife sitting at dinner, not saying a single word to each other. That is usually a sign that something is wrong with that relationship. A healthy relationship is verbal; people are talking, there is an exchange. Just like when you have a good relationship with God—you cannot help but want to declare, "God, You are good. I love You. Thank You for who You are!" Now what you must be careful of doing is living off cheat sheets. The song lyrics on the screen are your cheat sheet. Don't let the only thing you say to God be what you see on the screen.

Can you imagine if I woke up every morning and had to rely on a script in order to talk to my wife?

Good morning, Cindy. (Pause for response.)

It is so good to see you today.

My, you are looking good . . .

Even for this early in the morning.

I love you. (2x)

That's a cheat sheet. Just because you sang does not necessarily mean you praised. Your praise to God must come from your heart and soul. That means you need to build a praise vocabulary.

There is no such thing as praising God "your way." There is only God's way. Praise is declared; praise is not praise until it is vocal. You cannot praise with a closed mouth. You can pray or meditate with a closed mouth, but not praise. And no matter how many people praise God beside you and around you, they cannot praise God for you. You must praise God for yourself.

Praise and worship have gone awry today because we have focused on the wrong things. Many have been content to watch everyone on stage, never lifting their eyes higher. I am thankful for the tool that music can be, but singers and instruments and songs must not be our focus. We have been concerned about all the peripherals while missing the main attraction. God must be our one focus.

When we lived in Detroit and our children were young, the Detroit Zoo had just built a multimillion-dollar polar bear exhibit—one of the first of its kind in the country. We took our children to see it, and it did not disappoint. As you walked underneath a glass ceiling, you could see the giant paws of the polar bears as they swam over you. However, it was my son's response that was the most memorable. He was captivated by one thing: the four giant green rubber balls that the polar bears were playing with! All my son was interested in were those green balls and whether we could purchase them. Imagine that, walking through this multimillion-dollar exhibit, and he is fixated on four cheap green rubber balls!

Speaking of zoos, several years ago a German zoo was preparing to retire one of its faithful bears, Ziggy. Most of Ziggy's fifteen years had been spent walking back and forth in his four-by-twelve-foot cage. When the day came to release Ziggy into a fenced field where he could roam to his heart's content, something unexpected happened. As Ziggy's keepers tried to coax the old bear into exploring the boundaries of his new home, to their amazement he did what he had been conditioned to do: walk twelve feet forward, turn around and walk twelve feet in the opposite direction. With nothing obstructing Ziggy's vision, the animal keepers concluded that he was a prisoner to his own traditional perceptions!

Have we as the church grown so accustomed to worshiping on Sunday in our twelve-foot cage that we have forgotten worship is not about these four walls? You are not Ziggy! Your worship should not be confined to Sunday mornings in church. How can we worship the God of the universe and all look the same? We get stuck in twelve-foot churches, all doing the same thing—relegating worship to eighteen minutes so that people won't be stuck in church too long. It is time to bring praise and worship back to what the Bible says. Remember, we serve a God who knows no limitations, and we have the freedom to worship Him whenever we desire. Let's break the twelve-foot barrier and worship God for who He is and what He has done!

Let's now look at two things I want you to remember regarding the song God has put within you: the source and power of that song. We must recover the *source* of worship and remember the *weapon* of worship.

Recovering the Source of Worship

It is said that when Jesus is not wonderful, then men become clever. Men have to create gimmicks in order to draw people in. Welcome to the twenty-first-century church.

In contrast, look at the source of worship according to David:

> From You comes my praise in the great assembly. (Psalm 22:25)

I believe people know *how* to worship; they just don't know *who* to worship. The church must recover who the "You" is in Psalm 22. True praise has been lost because the "You" has been replaced with other things. We have somehow determined that the "You" is not big enough to keep people in awe during a Sunday service. And when the "You" is wrong, worship gets reduced to eighteen minutes.

When we can sit in the presence of God and not be overwhelmed by Him, it means we have lost who the "You" is. We have lost the focus of Him. You cannot be in the presence of God—the One who has put a new song in your heart—and be silent! In fact, the Bible tells us that *praiselessness* is an attitude and characteristic of the *unsaved*:

> They knew God but did not praise and thank him for being God. Instead, their thoughts were pointless, and their misguided minds were plunged into darkness. (Romans 1:21 GW)

On the other hand, when you are engulfed and enraptured with God as the "You," eighteen minutes is not enough. An hour or even a day is not enough.

Only eternity is enough! It is like the song goes: "I'm coming back to the heart of worship, and it's all about You, it's all about You, Jesus." When God is the source of our praise we have come back to the heart of worship. Why is this important? Because praise is not dependent on me, my church, the music, or my feelings. The circumstances of my days do not determine my praise. My days *call* for praise but are not the *cause* for praise. I do not need a good day or a good song to praise God. I just need a good God!

> Great is the LORD, and greatly to be praised. (Psalm 48:1)

If God is great, then my praise must be great. My praise must match His character. Who He is, not how I feel, determines how I praise. His greatness dictates my worship—not my personality, my preferences, or what I feel comfortable calling worship. My church denomination, my background, or my cultural history do not determine how I praise. If the Bible says to shout unto the Lord, then we shout unto the Lord! It is not a Pentecostal or Charismatic thing; it is a Bible thing. The bottom line is that God is great; therefore He is to be greatly praised. There is enough value in who God is to praise Him every day for all eternity!

In Psalm 22, David not only revealed the source of worship but also showed us that when you have the source right, you will understand that it does not matter what you are going through—God is always worthy of worship. Psalm 22 describes how David felt at his lowest time. And of the 2,461 verses in the book of Psalms, Jesus chose this one to articulate His pain from the cross.

> My God, my God, why have you abandoned me?
> > Why are you so far away when I groan for help?
> Every day I call to you, my God, but you do not answer.
> > Every night I lift my voice, but I find no relief.
> (Psalm 22:1–2 NLT)

Here we catch a glimpse of the sheer agony Jesus felt at His lowest moment. But then comes the incredible transition from these first two verses to verse 3, beginning with the powerful conjunction *yet*.

> Yet you are holy,
> > enthroned on the praises of Israel.

(Psalm 22:3 NLT)

Yet You are holy. Those transitional words pop off the page to me. Another way to say "yet" is "regardless of what is going on." It was a pronouncement of who God is despite what David was facing. Our changing circumstances do not change God. *Immutability* is a theological word that means "God does not change; He remains the same." It is just as it says in Malachi 3:6, "For I am the LORD, I do not change" (NKJV).

Despite how we feel, God remains the same—ever worthy of praise. We must praise God during the difficult times, knowing that He "inhabitest the praises" of His people (Psalm 22:3 KJV). The Hebrew word for *inhabit* means "to sit down; to recline and relax." God is saying, "When you praise, I find Myself wanting to sit and listen. I want to take it all in, recline, and enjoy it." The praise that goes up when your life is going down is a particular kind of praise that God takes special notice of. When you praise in tough times, God draws close and stays long.

I personally believe that God recognizes the songs sung by the saints on earth more than the songs sung to Him in heaven. Why? The songs of the redeemed sound different from the chorus of the cherubim and seraphim in heaven. While the angels of heaven sing in the presence of the glory of God, the redeemed can sing through pain on earth. The redeemed can sing songs with cancer in their body, with an unsaved spouse next to them in their bed, with fear of job security, with wayward children living a life of addiction. As these songs are sung, they are declaring, "My life is in trouble, but You are still the same!"

REMEMBERING THE WEAPON OF WORSHIP

Once we get the source of worship right, we equip ourselves not with lyrics but with fighting words. Someone once said, "When we lift our voice to worship Jesus, the devil loses his." This verse helps explain why:

The high praises of God shall be in their mouths,
And a two-edged sword in their hands.
(Psalm 149:6)

The psalmist likened high praises in our mouth to a weapon in our hand. Let me give you a picture of what happens when we praise Him. Some years ago, I was traveling by myself, preaching in a Midwest city. After I finished, a lady came up to me and began complimenting me a little too much. Every time I backed up—with nobody there to help me—she came closer and continued with the compliments. Suddenly I knew the Holy Spirit was helping me, for it dawned on me: Talk about my incredible wife, Cindy. The more I did, the more the lady backed off, until I "Cindy-ed" her out the door! At that point, it hit me: That is what praise is. As the enemy starts closing in on you, keep talking about God. It will change the environment. The high praises of God in our mouth are a double-edged sword in our hand!

The purpose of praise is that God would be glorified, the saints fortified, and the devil horrified. Because praise is a weapon, the enemy works hard to convince us that it is reserved for Sundays in a building. Satan's plot is to take six days of praise away and keep us singing only one day. He is distracting us from using this weapon all the time, everywhere. But David knew the secret:

> I will bless the LORD at all times;
> His praise shall continually be in my mouth.
> (Psalm 34:1 AMP)

At *all* times! Perhaps you have heard the saying: "There are two times to praise the Lord: when you feel like it, and when you don't." Praise is to be an everyday part of your life. In other words, God is worthy of your praise in the best of times as well as the worst. What happens if we don't feel like it? Let's take a tip from David who is known as *the* worshiper. He did not always feel like praising.

> Why, my soul, are you downcast?
>   Why so disturbed within me?
> Put your hope in God,
>   for I will yet praise him,
>   my Savior and my God.
>
> My soul is downcast within me;
>   therefore I will remember you.
> (Psalms 42:5–6 TNIV)

David had to talk to his soul and say, "You don't determine my obedience! If I am breathing, I have a job to do: Praise God!"

There is a fascinating story in Acts 16 that clearly demonstrates this weapon of worship. Paul and Silas had been arrested for preaching, and after being beaten, they were thrown in prison. But something happened at midnight when they began to sing:

> Now about midnight Paul and Silas were praying and singing hymns of praise to God, and the prisoners were listening to them; and suddenly there was a great earthquake, so that the foundations of the prison were shaken; and immediately all the doors were opened, and everyone's chains were unfastened. When the jailer awoke and saw the prison doors opened, he drew his sword and was about to kill himself, thinking that the prisoners had escaped. But Paul called out with a loud voice, saying, "Do not harm yourself, for we are all here!" (Acts 16:25–28)

The singing of Paul and Silas arrested the arrested! Don't you think those convicts wanted to escape? Yet not one of them left. The praises of Paul and Silas froze them. It is just as it says in Psalm 40: "Many will see and fear the LORD and put their trust in him" (verse 3 NIV). The prisoners saw something when those men sang in jail. Something else happened when the praises went up, and God took notice: The foundations were shaken, doors were opened, and chains were loosed!

Jesus' Worship Conference

The longest teaching on worship in the New Testament was from Jesus Himself, and it occurred in the most unexpected place. His audience? Not a single worship leader or musician. The Jesus' worship conference only had one person in attendance. This is what He taught: Praise and worship brings freedom. He used a verse we often associate with music and instruments, not with liberty. Jesus was reminding us that there is much more to worship than we often consider.

> But a time is coming, and even now has arrived when the true

worshipers will worship the Father in spirit and truth; for such people the Father seeks to be His worshipers. God is Spirit, and those
who worship Him must worship in spirit and truth. (John 4:23–24)

Why are these words significant? Keep in mind that Jesus was not speaking to musicians or singers to get them ready for Sunday church. Instead, He
was addressing an immoral woman who had to draw water during a certain
time of day in order to avoid the shame and chatter of the town ladies regarding her promiscuous lifestyle. It is astounding to think that Jesus was speaking
to not only a Samaritan woman but an immoral woman! She already had three
strikes against her: She was hated for her ethnicity, disrespected for being a
woman, and ostracized for her sin.

When Jesus spoke to her, He did not talk about moral living but about worship. Somehow it does not seem like a fitting conversation. Why not a sexual
purity conference or verses about holiness for her? It is because Jesus wanted to
teach her the source and the weapon of worship.

The source of worship: Regardless of what you have done and the person
you have become, God is God. To worship Him requires seeing Him as the
source, not your horrible lifestyle.

The weapon of worship: When you are fighting those horrible thoughts of
your sin, begin to speak about God. Talk out loud, make the enemy run. Jesus
was saying that if you can worship, you can face anything—your checkered
past, your sketchy present, and your troublesome future.

No matter what you have done or what you are going through, I encourage
you to worship God. Choose to praise Him at all times. You can begin by simply declaring who He is. God is love. God is great. God is faithful. Who He is
can overcome any current or future obstacle in your life.

You were created to praise and worship God. Not only does it put a weapon
in your hand, but you get to join the everlasting chorus of praise to a God who
is worthy.

Then I heard every creature in heaven and on earth and under the
earth and on the sea, and all that is in them, saying:

"To him who sits on the throne and to the Lamb
be praise and honor and glory and power,
    for ever and ever!"
(Revelation 5:13 TNIV)

QUESTIONS

1. How can you encourage yourself to praise when you don't feel like it?

2. When was the last time you worshiped God extravagantly? What was the reason?

3. Read Psalm 98:1; Psalm 63:4; Psalm 47:1; Psalm 149:3 (or find other verses on praise and worship). What does the Lord expect our praise and worship to look like? Does it look any different for those who are introverted, reserved, not musically inclined, or uncoordinated?

X CHROMOSOME

AND OTHER FALLACIES THAT TRY TO DICTATE MY FUTURE AND MY ETERNITY—AND THE FIGHT FOR TRUTH

When Truth Is Called Insanity

"Tolerance applies only to persons, but never to truth. Intolerance applies only to truth, but never to persons. Tolerance applies to the erring; intolerance to the error."
FULTON J. SHEEN[1]

I believe it was C. S. Lewis who once said, "When the whole world is running toward a cliff, he who is running the opposite direction appears to have lost his mind."[2] I am about to run the opposite direction of the masses. I may appear in this chapter to have lost my mind, but I am in good company.

Jeremiah told the truth, and the religious wanted him locked up.

> You are responsible to put into stocks and neck irons any crazy man who claims to be a prophet. (Jeremiah 29:26 NLT)

Jesus was the truth, and his family wanted to take charge of Him.

> When his family heard about this, they went to take charge of him, for they said, "He is out of his mind." (Mark 3:21 NIV)

The Apostle Paul preached the truth, and the government called it insanity.

> At this point Festus interrupted Paul's defense. "You are out of your mind, Paul!" he shouted. "Your great learning is driving you insane." (Acts 26:24 NIV)

Paul's response to the Roman governor was simply, "I am not insane, most excellent Festus. What I am saying is true and reasonable" (Acts 26:25 NIV). What may appear to be insanity today is actually true and reasonable. If we are "out of our mind," as some say, it is for God.

I am sure you have heard the phrase "the elephant in the room"—the glaringly obvious issue that exists but no one is dealing with. Nothing is more demoralizing to a marriage, a family, or a ministry than to have a herd of elephants running around with no one talking about them. God did not make elephants to live in rooms. They are meant for the wild. When you bring the wild into a room, chaos ensues, making it increasingly difficult to effectively deal with present issues. Nice talk with elephants present is not nice talk; it is a smoke screen. It takes courage to call out what is really there instead of dancing around it and assuming no one sees it.

So let me start with a big question: What do you do when God's Word contradicts your lifestyle or opinion? Who wins the fight?

When you do not obey what God says, you are claiming to know better than God. Do you know better than God on finances and tithing? On love and sex? On drinking and alcohol? On sexual identity?

There is an elephant in the room where tolerance and intolerance have been misunderstood. Liberal pulpits will affirm sinful lifestyles while the pulpits who ought to have a voice in our country remain silent.

It seems that during COVID, something crept into the American mindset as well as that of nations around the world. Not only did anxiety overwhelm minds and hearts, but somehow when America was left to her own thoughts with no church or Christian values, we ended up in a dangerous place. We have allowed biological men to play women's sports. We told our children to decide which gender they are by checking a box.

In this chapter, I want to speak to an elephant in the room and deal with the gender identity issue. I will be the crazy man running away from the cliff while society is running toward it. I want to deal with legislation that our courts have upheld. I want to challenge churches and pastors who have used their pulpits to uphold fallacies and sinful stances, pastors who no longer preach the Bible but pander to popular opinion while chastising those who stand for truth. I am not angry, but I feel an urgency. I want to be a soldier for truth and a shepherd for the hurting and the lost. My aim is not condemnation but revelation.

> But all things become visible when they are exposed by the light, for everything that becomes visible is light. For this reason it says,
>
> "Awake, sleeper,
> And arise from the dead,
> And Christ will shine on you."
> (Ephesians 5:13–14)

You can only fight woke America with an awakened church. And the only way the church will be awake is if it has a revival. A dead fish can float downstream, but it takes a live one to swim upstream. We must be alive in Christ because we need to swim upstream in this hour. For too long we have allowed others to tell us how to live and what to accept. It is time to return to the One who gave us life. Since God is the source, He knows how we work best.

> You let the world, which doesn't know the first thing about living, tell you how to live. (Ephesians 2:2 MSG)

Only God knows how life really works. That means when God defines something, let's go with His definition. Definitions do not come from politics, a court decision, or a majority. They come from God, who is omnipotent, omniscient, and omnipresent. We must be careful not to mistake government policy for God's truth. You can vote on policy, but you cannot vote on truth.

This chapter is called "X: The X Chromosome and Other Fallacies That Try to Dictate My Future and My Eternity—And the Fight for Truth" What science is saying—and our government and courts are affirming—is that a certain lifestyle is acceptable because of the way we are created with the Xq28 genetic marker. Studies of the X chromosome as well as the entire human genome have linked Xq28 to the heredity of homosexuality in human males. A molecular biologist offered the first direct evidence of a "gay gene" by identifying a stretch on the X chromosome likely associated with homosexuality.[3]

If this is true and God exists, then God cannot send anyone to hell because He is holding people responsible for doing what He forbids, though He Himself put the inclination inside of them. You cannot believe in God and His

Word while at the same time believe this sin is in our genes and therefore must not be called sin. Remember that what Festus called crazy, Paul called sober truth. Yet that governor in power could legalize insanity while criminalizing sober truth.

That is exactly what is happening today.

To redefine is to undermine. Marriage and sexuality have been redefined in our society because God's place has been redefined. A word to our judges and justices who are trying to "redefine"—a psalm that calls judges to account:

> God calls the judges into his courtroom,
>   he puts all the judges in the dock.
>
> "Enough! You've corrupted justice long enough,
>   you've let the wicked get away with murder.
> You're here to defend the defenseless,
>   to make sure that underdogs get a fair break;
> Your job is to stand up for the powerless,
>   and prosecute all those who exploit them."
>
> Ignorant judges! Head-in-the-sand judges!
>   They haven't a clue to what's going on.
> And now everything's falling apart,
>   the world's coming unglued.
>
> "I appointed you judges, each one of you,
>   deputies of the High God,
> But you've betrayed your commission
>   and now you're stripped of your rank, busted."
> (Psalm 82:1–7 MSG)

Just because something is legalized or permissible does not mean it is right and that you should do it. Consider the words of the Apostle Paul:

> Or do you not know that the unrighteous will not inherit the king-
> dom of God? Do not be deceived; neither the sexually immoral,
> nor idolaters, nor adulterers, nor homosexuals, nor thieves, nor the
> greedy, those habitually drunk, nor verbal abusers, nor swindlers,

will inherit the kingdom of God. Such were some of you; but you were washed, but you were sanctified, but you were justified in the name of the Lord Jesus Christ and in the Spirit of our God. All things are permitted for me, but not all things are of benefit. All things are permitted for me, but I will not be mastered by anything. (1 Corinthians 6:9–12)

We obey the law, but we are also to live by a higher law.

WHERE THE BATTLE BEGINS

I want you to understand that this battle we are facing today did not start in a courtroom or in D.C. It did not start on a university campus. This battle started in the minds of people. It went from the minds of people to a lifestyle and eventually to a law. We have made this about birth instead of a battle. The lifestyle did not come from a chromosome; it began as a battle in the mind.

The mind is Satan's battleground, and satanic questions are his strategy. The three times Satan talked in the Bible, he did not declare but instead imposed questions.

1. To Eve:

"Now the serpent was more cunning than any animal of the field which the LORD God had made. And he said to the woman, "Has God really said, 'You shall not eat from any tree of the garden'?" (Genesis 3:1)

2. Regarding Job:

Then Satan answered the LORD, "Does Job fear God for nothing?" (Job 1:9)

3. To Jesus:

And the tempter came and said to Him, "*If* You are the Son of God, command that these stones become bread." (Matthew 4:3, emphasis added)

These satanic attacks happen today to all of us. *Has God forgotten you? Is there a God? Are you really a man? Are you really a woman?* We are all constantly in that mind battle. Every Sunday service during worship, I pray four verses because of how intense the mind battle can get. I sit in the front row and, while everyone is singing the words on the screen, I am saying something different. I speak out these four passages of Scripture to those rogue thoughts:

Set your mind on things above, not on things on the earth. (Colossians 3:2 NKJV)

For as he thinks in his heart, so is he. (Proverbs 23:7 NKJV)

Finally, brethren, whatever things are true, whatever things are noble, whatever things are just, whatever things are pure, whatever things are lovely, whatever things are of good report, if there is any virtue and if there is anything praiseworthy—meditate on these things. (Philippians 4:8 NKJV)

Casting down imaginations, and every high thing that exalteth itself against the knowledge of God, and bringing into captivity every thought to the obedience of Christ. (2 Corinthians 10:5 KJV)

It is this last verse that I want us to focus on. Rogue thoughts often get lodged and then turn into lifestyles. They make their journey from people's heads to their feet. There is an Old Testament story that shows us even David the psalmist fought mind battles. After being anointed by Samuel, he killed a giant, dodged a spear-throwing boss numerous times, and then continued running from Saul for a decade. By 1 Samuel 27, David was nearing the fulfillment of the prophecy that he would be king—just a few chapters away from having a crown put on his head.

And then something goes wrong. Something gets in his head that literally could have derailed God's plan.

David experienced a miracle in 1 Samuel 26 where God put the whole enemy army to sleep. David then gathered spears and water jugs that were next to Saul while he and his men were in their deep sleep, and he showed them from afar. But suddenly something got into David's mind after this incredible moment, and it started to make its way to his feet.

> But David thought to himself, "One of these days I will be destroyed
> by the hand of Saul. The best thing I can do is to escape to the land
> of the Philistines. Then Saul will give up searching for me any-
> where in Israel, and I will slip out of his hand." So David and the
> six hundred men with him left and went over to Achish . . . king of
> Gath . . . David lived in Philistine territory a year and four months.
> (1 Samuel 27:1-2, 7 NIV)

Instead of praising God for the victory, David began to doubt whether he would even live to see tomorrow. Something in David's mind was now starting to move him in a wrong direction. The mind battles were stronger than the miracles he had experienced.

"David thought to himself"—that is the mind battle in verse 1. It is not that the mind battles won't come. There will always be battles of the mind. The fight we must focus on is stopping the thoughts from going from head to foot. Head for David was in 1 Samuel 27:1; foot was 1 Samuel 27:2. You lose when you act out what you were thinking.

Notice that when David was battling those rogue thoughts, he kept silent. What he should have done was confess them. People are afraid to tell others about their battles. But as the saying goes, "You are only as sick as your secrets." What was the magnitude of the damage of David's rogue thoughts? Not only did David cross over to Achish, but 600 men and their families went with him! When we have no one to stand with us, we end up bringing others into our battle. So either we confess to one godly person, or we take hundreds of unsuspecting people—perhaps our spouse, children, family members, friends—into crazy regions like Gath. Do you know what Gath is? Do you remember the name of the giant that David defeated? Goliath. But that was not his full name; he was called Goliath of Gath. David's thoughts took him and 600 families to Gath—the home of the Philistines and Goliath! The murderer and decapitator of Goliath was now residing in his neighborhood, all because he wouldn't confess a rogue thought! Our struggles bring others along. That is why it is essential that we fight the thoughts before they go from our head to our feet.

Are you aware that when you became a Christian, you were adopted *and* enlisted at the same time? You were adopted into God's family and enlisted into God's army. The church that is ignorant about weapons and warfare is a weak and defeated church. Because we are engaged in a war, we will have difficulty. War demands courage, persistence, and discipline.

When you enter an army, do you tell them, "I would like to wear something with a swoosh on it" or "Do you have the new Jordans for my boots?" Do you say, "I don't like broccoli; I would like pizza every Thursday night"? Absolutely not! Do you explain that you are a night person, so you will not be getting up early in the morning? Of course not. You do what that army commander wants you to do. Wartime does not allow for personal preferences.

When you become a soldier, your agenda changes. Many have accepted that they are a Christian but not that they are a soldier. In order for us to be victorious, we must understand the ongoing war that we are engaged in. Satan's major strategy is to get you to believe that your problem is flesh and blood rather than the forces behind the flesh and blood. You cannot fight a spiritual battle unless you have spiritual tools.

So how do we win the battle of the mind? We must learn how to attack the meditation before it becomes a manifestation.

> May the words of my mouth and the meditation of my heart
> Be acceptable in Your sight,
> Lord, my rock and my Redeemer."
> (Psalm 19:14)

Don't miss the words *think* and *knowledge of God* in the following passage. The battleground becomes evident:

> Furthermore, just as they did not think it worthwhile to retain the knowledge of God, so God gave them over to a depraved mind, so that they do what ought not to be done. They have become filled with every kind of wickedness, evil, greed and depravity. They are full of envy, murder, strife, deceit and malice. They are gossips, slanderers, God-haters, insolent, arrogant and boastful; they invent ways of doing evil; they disobey their parents; they have no understanding, no fidelity, no love, no mercy. Although they know God's righteous decree that those who do such things deserve death,

they not only continue to do these very things but also approve of those who practice them. (Romans 1:28–32 NIV)

There are two dangerous mindsets happening in Christianity. *Deconversion*—Christians turning into atheists. This is not theological but emotional. Their stories are all the same. Tragedy strikes, and their anger at God turns into disbelief.

However, even more dangerous is *deconstruction*—editing truth. It is removing and adding to the Word. Today we have preachers editing the Bible. Jeremiah 36 tells us of Jehoiakim, who was king during the Babylonian takeover. What did King Jehoiakim do when Jeremiah preached a message he did not like? He cut up parts of the Bible and threw them in the fire (see Jeremiah 36:23)! Jeremiah 36 is not only scary but contemporary. King Jehoiakim exists today in the form of politics, courts, and public opinion. However, after God's Word was thrown in the fire, God immediately instructed Jeremiah to take another scroll and write out His words again. It goes to show that you can try to edit the Bible and cut out passages, but one thing will always be true: "Heaven and earth will pass away, but My words will not pass away" (Matthew 24:35).

For those who insist on editing the Bible, the book of Revelation says they we be under a curse:

I testify to everyone who hears the words of the prophecy of this book: if anyone adds to them, God will add to him the plagues that are written in this book; and if anyone takes away from the words of the book of this prophecy, God will take away his part from the tree of life and from the holy city, which are written in this book. He who testifies to these things says, "Yes, I am coming quickly." Amen. Come, Lord Jesus. The grace of the Lord Jesus be with all. Amen. (Revelation 22:18–21)

The Bible's final message: Do not add or subtract from the Bible. Jesus is coming. Grace is here for everyone. If you want to remove or add, do not call it Christianity. Deconstructionists do not believe God; they believe themselves.

The president of a Christian university recently sent me an article on a new AI commentary that affirms sinful sexual lifestyles, generated by ChatGPT. It said that Jesus accepts trans-identifying individuals, stating "there is no man nor woman." The passage continued: "Jesus looked upon her with kindness, replying, 'My child, blessed are those who strive for unity within themselves, for they shall know the deepest truths of my Father's creation . . . Be not afraid, for in the kingdom of God, there is no man nor woman, as all are one in spirit. The gates of my Father's kingdom will open for those who love and are loved, for God looks not upon the body, but the heart."[4]

If the church approves and does not speak out against this personal choice of gender identity, what we are doing is removing God. We now have a god who makes mistakes. Second, we are denying the inerrancy of the Bible. You cannot say God does not speak to this issue without deconstructing the Bible (see 1 Corinthians 6:9–10; Romans 1:24–26). Any pastor or church who supports personal choice of gender identity does not believe in God or His Word. It's as simple as that.

THE ISSUE OF HOMOSEXUALITY

Let me specifically address the issue of homosexuality for a moment. F. W. Boreham, one of the great preachers of the past, made it his aim never to condemn when he preached. His rule was that "the best way to prove a stick is crooked is to lay a straight one beside it."[5] The job of the preacher is to put down the straight stick.

For those who struggle, for those who have family or friends who struggle, for those who want to know how to minister, and for those who want to be free—let's start with three important verses.

> The disciples said to Him, "If the relationship of the man with his wife is like this, it is better not to marry." But He said to them, "Not all men can accept this statement, but only those to whom it has been given. For there are eunuchs who were born that way from their mother's womb; and there are eunuchs who were made eunuchs by men; and there are also eunuchs who made themselves eunuchs for the sake of the kingdom of heaven. The one who is able to accept this, let him accept it." (Matthew 19:10–12)

> But I want you to be free from concern. One who is unmarried is

concerned about the things of the Lord, how he may please the Lord; but one who is married is concerned about the things of the world, how he may please his wife, and his interests are divided. The woman who is unmarried, and the virgin, is concerned about the things of the Lord, that she may be holy both in body and spirit; but one who is married is concerned about the things of the world, how she may please her husband. I say this for your own benefit, not to put a restraint on you, but to promote what is appropriate and to secure undistracted devotion to the Lord. (1 Corinthians 7:32–35)

But an angel of the Lord spoke to Philip, saying, "Get ready and go south to the road that descends from Jerusalem to Gaza." . . . So he got ready and went; and there was an Ethiopian eunuch, a court official of Candace, queen of the Ethiopians . . . He had come to Jerusalem to worship, and he was returning and sitting in his chariot, and was reading Isaiah the prophet. Then the Spirit said to Philip, "Go up and join this chariot." Philip ran up and heard him reading Isaiah the prophet, and said, "Do you understand what you are reading?" And he said, "Well, how could I, unless someone guides me?" . . . Then Philip opened his mouth, and beginning from this Scripture he preached Jesus to him. As they went along the road they came to some water; and the eunuch said, "Look! Water! What prevents me from being baptized?" [And Philip said, "If you believe with all your heart, you may." And he answered and said, "I believe that Jesus Christ is the Son of God."] And he ordered that the chariot stop; and they both went down into the water, Philip as well as the eunuch, and he baptized him. (Acts 8:26–31, 35–38 NASB)

1. The Origin of the Thoughts (Matthew 19:10–12)

This passage defines and speaks about the origin of the thought, "I don't like women." This thought may come from God Himself. The thoughts do not define you; they are for a future that God is leading you to—not to a sexual future but a ministry future. Jesus spoke about celibacy as a gift and something that God puts in a man.

Homosexuality is a rogue thought trying to redefine God's intention.

There are men to whom God has given the desire to not want to be with a woman. That does not mean they should marry or have sex with a man. If God has pronounced homosexuality to be wrong in His Word, then there is another alternative: celibacy. Why do we not speak about celibacy?

2. The Purpose of Celibacy (1 Corinthians 7:32–35)

Paul spoke about the purpose and benefits of celibacy. We have overemphasized marriage because most people want to be married. We have not only undervalued celibacy and singleness, but we have deemed it undesirable and created this second lane, therefore making it easy for many to embrace the lie: *Because I don't want to marry a woman, it means I am a homosexual.* That is not a biblical option.

Singleness is celebrated and encouraged in the Scriptures. Yet we have discouraged people from wanting to be single, regarding older single people as "less than" when the Bible sees them as the opposite. We encourage divorced people to get remarried. But God says, "Are you single? Stay that way. Are you married? Stay in it."

3. The Rewards of Celibacy (Acts 8:26–38)

Let's take a case study of a man who has a celibate thought, chooses it, and wins as a celibate. It is a story of a man who never had earthly children, but his clock is still ticking for spiritual children. Some of you need to forget your biological clock and focus on your spiritual kid clock. So far, this man is presently up to half a billion spiritual children and counting.

He is the Ethiopian eunuch—the one who is considered to be the key to the gospel going into Africa! God's purposes are always greater than we can fathom. That is why the enemy works hard to get people to buy into his lies, particularly regarding identity.

A note on rainbows and pride: No matter what I see in our society today, I always remember that the first rainbow was given by God—a promise that He would never again destroy the earth with a flood. The desire of His heart is to show mercy. When I see the rainbow, I do not see a select group of people. I see humanity, and I see a merciful God who passionately loves this world. No one is more inclusive than God. He tells us, "For *all* have sinned" (Romans 3:23, emphasis added). He does not single out homosexuality as the only sin that separates humanity from Himself. But God so loved the world—the *whole* world—that He made a way through His Son, Jesus, for us to come back to Him. He says, "The one who comes to Me I will most certainly not cast out [I will never, never reject anyone who follows Me]" (John 6:37 AMP). God "wants all people to be saved and to come to the knowledge of the truth" (1 Timothy 2:4).

Renewing Your Mind

God is inclusive, but definitions and our view of God have become blurred. The enemy is always attacking minds. A. W. Tozer said, "Ten thousand thoughts a day pass through our minds, and they try to predict what we will become."[6] Ten thousand negative thoughts try to predict who you will become. I want to stop those predictions from coming true. That is why I fight them every day.

Remember this important tip: Don't believe everything you think!

It is within the mind that the new nature and the old nature are constantly at war. How do we get the victory? It comes by the renewing of our mind. Paul said in Romans:

> And do not be conformed to this world, but be transformed by the renewing of your mind, so that you may prove what the will of God is, that which is good and acceptable and perfect. (Romans 12:2)

The word *renewal* means renovation. Anyone who has ever renovated something knows this to be true: renovation costs more and takes longer than you expected. Paul further explained:

> For though we walk in the flesh, we do not war according to the flesh. For the weapons of our warfare are not carnal but mighty in God for pulling down strongholds, casting down arguments and every high thing that exalts itself against the knowledge of God, bringing every thought into captivity to the obedience of Christ. (2 Corinthians 10:3–5 NKJV)

How do we renew our minds? By pulling down strongholds and casting down arguments. A stronghold is a fortress—a wall intended to keep things out. In this case, the stronghold is trying to keep out God's truth. The messages of our culture are trying to build fortresses of belief that will remain for a long time—thoughts about God, money, marriage, sexuality. Society wants you to sort them out by your political affiliation or by whether you watch Fox News or CNN. But that has nothing to do with us as Christians.

We all face rogue thoughts—thoughts that are not God thoughts. People assume that once you become a Christian, you do not have ungodly thoughts anymore. That is simply not true. Each of us will continue to fight lies and fleshly thoughts—whether we are heterosexual or homosexual. But just because you think a crazy thought does not mean you have to fulfill or become it.

How is it that some of those thoughts end up winning and becoming strongholds that keep God's Word out? It happens when the thought is raised higher than the knowledge of God. Remember, it says in 2 Corinthians 10:5 that we are to cast down "every high thing that exalts itself against the knowledge of God" (NKJV).

In order to fight the strongholds, we must renew our minds with the knowledge of God. Where do we get the knowledge of God? From the Word of God. Peter exhorted us to "grow in the grace and knowledge of our Lord and Savior Jesus Christ" (2 Peter 3:18). I have found that as I get older, the battles get more intense; therefore, I must constantly be growing in my knowledge of God. Knowing God is my weapon.

Now the renewal of your mind involves not only the Word of God but the Spirit of God. The Spirit of God uses the Word of God to convict us when a thought contradicts God's truth. Here is how it works: As you continually fill your mind with God's Word, when the time comes that you are faced with an outside mindset that is trying to conform you, an alarm will go off. It is the Holy Spirit telling you, "This is stinkin' thinkin.' Don't let these statements conform you!" It is just like being stopped at a TSA checkpoint at the airport and being told you cannot take an item through on your journey. When the Holy Spirit says, "That is not God's truth," you must immediately pull that thought out and dispose of it. We have power by the Holy Spirit to refuse to carry out ungodly thoughts in the mind. Just because you think it does not mean you have to do it!

As a test case, let's put the knowledge of God over a rogue thought—a question regarding your birth and how God made you. Begin to attack those thoughts with God's truth:

- I am who God created me to be.

  > He answered and said, "Have you not read that He who created them from the beginning MADE THEM MALE AND FEMALE?" (Matthew 19:4)

- I don't choose my gender; God already chose it for me.
- I trust God more than the checked box at my educational institution.

When you fill your mind and your mouth with God's Word, there will be no more room for Satan's lies!

Clarence Macartney was a powerful preacher in the early 1900s whose books have greatly influenced me. I found his book *The Greatest Words in the Bible and in Human Speech* to be particularly powerful. In this work he wrote about the time when the world was intrigued with transatlantic flight. Charles Lindbergh left Roosevelt Field in Long Island, New York, in his plane called the *Spirit of St. Louis* and flew for thirty-three hours all the way to Paris. Many others attempted this amazing feat but failed.

Macartney told the story of a pilot who took off on a transatlantic flight and was just a few minutes in the air when he heard some sounds in the cockpit. Looking down at his feet, he saw a rat just out of reach—gnawing on the coils of some wires. He couldn't fight the gnawing rat, but he knew that if he didn't do anything, the rat would gnaw his way through the control panel, and he would surely die in the cold waters of the Atlantic. What should he do? The pilot brilliantly decided to take the plane *higher*—to an altitude where a rodent could not live and breathe![7]

In the same way, we all have rats nibbling at our minds every single day. *You're a failure. Nobody really cares about you. You're not going to make it. You're not good enough to be a Christian.* When you feel the rogue thoughts gnawing at you, it is time to go up higher! Place the Word of God over the thoughts, bringing them to an atmosphere where lies can no longer exist. Remember, do not be caught off guard or condemned when the thoughts come—just be prepared to throttle up, and let God take you to new heights!

QUESTIONS

1. Write down at least five verses that you can have ready for when you need to "throttle up."

2. How have your ways of thinking already been renewed since meeting Jesus?

3. Who are the people in your life with whom you can confess "rogue thoughts"?

YOUNG AND OLD

Bridging the Church's Generational Gap

"When sinners are careless and stupid, and sinking into hell unconcerned, it is time the church should bestir themselves. It is as much the duty of the church to awake, as it is for the firemen to awake when a fire breaks out in the night in a great city."

Charles Finney[1]

When you ask God to send revival, you are presupposing that the church is in decline, dormancy, and stagnation. Something has gone wrong, and we need Someone to make it right. Yet in order for revival to come, it must first begin in the church. According to J. I. Packer, "Revival is the visitation of God which brings to life Christians who have been sleeping and restores a deep sense of God's near presence and holiness. Thence springs a vivid sense of sin and a profound exercise of heart in repentance, praise, and love, with an evangelistic outflow."[2]

Why does revival start in God's church and then move outside the doors? It is because the Lord needs a holy, on-fire, Spirit-filled church to send the newly saved to. Nothing could be worse than God setting people free from bondage only to put them in a church full of religious bondage. People need to experience Jesus, not church.

If you want a last-days revival, you need a last-days church. G. Campbell Morgan said, "Revival cannot be organized, but we can set our sails to catch the wind from heaven when God chooses to blow upon His people once again."[3] The book of Acts shows us where the wind from heaven is blowing and where the church must hoist its sails:

> "AND IT SHALL BE IN THE LAST DAYS," God says,
> "THAT I WILL OUT MY SPIRIT ON ALL MANKIND;
> AND YOUR SONS AND YOUR DAUGHTERS WILL PROPHESY,
> AND YOUR YOUNG MEN WILL SEE VISIONS,
> AND YOUR OLD MEN WILL HAVE DREAMS;
> AND EVEN ON MY MALE AND FEMALE SERVANTS
> I WILL POUR OUT MY SPIRIT IN THOSE DAYS,
> and they will prophesy.
> (Acts 2:17–18)

Do you consider yourself old, or do you consider yourself young? (I would love to see your criteria for how you answered.) No matter what your age, you are a critical part of God's last-days plan. In order for a bullet to hit a target, you need crosshairs comprised of two axes. Our target is a last days revival, and the two axes of the crosshairs are the old and the young. The last-days church needs both dreamers and visionaries working together.

Bringing these two groups together is not only vital but supernatural, for each group has unique gifts as well as unique battles. The great reformer Martin Luther said, "Where God builds a church, Satan builds a chapel."[4] Satan's chapel has done a lot of damage to God's church, keeping the dreamers and the visionaries apart.

If you have dreamers without visionaries, you get a bunch of people who protect the past and become irrelevant for the future. They shrivel up. On the other hand, if you only have visionaries, you get excitement and creativity without roots and stability. They eventually implode because their outside is bigger than their inside. Dreamers consider everything sacred; visionaries think nothing is sacred. Dreamers get stuck and stale; visionaries get oblivious and imprudent. Dreamers are stagnant; visionaries are in contempt.

So let me address both the young and the old and get us ready for a last-days church.

The last-days revival will need four key elements in the church: *fearlessness and patience; wisdom and testimony.* The dreamers provide wisdom and testimony. The visionaries provide fearlessness and patience.

THE DREAMER'S WISDOM AND TESTIMONY

What is a testimony? A testimony is different than a biography. A biography always ends with a person and what they did. A testimony ends with God and what *He* did. God is the star of a testimony; a person is the star of a biography.

The old saints used to say, "No test? Then no testimony." The test is what gives us the testimony. I grew up always hearing the word *testimony.* It seems we don't hear that very often anymore. We used to have "testimony services" in my church where we had a chance to hear people's stories. The basic plotline to a testimony is this: "It was bad, really bad. I was at the end of my rope. But in the last hour, Jesus stepped in, and this is what He did. He rescued me."

When I was twenty-seven years old and starting a church, David Wilkerson told me to pray for grayheads, or "cotton heads" as he called them—people who know God and have seen God work. Now I am a grayhead. Grayheads have stories of miracles. David Wilkerson knew I needed grayheads in my life who would testify, "Let me tell you what God did!" That is where wisdom comes from.

I was recently calculating the ages of some of my closest friends—the grayheads God has brought into my life. One is seventy-six; the others are seventy-three, eighty-two, eighty-eight, and the youngest is seventy. The average age of these men is seventy-seven! I need their testimonies and wisdom in order to fight this battle. Pastor and author Tan Seow How said, "Our next-generation leaders should walk in our footsteps, not in our shadow."[5] I am grateful that all these men have given me footsteps to walk in.

THE VISIONARY'S FEARLESSNESS AND PATIENCE

In 2023, the release of two incredible Christian movies caught the world's attention: *Sound of Freedom* and *Jesus Revolution.* The critics were shocked when *Sound of Freedom* even surpassed *Indiana Jones and the Dial of Destiny* at the box office.

Both of these Christian movies were speaking to something bigger. *Sound of Freedom*'s message was that a fearlessness is required in order to be a part of something that others are reluctant to touch—rescuing the helpless from sex trafficking. *Jesus Revolution* gave us a glimpse of the "Jesus People Revival" that happened fifty years ago. I believe it is a prophetic cry to the church that people are coming, and they will not look like Sunday morning Christians.

The church is about to change dramatically with the next harvest. Masses of people will get saved and enter the church, and it will call for patience from the congregation as they grow. Remember, we want people to grow and look like Jesus—not like you and me, or like our church or denomination. God is going to start saving people who are totally different—rescuing them from the bowels of hell—but it will be a genuine work of the Holy Spirit. Many will have grown up as atheists; some may still smell like smoke and weed when they come into church. The present-day church will soon be worshiping next to people with whom they will be uncomfortable, and an unprepared church will be a judgmental church. God is calling us to have the patience but also the fearlessness to see them rescued.

Understanding Romans 14 and 15 is key for handling the end-times harvest. A harvest of souls is always a disruption for the status quo and the comfortable. Winkie Pratney, a youth evangelist from New Zealand, said, "Revival brings back a holy shock to apathy and carelessness."[6] Romans 14 and 15 was a shock to the first century-church as it issued a challenge. At the time, the church was facing a huge hurdle—one that we might expect to face in our day.

> Now we who are strong ought to bear the weaknesses of those without strength, and not just please ourselves. (Romans 15:1)

Paul described two kinds of people who will be in this new church: the strong and the weak. The strong will have the biggest weight of responsibility with the harvest. Here is Paul's challenge to the strong:

> Therefore, accept one another, just as Christ also accepted us, for the glory of God. (Romans 15:7)

The Bible's "just as Christ" challenges are simple, but they are sledgehammers. When you read about the life of Jesus, it seems that the worse the people are, the more at ease they feel around Jesus. On the other hand, Jesus received a chilly response from the religious crowd.

The Gospels mention eight dinner parties Jesus was invited to, and only three were with friends; the other five were what I would label "sinner dinners." Jesus never met a disease He could not cure, a birth defect He could not reverse, a demon He could not exorcise. But He did meet the religious, whom He could not convince.

Because judgment is coming, a remnant is rising so that the church will be cleansed for revival. How does fearlessness, patience, wisdom, and testimony develop? In order to see these key elements develop, both the young and the old most overcome a challenge. For the visionaries, there are three people you must meet. For the dreamers, there are two trees you must know.

A CHALLENGE TO THE VISIONARIES: THREE PEOPLE YOU MUST MEET

There is a horrible poison seeping into our society and, in fact, is already here in great measure.

> But realize this, that in the last days difficult times will come. For men will be lovers of self, lovers of money, boastful, arrogant, slanderers, disobedient to parents, ungrateful, unholy, unloving, irreconcilable, malicious gossips, without self-control, brutal, haters of good, treacherous, reckless, conceited, lovers of pleasure rather than lovers of God, holding to a form of godliness although they have denied its power; avoid such people as these. (2 Timothy 3:1–5)

As Satan unleashes his worst, God will unleash His best. Look once again at the verse from Acts 2:

> "AND IT SHALL BE IN THE LAST DAYS," God says,
> "THAT I WILL POUR OUT MY SPIRIT ON ALL MANKIND;
> AND YOUR SONS AND YOUR DAUGHTERS WILL PROPHESY,
> AND YOUR YOUNG MEN WILL SEE VISIONS,
> AND YOUR OLD MEN WILL HAVE DREAMS."
> (Acts 2:17)

To the visionaries: Jesus did not save you just so that you can go to church. He did not come down to earth and die the death He did in order to secure you a seat for two hours on a Sunday. If you want to do what God has called you to do in life, you must meet three people.

The best person to help us toward our calling is David. There is more about David in the Bible than any other person, except for Jesus. The Scriptures show us how he went from teen to God-appointed destiny. David surpassed platinum status (which is one million units sold) as a songwriter and musician, for he has had billions of sheet music sold—called the Psalms. He was royalty, an army general, a politician, a national leader, a shepherd, an armor-bearer—and above all, a lover of God while he accomplished all of this. It is evident through his life that David needed three people to make him who he was and to do what God called him to do: a Samuel to listen to, a Goliath to conquer, and a Saul to forgive.

1. A Samuel to Listen To (1 Samuel 16)

Samuel is the one who found, identified, and called David when his own father forgot about him. Samuel is the godly voice in your life; Samuel sees future in you before you do.

> Ask the former generation
> > and find out what their ancestors learned,
> for we were born only yesterday and know nothing,
> > and our days on earth are but a shadow.
> Will they not instruct you and tell you?
> > Will they not bring forth words from their understanding?
> (Job 8:8–10 NIV)

Who in your life do you process with? Where do you get wisdom from?

2. A Goliath to Conquer (1 Samuel 17)

This is tough for today's younger generation because we as the older generation often try to fight their Goliaths for them. Parents and teachers have fostered environments where everyone wins. Everyone gets a trophy; no one gets cut from the team. I was once looking through my youngest daughter's closet and found that she had seventeen trophies! When I asked her where she got all of them, she proceeded to explain, "This one was just for participating; this one was from getting eighth place . . ." In my day, eighth place was called "loser"!

Our government is even trying to pass new legislation called the "equitable grading scale." Nobody gets zeros anymore, and students can retake tests that they failed. I am wondering where they were when I was in school! When we did badly on a test, it was because we didn't study.

You need to face something bigger than you so that you can learn to depend on God. Goliath means a cause greater than you, a challenge that needs God to show up. Something huge will call your name—perhaps it will be poverty, racial injustice, sex trafficking, orphanages, inner-city youth, a soup kitchen, missions, or working with the migrant problem. Those who answer that call will quickly learn to depend on God.

3. A Saul You Must Forgive (1 Samuel 18)

Saul was a bigger threat to David's future than Goliath was. Goliath could have taken his life, but Saul could have destroyed his soul. Forgiveness is a hurdle that sits on the pathway to greater influence and effectiveness. In this journey called life, you are going to be hurt, offended, and crushed. It is an inevitable part of character formation. You do not fight Saul but fight *through* Saul.

The man who was promoting David eventually grew jealous and tried to kill him. David faced Goliath for one day, but he faced Saul for almost thirteen years *every day*. Character is not made by defeating a giant once but by defeating Saul every day through forgiveness. I have seen more people hurt, scarred, and crushed in recent years. I think God is teaching us something through this—to learn to let go of vengeance and grip hold of forgiveness in order to be part of this last-days church.

Visionaries need to say today:
- Samuel, I am going to find you.
- Goliath, look out, here I come!
- Saul, I forgive you. You won't control me anymore!

A CHALLENGE TO THE DREAMERS: TWO TREES YOU MUST KNOW

A milestone recently happened in America, albeit one which passed very quietly. For the first time in the history of our nation, there were more people in our society age sixty-five and older than those who were eighteen and younger. Did you know that two-thirds of all the people who have lived beyond sixty-five in the entire history of the world are alive today? The over-sixty-five crowd now constitutes 14 percent of our nation's population.[7]

I was reading Billy Graham's last book, *Nearing Home*, when I was a visionary, approaching dreamer status.

> Old age is not for sissies. But that isn't the whole story, nor did God intend for it to be. While the Bible doesn't gloss over the problems we face as we grow older, neither does it paint old age as a time to be despised or a burden to be endured with gritted teeth (if we still have any). Nor does it picture us in our latter years as useless and ineffective, condemned to spend our last days in endless boredom or meaningless activity until God finally takes us home. Instead, the Bible says that God has a reason for keeping us here; if He didn't, He would take us to Heaven far sooner.[8]

Your second half is important. Finishing well is vital. You are never safe until you are home because there will always be battles. Detours will always abound.

I remember the story of the 1968 Olympics in Mexico City. John Stephen Akhwari from Tanzania competed with seventy-four other world-class runners. Akhwari ended up coming in last. He fell during the race and dislocated a joint, but he continued to run. By the time he entered the stadium, the medal ceremony had already been completed, and there were only a few thousand people left in the crowd. It was dark, but he finished. When asked why he had continued, he responded, "My country did not send me 5,000 miles to start the race. My country sent me 5,000 miles to finish the race."[9] We are called to finish this race and do what God has asked us to do.

There is a description of Jesus in the book of Revelation that each of us ought to aspire to:

His head and His hair were white like white wool, like snow; and
His eyes were like a flame of fire. (Revelation 1:14)

White hair and fiery eyes—this represents wisdom and zeal, experience and excitement. What a great challenge for those of us who are older. Do not simply rely on your white hair of experience; get a fire in your eyes again! Stir up the gift. For those who have been in the church for a number of years, how do you rekindle that fire?

Here is my challenge to the dreamers: You need to become palm trees and cedar trees:

The righteous person will flourish like the palm tree,
He will grow like a cedar in Lebanon.
Planted in the house of the Lord,
They will flourish in the courtyards of our God.
They will still yield fruit in advanced age;
They will be full of sap and very green,
To declare that the Lord is just;
He is my rock, and there is no malice in Him.
(Psalm 92:12–15)

The righteous are like the palm tree and the cedar. What are the characteristics of these trees?

Palm Trees

Palm trees grow in harsh environments. A palm tree can survive in a desert because its roots go deep into the ground, searching for water. They are always green and always producing, regardless of where they are planted.

In storms, palm trees bend, but they do not break. In a desert, sandstorms are inevitable. A palm tree will be bent down, but when the storm is over, it gets back up again. They have an elasticity about them, enabling them to withstand hardship rather than break under pressure.

The Cedars of Lebanon

The cedars of Lebanon have such extraordinary power of life that instead of nourishing parasites, they actually kill them! Their bark, wood, cones, and leaves are completely saturated with sap. When parasites come to suck it up, they literally die because of the richness of it. Instead of feeding, the parasites choke.

May God grant that we, too, be so filled with His life. Imagine having so much of Jesus in you that when people try to "take a bite" out of you, rather than affecting you, they end up with what is in you!

For the cedars, what is on the inside is greater than what attacks them from the outside. Bite into them, and you do not hear a bitter story. Life comes out. They may have gray hair, but fire is in their eyes!

What is the testimony of the old cedars and the palm trees?

> I have been young and now I am old,
> Yet I have not seen the righteous forsaken
> Or his descendants begging bread.
> (Psalm 37:25)

What David is saying here is the story of the cedars and the palms. God will never fail you. He is always there. He will always provide.

My son sent me a text not too long ago asking what to do when someone is angry with God because of their circumstances. I told him that they are not old enough to have the margin between their hard life and why it happened. It is easy for the young person to conclude, "God is not good." But the old person declares, "He is my rock; there is no unrighteousness in Him!" People need some distance before they can understand, "Now I see what God is doing. He was there the whole time."

I encourage all who are old to start a small group for teens and impart your wisdom. Don't fight for old trophies. Help the next generation get new trophies. And to the young people, I encourage you to start a small group for old people and gather stories and testimonies. Everyone has a critical part to play.

Gerald Sittser explained the dangers of a one-generational church in *Water from a Deep Well*:

> A one-generational church is capable of generating energy but there
> are no roots. When emotions wear off or difficulty arrives it withers.
> Soon there is nothing to show for it. Without a cultivated memory

we live from hand to mouth on fad and novelty. But Christians don't sprint out of starting blocks in each generation in a race for heaven. We are on a relay team. We have a heritage , a richly composted family history. We need to know these members of our family who lived lives similar to what we are living and lived them well. As we get to know them, we are less isolated, less alone. We are not orphans."[10]

I love that picture: We are on a relay team. The baton we hand to the next generation is the story of what God can do. This reminds me of one of my life verses, found in Psalm 71:

God, You have taught me from my youth,
And I still declare Your wondrous deeds.
And even when I am old and gray, God, do not abandon me,
Until I declare Your strength to this generation,
Your power to all who are to come.
(Psalm 71:17–18)

May the old be ready to declare and impart and the young be ready to receive and press on. May the fearlessness of the young inspire a rekindling of fire in the eyes of the old. And by God's grace, we will finish this race triumphantly—young and old, together as the last-days church.

QUESTIONS

1. Are you content with the average age of your closest friends?

2. What words of wisdom would you give to yourself if you could go back in time to when you were half the age you are now? Who in your life also needs to hear this wisdom?

3. What is a challenge you are currently facing that you think someone ten years older than you has never experienced? What about a challenge in your life that most people ten years older *have* experienced?

4. Is there a "Goliath-sized" issue that has gripped your heart—one that you know will require dependence on God?

ZEAL

When Something Is Over, Something Better Is Coming

*"If sinners are zealous in their sins, should not saints be
zealous for their God? If the things of time can stir the human
passions, should not the realities of eternity have a greater and
more tremendously moving force in us?"*
CHARLES SPURGEON[1]

Coming to the end of something significant will often bring about a desire
to extend the experience. Our tendency to want to extend it simply reminds us that we have a remnant of the Apostle Peter within us. Look at what
Peter said at the top of the Mount of Transfiguration when he saw Jesus speaking to Moses and Elijah:

> Peter exclaimed, "Lord, it's wonderful for us to be here! If you want,
> I'll make three shelters as memorials—one for you, one for Moses,
> and one for Elijah." (Matthew 17:4 NLT)

Peter was saying in essence, "Let me leave the fishing business and go into
the home construction business. I'll build three homes so we can camp here
and keep talking to Moses and Elijah. Let's never leave!"

There is always something in us that does not want something good to end,
so we figure out a way to extend it—a book, a movie, a lunch, even building
shelters at the Mount of Transfiguration. But there was a problem brewing
elsewhere which Jesus was aware of, though Peter wasn't. Peter did not realize

that at the *bottom* of the Mount of Transfiguration was a little boy under demonic influence—being burned and drowned by demons—and a father desperate to see him delivered.

What was happening at the bottom of the hill was just as important as what was happening on top of the hill.

The question on the floor at the Mount of Transfiguration was: Do we continue to stay and talk with Elijah and Moses, or do we go down and see a child set free? Peter already turned in his vote, but Jesus had the majority vote.

> At the foot of the mountain, a large crowd was waiting for them. A man came and knelt before Jesus and said, "Lord, have mercy on my son. He has seizures and suffers terribly. He often falls into the fire or into the water." (Matthew 17:14–15 NLT)

I like that the crowd was "waiting for them." Somehow the crowd knew that Jesus was coming down for them.

Much later, Jesus faced something similar and even more important with His disciples. Jesus announced that His time with them was coming to an end. The disciples were saddened that He was speaking about the conclusion of His earthly ministry. Jesus tried to explain to them that it was for the better:

> But in fact, it is best for you that I go away, because if I don't, the Advocate won't come. If I do go away, then I will send him to you. (John 16:7 NLT)

In other words, here is the message: *When something is over, something better is coming.*

I believe this same principle held true even on the day of Pentecost. The disciples went to an upper room, heaven opened, the Holy Spirit came down with fire, and they were all filled. However, there would be no camping in the upper room—no invites to special services or posting pictures of fire on heads on Instagram. God was not done in Acts 2. He would not allow them to stay in the upper room.

In fact, they never returned to the upper room in the book of Acts, yet the results of the upper room were felt all over the world. Something was ignited in the hearts of the 120 who were gathered in that upper room. You, too, have been equipped by God. You have been given all that you need, and now it is time to leave the upper room—to come down from the mountaintop and get in the game. Titus spoke of the way God has equipped us:

> For the grace of God that brings salvation has appeared to all men, teaching us that, denying ungodliness and worldly lusts, we should live soberly, righteously, and godly in the present age, looking for the blessed hope and glorious appearing of our great God and Savior Jesus Christ, who gave Himself for us, that He might redeem us from every lawless deed and purify for Himself His own special people, zealous for good works. (Titus 2:11–14 NKJV)

This amazing list of what God has done for us indicates that a response is required on our end. Something happens when we grasp the reality of this passage. It is the outcome in every true Christian's life: *zeal*. Christ delivered us so that we would in turn see others delivered. We were redeemed and purified so that we would become a people zealous for good deeds.

Let me describe zeal another way:

- Zeal will respond to what it saw on a mountaintop and go down.
- Zeal will respond to what it experienced in an upper room and go down the steps to the streets.
- Zeal does not say, "Let's keep it going," but rather, "Now what do we do with what just happened?"

Nineteenth-century English author J. C. Ryle described zeal this way in his book *Practical Religion*:

> Zeal in Christianity is a burning desire to please God, to do His will, and to advance His glory in the world in every possible way. It is a desire, which is not natural to men or women. It is a desire which the Spirit puts in the heart of every believer when they are converted to Christ, however, a desire which some believers feel so much more strongly than others that they alone deserve to be called "zealous" men and women.
>
> A zealous person in Christianity is preeminently a person of one thing. They only see one thing, they care for one thing, they live for

one thing, they are swallowed up in one thing; and that one thing
is to please God.[2]

By definition, zeal is a burning fire in the soul of man. It is fervent and
fierce. Just as fire consumes and spreads, zeal is both contagious and consuming. I believe the list in Titus 2 is kindling wood to ignite a fire in our soul to be
zealous for good works. It reminds us to thank God for His grace, for godliness
that instructs us to deny ungodliness, and that we serve a King who is coming
again. It causes us to become zealous to worship, zealous to witness, and zealous to pray. The Corinthian church burned with zeal.

Your zeal has stirred up most of them. (2 Corinthians 9:2)

Zeal is a fire to advance as well as a jealousy to defend. Jesus was consumed
by zeal when He walked in and cleansed the temple from money changers.

ZEAL FOR YOUR HOUSE WILL CONSUME ME. (John 2:17)

Recovering zeal was even a part of Jesus' instructions to a lukewarm church
called Laodicea. It was a church that did not do anything because it was stuck.
Lukewarm does nothing.

As many as I love, I rebuke and chasten. Therefore be zealous and
repent. (Revelation 3:19 NKJV)

There is a name in the Bible that intrigues me. This man is not part of
any story. Every time he appears in the Word, he is just a name on the list.
However, I believe the title attached to his name tells a story in itself. This disciple of Jesus had "zeal" attached to his name. He is mentioned three times
with this tagline: Simon the Zealot.

Why was he called Simon the Zealot? Historians agree on three possible
reasons: (1) He was associated with the Zealots, a sect of radicals who hated
the Romans being in power and wanted them removed; (2) He was being dis-
tinguished from Simon Peter; (3) He was extremely passionate for Christ—a
radical. The word next to his name means "burning with zeal, boiling over."
Tradition says that he died a martyr, preaching the gospel in Egypt, Iran, and
throughout the Middle East.

I believe all three reasons are true. But what I find important is that Jesus took this man's misdirected zeal and made Simon passionate about Himself. Simon the Zealot was a man whose whole life was given to politics. He did not like who was in charge in government, so he spent all his time and energy trying to figure out how to get his own group back in the seat of government. He assumed politics could change his city and solve all their problems—a trap that still ensnares many to this day. But Jesus ended up taking this man's zeal for a political party and exchanging it for a much greater passion—a kingdom passion!

Years ago, I became a tennis fan because my wife was a tennis player. Before Federer and Djokovic and Nadal, there was an American tennis player we used to love—the first one to break the Grand Slam record. His name was Pete Sampras. I read an article about him after he retired from tennis with fourteen Grand Slams. Before he would go out for a tennis match, he would be in the locker room getting ready. After lacing up his tennis shoes, he would then take both hands and slap the floor. That was his way of saying, "Okay, it's time!"

Sampras said, "I always told myself, if you quit slapping, it's time to retire." Eventually he found that he had stopped slapping the floor. There was a point when it had become just a job and a paycheck, and he knew it was time to retire.[3]

I am still slapping. I slap the floor (maybe not literally) every time I get ready to preach or create books or write messages. I get genuinely excited. Something inside me says, "We have a billion souls to win—lives that need to be changed!" I do not show up simply out of religious obligation. We should all be coming to the house of God with an excitement and a zeal burning deep inside because God has saved us, changed us, and filled us! We slap the floor, saying, "We get to worship today! We get to give God glory for all He has done!" Floor slapping is zeal.

The world is not moved by mildly interested people but by floor slappers. I am more afraid of indifference in the church than persecution of the church. Persecution fires me up because when the church is under attack, that means we are doing something. Sadly, it seems much of the church has lost its zeal while the world's is increasing. The church used to be a lifeboat rescuing the perishing. Now she is a cruise ship promising rest and vacations for all who sign up. We lose the fire when we forget how we got here and the reason we are here. We cannot make a difference by being indifferent.

Jesus wrapped Himself in zeal when He came to this planet.

> And he saw that there was no man, and wondered that there was
> no intercessor: therefore his arm brought salvation unto him; and
> his righteousness, it sustained him. For he put on righteousness
> as a breastplate, and an helmet of salvation upon his head; and he
> put on the garments of vengeance for clothing, and was clad with
> zeal as a cloak. (Isaiah 59:16–17 KJV)

According to Peter, Jesus left us "an example, so that you would follow in
His steps" (1 Peter 2:21). We get uncomfortable when people follow in Jesus'
footsteps and put on the same clothing of zeal. Extremely sold-out Christians
cause much discomfort to the casual Christian. I remember once hearing the
definition of a fanatic: It is someone who loves Jesus more than you do. That is
why they bother you.

So why have many people lost the fire? Proverbs tells us that "for lack of
wood the fire goes out" (Proverbs 26:20). We must add wood to the fire every
day to keep it burning. Your fire may have died because you were only adding
wood on Sundays. The best wood to ignite zeal is when you are reaching people—living not for your own comfort but for the benefit of others.

WHAT GOES UP MUST COME DOWN

What would have happened if the disciples had decided not to come down
from the mountain? They needed to come down not only from the Mount of
Transfiguration but from another mountain as well. In Matthew 5–7, Jesus
taught the Sermon on the Mount—the greatest sermon ever preached. When
He was done, I imagine there were many who urged Him to preach just one
more message! But the Sermon on the Mount needed to become the power on
the ground. Waiting for Jesus in Matthew 8 were four people who did not need
a sermon but a miracle: A leper needed to be healed, a Roman captain had a
paralyzed staff member, Peter had a sick mother-in-law, and there were two
graveyard demoniacs wreaking havoc in town.

Here is the challenge for us: Acts 3 must come after Acts 2. That may not sound profound, but it is important. Acts 2 was the day of Pentecost; Acts 3 determined if Pentecost was real.

It was in Acts 2 that the Holy Spirit came down. Fire touched the disciples. The church was birthed, and people were changed. God was doing something incredible. But remember, when something is over, something better is coming.

What happens next? Here is Acts 3:

> Now Peter and John were going up to the temple at the [a]ninth hour, the hour of prayer. And a man who had been unable to walk frombirth was being carried, whom they used to set down every day at the gate of the temple which is called Beautiful, in order for him to beg for charitable gifts from those entering the temple grounds. When he saw Peter and John about to go into the temple grounds, he began asking to receive a charitable gift. But Peter, along with John, looked at him intently and said, "Look at us!" And he gave them his attention, expecting to receive something from them. But Peter said, "I do not have silver and gold, but what I do have I give to you: In the name of Jesus Christ the Nazarene, walk!" And grasping him by the right hand, he raised him up; and immediately his feet and his ankles were strengthened. And leaping up, he stood and began to walk; and he entered the temple with them, walking and leaping and praising God. And all the people saw him walking and praising God; and they recognized him as being the very one who used to sit at the Beautiful Gate of the temple to beg for charitable gifts, and they were filled with wonder and amazement at what had happened to him. (Acts 3:1–10)

After the most powerful move of God in the church, the church left the upper room and went public. The 120 needed to come down from the upper room. People needed them to; God needed them to. Zeal compelled them to come down.

Acts 3 will determine if Acts 2 was real; real life will determine if what you have is real. There comes a time when you must leave practice and actually get in the game. You have to leave the weight room to see if what you have really works. In Acts 3, the first miracle after the upper room involved a lame man. Why is this significant? The lame man could not walk up the stairs to the upper room. While the church is shouting upstairs, that lame man does not get set free—unless they realize that when something good is over, something better is coming. The church needed to come down the stairs for the miracle to take place!

Look at verse 1 again:

> Now Peter and John were going up to the temple at the ninth hour, the hour of prayer. (Acts 3:1)

The ninth hour is 3 p.m. in the afternoon. The ninth hour was the normal hour of prayer in Jewish culture. This means that after God touched and equipped the disciples, He put them right back on their regular schedule. They started attending the normal prayer meeting again. That is insightful. They became 3 p.m. Christians once again, and God is calling us to do the same.

What Is a 3 p.m. Christian?

A 3 p.m. Christian is one who was touched by the Holy Spirit in a special setting and then takes that new fire to his or her everyday environment. Different person, same setting. Three p.m. Christians come to their usual places, but with a different heart and a different perspective. God does not change places; He changes people, and then He sends them back to those places to bring transformation. According to George Campbell Morgan, "If you cannot be a Christian where you are, you cannot be a Christian anywhere. It is not place but grace."[4]

Let's look at four things that describe a 3 p.m. zealous Christian:

1. Every day of the week replaces one day of the week

Sunday is not the only day you can get happy; you can have zeal every day. You don't need the pastor and the choir coming with you to school or to the office in order to get you excited—you can shout, sing, and worship every day because of who God is and the fire He has put in your soul!

The Bible tells us that the disciples were in the upper room for ten days. God does not want to be limited to ten days in the upper room; He wants every day to be a candidate for the supernatural to happen. God put them back on schedule for that to happen.

2. Slowing down allows time for God to intervene

I always thought the most expensive place on the planet to advertise was Times Square. Actually, the most expensive place in the world to advertise is NASCAR, and there is one key artist who does it: Sam Bass. He has designed over 350 paint schemes for drivers like Bobby Allison, Dale Earnhardt, and Jeff Gordon. Bass views his job as that of an artist, considering that "these cars are really 200-mph paintings." Others have called the cars 200-mph billboards. In fact, you cannot even see them live but only on television when they slow it down! When a company sponsors a NASCAR vehicle, it is investing between $15 and $20 million for hood placement of their ad. In return, it expects the race car to effectively advertise its brand.

If you were a walking advertisement for the Lord, what would people learn about Him? If God's blessings on your life were emblazoned on you like decals on a NASCAR race car, what would people see? Sometimes it is as if we are zooming through life at 200 mph, passing right by neighbors, coworkers, or people in the streets. We are going so fast and do not slow down for people anymore. It would have been so easy for Peter and John to hurry past the lame man so they wouldn't be late for church. I believe God is asking us to downshift or pause instead of whipping right by people. As we do so, it will lead us to the next point.

3. The ordinary starts to looks like a candidate for the extraordinary

The upper room helped the disciples notice people and believe for miracles for them. That lame man at the temple gate was not a new scene. He had been put there every day since he was a child. The disciples must have passed that guy countless times, but on this day, he looked different. He looked like a candidate for a miracle.

You get new eyes and a new voice when God touches you. You begin to slow down and pause, and you start to notice people you never noticed before. You not only have a greater love for God, you have a greater love for people as well. It is not a true work of God if it does not change the way you see and treat people. The ordinary and the common should start looking different—from Starbucks regulars to your spouse, your kids, your coworkers, and people on the street.

What is a practical way to make that happen? Begin to pray with people as often as you can. Ask this simple question: "Can I pray with you?" I have found it to be the most helpful phrase for taking the gospel outside the church. You will be surprised at how willing people are to receive prayer.

4. A testimony can have more power than a sermon

The Bible tells us in the book of Revelation:

> And they overcame him because of the blood of the Lamb and because of the word of their testimony, and they did not love their life even when faced with death. (Revelation 12:11)

The Bible does not say that they overcame by "the word of the pastor." Look at what happened because of this miracle—because they chose to come down from the upper room.

> And leading up, he stood and began to walk; and he entered the temple with them, walking and leaping and praising God. And all the people saw him walking and praising God; and they recognized him as being the very one who used to sit at the Beautiful Gate of the temple to beg for charitable gifts, and they were filled with wonder and amazement at what had happened to him. (Acts 3:8–10)

> But many of those who had heard the message believed; and the number of the men came to be about five thousand. (Acts 4:4)

I can see Peter and John walking, and this man who used to be lame is leaping and dancing next to them! Sometimes the greatest apologetic is a walking and leaping man. The greatest proof that God is alive is a changed life.

> And seeing the man who had been healed standing with them, they had nothing to say in reply. (Acts 4:14)

The late British evangelist Gipsy Smith once quipped, "There are five Gospels: Matthew, Mark, Luke, John and the Christian, but most people never read the first four."[5] Guess who they are looking at! Remember, God did not change you for church; God changed you for life. You are His living witness—every day of the week!

I am so glad that you made this journey with me from A to Z. Remember, zeal takes the twenty-six letters and does not merely say, "Let's start all over again." Rather, zeal boldly declares, "It is now time to go and do what God is asking us to do."

I would like to commission you today. I pray that God would ignite a fresh fire in your soul, causing you to be zealous for good works. I commission you to go back to your family, your school, your workplace, your neighborhood, your city—and for the ordinary to suddenly look like a candidate for the extraordinary. May you enter places and see the lame walk, the lost found, and miracles abound. May you speak and bring truth, walking with new courage and confidence. Through it all, continually embrace what God has done and is doing in your life, knowing that when something is over, something better is coming!

QUESTIONS

1. What Acts 2 moments have you experienced in your life, and what Acts 3 events followed them?

2. In Revelation 2:1–5, Jesus addresses another church that is no longer as zealous as it once was. Was there a time in your life when you loved Jesus more than you do now? What were you like? How can you apply His instructions to the church at Ephesus to your own life?

3. Looking back from A to Z, which topics were surprising to you? Which do you find to be the most difficult to live by? How can you specifically pray for God's help in these areas?

4. Now that our journey through the alphabet is over, what is one thing God has put on your heart to do as a step forward into the "something better" that is coming?

How Do You Get to Heaven?

The most important question anyone can ever ask you is: "Have you been born again?" These were the directions that Jesus gave us to get to heaven.

What is amazing is that if you ask 100 people how to get to heaven, you just might get 100 different answers. But what makes the 100 answers stunning is that everyone seems to know how to get to a place they have never been before!

If anyone knows how to get to his own home, it would have to be Jesus.

And Jesus gave the directions to His home. He said, "Unless someone is born again he cannot see the kingdom of God" (John 3:3). Again, He repeated, "You must be born again" (John 3:7).

"Born again" are Jesus' words, not religious words. What Jesus was saying is that just as you had a first birth *physically*, you need a second birth *spiritually*. Just as you have a birth date for your physical birth, you need a birth date for your spiritual birth. Today can be that day. In fact, the Bible says, "Now is the day of salvation" (2 Corinthians 6:2 NKJV).

So how does one become "born again"? It is as simple as A-B-C.

A = Admit I Am a Sinner

We are all broken. All of us have a condition called sin. There is not a promise, priest, pastor, or program that can fix us. We need to be fixed on the *inside*. So the first thing I must do is get honest with God and admit I am a sinner.

One pastor said it this way: "We are not mistakers in need of correction. We are sinners in need of a Savior. We need more than a second chance; we need a second birth!"

B = Believe That Jesus Died in My Place

The sin issue is a big issue. God sent His Son to fix our sinful condition because we could not fix ourselves. If we could fix it ourselves, then God putting His Son through the suffering He went through is the ultimate case of child abuse. If I could get to heaven simply by being good, then Jesus would never have had to come die on the cross for me.

I must believe that Jesus' death was Him being my sin bearer. He lived a life I could not live; He died a death I should have died. And then He gave me a reward—heaven—that I did not deserve.

C = Confess Jesus as Lord

Do you think God sent Jesus to die on a cross just to get you to sit in church for an hour every Sunday? No! He died for you because He wants a relationship with you! Coming to church on Sunday is religion; being born again is a relationship. Christianity is coming to a Person, not a place. And that Person is in charge.

> If you confess with your mouth Jesus as Lord, and believe in your heart that God raised Him from the dead, you will be saved; for with the heart a person believes, resulting in righteousness, and with the mouth he confesses, resulting in salvation. (Romans 10:9–10)

Confessing Jesus as "Lord" means Jesus is the boss now. I don't do what God wants merely for an hour on Sunday. God gets every day. That's called lordship.

If it is your desire, you can be born again right now. I invite you to pray this prayer:

> Dear Lord Jesus, I believe that You are the Son of God. I believe that on the cross, You took my sin, my shame, and my guilt, and You died for it all. I believe that You faced hell for me so that I would not have to go. You rose from the dead to give me a place in heaven, a purpose on earth, and a relationship with Your Father. Today, Lord Jesus, I turn from my sin to be born again. God is my Father, Jesus is my Savior, the Holy Spirit is my Helper, and heaven is now my home . . . in Jesus' name! Amen.

ENDNOTES

Introduction

1   William Laurence Sullivan, *Epigrams and Criticisms in Miniature* (Philadelphia: University of Pennsylvania Press: 2017), 96.

2   "Research," Arizona Christian University Curtural Research Center, November 18, 2022, https://www.arizonachristian.edu/culturalresearchcenter/research.

3   "A Quote by Augustine of Hippo.," Goodreads, accessed October 26, 2023, https://www.goodreads.com/quotes/110766-if-you-believe-what-you-like-in-the-gospel-and.

A: The Atonement

1   C. S. Lewis, *A Grief Observed* rev. ed. (1961, repr., San Francisco: HarperOne, 1996).

2   Oswald Chambers, *Our Ultimate Refuge* (Grand Rapids, MI: Our Daily Bread Publishing, 2015).

3   G. K. Chesterton, *The Everlasting Man* (London: Hodder & Stoughton, 1925).

4   R. T. Kendall, *Unashamed to Bear His Name: Embracing the Stigma of Being a Christian* (Grand Rapids MI: Baker Publishing Group, 2012), 53.

5   C. S. Lewis, *Mere Christianity* (New York: HarperCollins, 2007), 126.

B: The Bible

1   "A Quote by Charles Haddon Spurgeon," Goodreads, accessed February 25, 2023, https://www.goodreads.com/quotes/397346-a-bible-that-s-falling-apart-usually-belongs-to-someone-who.

2   Billy Graham, *Just as I Am: The Autobiography of Billy Graham* (New York: HarperCollins, 2011).

3   Søren Kierkegaard and Charles E. Moore, ed., *Provocations: Spiritual Writings of Søren Kierkegaard* (Walden, NY: Plough Publishing House, 2002).

4   Alex McFarland, *The 10 Most Common Objections to Christianity* (Bloomington, MN: Bethany House Publishers, 2007).

5   Jennie Cohen, "6 Things You May Not Know About the Dead Sea Scrolls," History.com, May 7, 2013, https://www.history.com/news/6-things-you-may-not-know-about-the-dead-sea-scrolls.

6   Bryan Windle, "Pontius Pilate: An Archaeological Biography," Bible Archaeology Report, October 11, 2019, https:// biblearchaeologyreport.com/2019/10/11/pontius-pilate-an-archaeological-biography.

7 Biblical Archaeology Society Staff, "The Bethesda Pool, Site of One of Jesus' Miracles," Biblical Archaeology Society, February 13, 2023, https:// www.biblicalarchaeology.org/ daily/biblical-sites-places/jerusalem/the-bethesda-pool-site-of-one-of-jesus-miracles.

8 Adrian Rogers and Steve Rogers, *What Every Christian Ought to Know: Solid Grounding for a Growing Faith* (Nashville, TN: B&H Publishing Group, 2012).

9 Richard C. Frank, *Fighting Cancer with Knowledge and Hope*, (New Haven, CT: Yale University Press, 2015); Dr. Richard Frank, "Bloodletting and The Death of George Washington: Relevance to Cancer Patients Today," Yale University Press, March 1, 2015, https://yalebooks.yale.edu/2015/03/01/bloodletting-and-the-death-of-george-washington-relevance-to-cancer-patients-today/.

10 Alfred Edersheim, *The Life and Times of Jesus the Messiah* vol. 1 (Cambridge, MA: Harvard University Press, 1912).

11 McFarland, *The 10 Most Common Objections to Christianity*.

12 Tim Challies, *Knowing and Enjoying God* (Eugene, OR: Harvest House Publishers, 2021), 97.

13 Todd Hampson, *The Non-Prophet's Guide to Spiritual Warfare*, (New York: Harvest House Publishers, 2020), 176.

14 Charles Colson and Harold Fickett, *The Faith: What Christians Believe, Why They Believe It, and Why It Matters* (New York: HarperCollins, 2008).

15 Gabe Habash, "How Many Copies Does It Take to Be an Amazon Bestseller?" Publishers Weekly, March 10, 2013, https://www.publishersweekly.com/pw/by-topic/industry-news/bookselling/article/56284-how-many-copies-does-it-take-to-be-an-amazon-bestseller.html.

16 John Riches, ed., *The New Cambridge History of the Bible: Volume 4, From 1750 to the Present* (Cambridge, United Kingdom: Cambridge University Press, 2015).

17 "2022 Global Scripture Access," Wycliffe Global Alliance, accessed October 18, 2023, https://www.wycliffe.net/resources/statistics2022/.

18 "Mind-Blowing Statistics About Christianity You Need to Know," Holyart.com, accessed November 8, 2023, https://www.holyart.com/blog/mind-blowing-statistics-christianity-need-know/.

19 Jeremy Wells, "Ethiopia: 'The Country Blessed of God'", *Christianity Today*, July 1, 2005, https:// www.christianitytoday.com/history/issues/issue-87/ethiopia-country-blessed-of-god.html.

20 "A Quote by Charles Haddon Spurgeon," Goodreads, accessed February 25, 2023, https://www.goodreads.com/quotes/8561226-the-word-of-god-is-like-a-lion-you-don-t.

C: The Church

1 Josh McDowell and Sean McDowell, *Evidence That Demands a Verdict: Life-Changing Truth for a Skeptical World* (Nashville, TN: Thomas Nelson, 2017).

2 R. Kent Hughes, *Disciplines of a Godly Man* (Wheaton, IL: Crossway, 2019).

3 Tyler J. VanderWeele, "Religion and Health: A Synthesis," in *Spirituality and Religion Within the Culture of Medicine: From Evidence to Practice*, ed., Michael J. Balboni and John R. Peteet (New York: Oxford University Press, 2021).

4 D. Martyn Lloyd-Jones, *Studies in the Sermon on the Mount* (Downers Grove, IL: InterVarsity Press, 1971).

5 Thom S. Rainer, "The Once-a-Month Churchgoers Are Becoming More Common," Church Answers, May 24, 2021, https://churchanswers.com/blog/the-once-a-month-churchgoers-are-becoming-more-common/.

6 Charles H. Spurgeon, "The Church, the World's Hope," sermon, Metropolitan Tabernacle, March 1, 1863.

7 "Don't Forget Your Purpose," Ministry127, accessed March 4, 2023, https://ministry127.com/resources/illustration/don-t-forget-your-purpose.

8 Georgia Dullea, "Ebony and Ivory: 1 Keyboard, 2 Good Hands," *The New York Times*, September 28, 1987, https://www.nytimes.com/1987/09/28/style/ebony-and-ivory-1-keyboard-2-good-hands.html.

9 Oswald Chambers, "The Assigning of the Call," *My Utmost for His Highest*, September 30, https://utmost.org/the-assigning-of-the-call/.

10 "Polycarp," *Christianity Today*, August 8, 2008, https://www.christianitytoday.com/history/people/martyrs/polycarp.html.

11 Peter J. Madden, *The Wigglesworth Standard* (New Kensington, PA: Whitaker House, 1993).

12 *Gladiator*, directed by Ridley Scott (Universal Pictures, 2000).

D: Discipleship

1 A.W. Tozer, *Renewed Day by Day, Volume 1: Daily Devotional Readings* (Chicago: Moody Publishers, 2011).

2 C. S. Lewis, *God in the Dock* (Grand Rapids, MI: Eerdmans, 1970), 58.

3 Elisabeth Elliot, *Through Gates of Splendor: The Event That Shocked the World, Changed a People, and Inspired a Nation* (Peabody, MA: Hendrickson Publishers, 2010).

4 Watchman Nee, *The Normal Christian Life* (Peabody, MA: Hendrikson Publishers, 2006), 31.

5   Winston A. Reynolds, "The Burning Ships of Hernán Cortés," *Hispania* 42, no. 3 (1959): 317–24, https://doi.org/10.2307/335707.

6   *A League of Their Own*, directed by Penny Marshall (Columbia Pictures, 1992).

7   "The Lives of Missionaries: William Borden," International Missions Project, February 5, 2014, https://www.intlmissions.org/?p=2479.

8   Brennan Manning, *The Signature of Jesus* (Colorado Springs, CO: Multnomah, 2011).

E: Eternity

1   C. S. Lewis, *Mere Christianity* (New York: HarperCollins, 2007).

2   "Life Expectancy," Worlddata.info, accessed November 7, 2023, https://www.worlddata.info/life-expectancy.php.

3   David Jeremiah, "What's Up with Heaven?" accessed October 20, 2003, https://sermons.love/david-jeremiah/1249-david-jeremiah-whats-up-with-heaven.html.

4   Alex Colville (@AlexJColville), "By comparison, the division of the US National Institute on Aging that . . . biology of aging spends about $325 million a year," Twitter, June 7, 2022, 11:03 am, https://twitter.com/AlexJColville/status/1534189266150084609.

5   Antonio Regalado, "Saudi Arabia Plans to Spend $1 Billion a Year Discovering Treatments to Slow Aging," *MIT Technology Review*, August 8 2022, https://www.technologyreview.com/2022/06/07/1053132/saudi-arabia-slow-aging-metformin.

6   Leon Morris, "The Dreadful Harvest," *Christianity Today,* May 27,1991, https://www.christianitytoday.com/ct/1991/may-27/dreadful-harvest.html.

7   Jerry Miles Humphrey, *The Lost Soul's First Day in Eternity* (1918).

F: Forgiveness

1   "School Shootings in 2022: How Many and Where," Education Week, January 5, 2022, https://www.edweek.org/leadership/school-shootings-this-year-how-many-and-where/2022/01.

2   C. S. Lewis, *The Weight of Glory: And Other Addresses* (New York: HarperCollins, 1949).

3   Corrie Ten Boom, *The Hiding Place* (Peabody, MA: Hendrickson, 1971, 1984).

4   Winkie Pratney, "Hurt and Bitternes: Complete 2 Sessions," YouTube, accessed November 7, 2023, https://www.youtube.com/watch?v=naYGwNv0kHs.

5   "Dr Karl Menninger, The Famed Psychiatrist, Once . . ." Sermon Central, January 2, 2001, https://www.sermoncentral.com/sermon-illustrations/347/dr-karl-menninger-the-famed-psychiatrist-once-by-ernest-canell.

6   Comprehensive Annual Financial Report (CAFR), published by the city of Chicago, https://www.chicago.gov/content/dam/city/depts/fin/supp_info/CAFR/2022CAFR/OHare2022.pdf, accessed October 20, 2023.

7   "What Are the Chances of Your Mail Being Lost?" The Donut Whole, February 4, 2023, https://www.thedonutwhole.com/what-are-the-chances-of-your-mail-being-lost/.

8   According to the United States Postal Service's 2022 Annual Report, the USPS successfully delivered 99.1percent of all first-class mail and 97.4 percent of all packages in 2022.

9   "One Day in the Postal Service," Postal Facts, accessed November 8, 2023, https://facts.usps.com/one-day/.

10 Charles H. Spurgeon, *Spurgeon's Sermons,* Volume 19 (1873).

11 Ron Lee Davis, *A Forgiving God in an Unforgiving World* (Irvine, CA: Harvest House Publishers, 1984).

12 C. S. Lewis, *Reflections on the Psalms* (San Francisco: HarperOne, 2017).

13 Cha Chong-Soon, *Son Yang-Won: Aeyangwon and Martyr of Love* (2008).

G: God

1   N. T. Wright, *Luke for Everyone* (Louisville, KY: Westminster John Knox Press, 2004), 200.

2   A.W. Tozer, *Knowledge of the Holy* (San Francisco: HarperOne, 2009).

3   Wilbur E Rees, *$3.00 Worth of God* (King of Prussia, PA: Judson Press, 1971).

4   Herblock, "Do we have to invite Him as well?" *Washington Post*, October 24, 1945.

5   John Lloyd and John Mitchinson, *The Book of General Ignorance* (New York: Crown, 2007).

6   "How Big Is the Solar System?" NASA Science, February 1, 2020, https://science.nasa.gov/learning-resources/how-big-is-the-solar-system/.

H: Holy Spirit

1   "Holy Spirit," Ministry127, accessed April 29, 2023, https://ministry127.com/resources/illustrations/holy-spirit.

2   Thom S. Rainer, "The Once-a-Month Churchgoers Are Becoming More Common," Church Answers, May 24, 2021, https://churchanswers.com/blog/the-once-a-month-churchgoers-are-becoming-more-common/.

3   E. M Bounds, *Power Through Prayer* (Radford, VA: Wilder Publications, 2008).

4   "A Quote by A.W. Tozer," Goodreads, accessed November 7, 2023, https://www.goodreads.com/quotes/964813-if-the-holy-spirit-was-withdrawn-from-the-church-today.

5   C. S. Lewis, *The Four Loves* (Boston: Houghton Mifflin Harcourt, 1971).

6   Frederick Edward. *Emblems of the Holy Spirit* (London: John F. Shaw & Co., 1974).

7   Gordon Dalbey, *Healing the Masculine Soul* (Nashville, TN: Thomas Nelson, 2003), 124.

8   Judge Judy, http://www.judgejudy.com, accessed November 7, 2023.

I: Israel

1   Mae Elise Cannon, ed., *A Land Full of God: Christian Perspectives on the Holy Land* (Eugene, OR: Cascade Books, 2017).

J: Jesus

1   "Top 90 Billy Sunday Quotes," QuoteFancy, accessed October 27, 2023, https://quotefancy.com/billy-sunday-quotes.

2   "Primary Homework Help for Kids," accessed October 27, 2023, https://primaryhomeworkhelp.co.uk/.

3   "How Do Burglars Break into Houses?" ADT, accessed May 20, 2023, https://www.adt.com/resources/how-do-burglars-break-into-houses.

4   In 2016, an airline company was boasting that they were 99 percent safe when it came to flying their aircraft. The airline was Qantas, and they released a safety video to promote their claim.

5   "Whoever Takes the Son Gets It All," Tony Cooke Ministries, October 15, 2014, https://tonycooke.org/stories-and-illustrations/son-gets-it-all/.

K: Knowledge

1   Joni Eareckson Tada, *Glorious Intruder: God's Presence in Life's Chaos* (Colorado Springs, CO: Crown Publishing Group, 2011), 94.

2   Kristine Parks, "Target Customers Shocked After Company Features Pride Items by Satanist Partner: Devil Is 'Hope' and 'Love,' Fox News, May 24, 2023, https://www.foxnews.com/media/target-customers-shocked-company-features-gay-pride-items-satanist-partner-devil-hope-love.

3   Ann Loades, "C. S. Lewis: Grief Observed, Rationality Abandoned, Faith Regained," *Literature and Theology*, 3, no. 1 (Oxford UP, March 1989): 107–21, https://doi.org/10.1093/litthe/3.1.107.

4   Edward Mote, "My Hope Is Built on Nothing Less," 1824.

5   Charles Duhigg, *The Power of Habit: Why We Do What We Do in Life and Business* (New York: Random House, 2012).

6   Philip Yancey, and Tim Stafford, *Unhappy Secrets of the Christian Life* (Grand Rapids, MI: Zondervan Publishing Company, 1979).

L: Love

1   "A Quote by David Wilkerson." accessed October 27, 2023, https://www.goodreads.com/quotes/814824-love-is-not-only-something-you-feel-it-is-something.

2   Thomas Kempis, *The Imitation of Christ* (Milwaukee, WI: Bruce Publishing Company, 1940).

3   "Send a Great Revival," Preaching Point, accessed June 10, 2023, https://preachingpoint.org/send-a-great-revival/.

4   Henry H. Meyer, ed., *The Sunday School Journal*, Uniform Lessons Edition 47, no. 1 (Cincinnati: The Methodist Book Concern, January 1915), 41.

5   Ken Haddad, "34 Years Ago: Northwest Flight 255 Crashes After Takeoff from Detroit Metro Airport," ClickOnDetroit, August 16, 2021, https://www.clickondetroit.com/all-about-michigan/2019/08/15/32-years-ago-northwest-flight-255-crashes-after-takeoff-from-detroit-metro-airport/.

6   C. S. Lewis, *The Problem of Pain* (San Francisco: HarperSanFrancisco, 2001).

7   Fyodor Dostoevsky, *The Brothers Karamazov, A New Translation by Michael R. Katz* (New York: Liveright Publishing Corporation, 2023).

M: Money

1   Billy Graham, *Billy Graham in Quotes* (Nashville, TN: Thomas Nelson, 2011).

2   Janet Lowe, *Billy Graham Speaks: Insight from the World's Greatest Preacher* (New York: John Wiley & Sons, 1999).

3   Paul Bunyan, *Pilgrim's Progress* (Oxford, England: Oxford University Press, 1998).

N: New Birth

1   "The Quotable Moody," D. L. Moody Center, accessed October 27, 2023, https://moodycenter.org/the-quotable-moody-d-l-moody-quotes/.

2   American Bible Society Record, March 1990, submitted by the homiletics class of West Coast Baptist College.

3   Wikipedia, s.v. "Titan Submersible Implosion." last modified October 30, 2023, https://en.wikipedia.org/w/index.php?title=Titan_submersible_implosion&oldid=1182627925.

4   Robert Bennett, *Is There Hope for the Unsaved? The Biblical Truth about Salvation You (Probably) Won't Hear in Church* (Independently Published, 2022).

O: Obedience

1   Kath Walden, "Joy Dawson," Daily Christian Quotes, accessed April 1, 2022, https://www.dailychristianquote.com/joy-dawson-5/.

2   "E. Stanley Jones Tells of the Time He Was About . . ." Sermon Central, May 16, 2004, https://www.sermoncentral.com/sermon-illustrations/16480/e-stanley-jones-tells-of-the-time-he-was-about-by-rodney-buchanan.

3   Jerry Vines, "Backslidden Believers," sermon.

4   Catherine Marshall, *A Man Called Peter* (Lincoln, VA: Evergreen Farm, 2021).

P: Prayer

1   F. B. Meyer, *The Secret of Guidance* (Chicago: Moody Publishers, 2010).

2   Max Lucado, *Discovering the Power of Prayer* (Colorado Springs, CO: Integrity House, 2007).

3   Joel Osteen, *Your Best Life Now* (Anderson, IN: Warner Faith, 2004).

4   "How Mail-In Rebates Rip You Off," Investopedia, accessed October 27, 2023, https://www.investopedia.com/financial-edge/0810/how-mail-in-rebates-rip-you-off.aspx.

5   Francis Chan, *Crazy Love: Overwhelmed by a Relentless God* (Colorado Springs, CO: Cook Communications, 2008).

6   James Dobson, AZ Quotes, accessed October 23, 2023, https://www.azquotes.com/quote/952000.

7   George Müller, *The Autobiography of George Müller* (Louisville, KY: GLH Publishing, 2015).

Q: Quarrels, Conflicts, and Divisions

1   John MacArthur, *1 Corinthians: MacArthur New Testament Commentary* (Chicago: Moody Publishers, 1984).

2   Craig S. Keener, *The IVP Bible Background Commentary: New Testament* (Downers Grove, IL: InterVarsity Press, 2014).

3   A. W. Tozer, *The Pursuit of God* (Grand Rapids: MI: Baker Books, 2013).

4   R. Kent Hughes, *Acts* (Wheaton, IL: Crossway Books, 1996), 76.

5   "A Quote from The Grand Weaver," Goodreads, accessed November 7, 2023, https://www.goodreads.com/quotes/7356296-thomas-merton-once-said-we-cannot-be-at-peace-with.

R: Repentance

1   Eugene H Peterson, *A Long Obedience in the Same Direction: Discipleship in an Instant Society* (Downers Grove, IL: InterVarsity Press, 2000).

2   Ken Weliever, "Admission of Wrong or Change of Heart," ThePreachersWord, January 26, 2013, https://thepreachersword.com/2013/01/26/admission-of-wrong-or-change-of-heart/.

S: Sin

1   J. John and Mark Stibbe, *A Box of Delights* (Oxford, England: Monarch Books, 2001).

2   "Ignatius of Loyola Quote: 'Sin Is Unwillingness to Trust That What God Wants for Me Is Only My Deepest Happiness,'" QuoteFancy, accessed November 7, 2023, https://quotefancy.com/quote/1303323/Ignatius-of-Loyola-Sin-is-unwillingness-to-trust-that-what-God-wants-for-me-is-only-my.

3   A. W. Tozer, *The Root of the Righteous* (Chicago, Moody Publishers, 2015).

4   A. W. Tozer, "The Hunger of the Wilderness, 1955," https://minds2mentes.wordpress.com/2016/04/27/the-hunger-of-the-wilderness-by-a-w-tozer-1955/.

5   James Stuart Stewart, *The Strong Name* (London: T&T Clark, 1940).

6   C. F. W. Walther, *The Proper Distinction Between Law and Gospel* (Brighton, IA: Just and Sinner Publications, 2014).

7   "Sir Anthony Hopkins: Atheist Turned Christian Credits God for 45 Years of Sobriety," *Charisma*, December 30, 2020, https://mycharisma.com/spiritled-living/supernaturaldreams/atheist-turned-christian-credits-god-for-45-years-of-sobriety/.

8   Brennan Manning, *The Ragamuffin Gospel: Good News for the Bedraggled, Beat-Up, and Burnt Out* (Colorado Springs, CO: Multnomah, 2005).

T: Temptation

1   John Piper, "How Dead People Do Battle with Sin," desiringGod.org, January 1, 1995, https://www.desiringgod.org/articles/how-dead-people-do-battle-with-sin.

2   Alan Stewart, "Giving Place to the Devil," PastorLife, accessed November 7, 2023, https://www.pastorlife.com/members/sermon.asp?SERMON_ID=2706&fm=authorbio&authorid=3381#:~:text=J.,door%20we%20have%20left%20open.

3   I. D. E. Thomas, *The Golden Treasury of Puritan Quotations* (Edinburgh: Banner of Truth Trust, 2000).

4   Robert Simmons, "Where Lions Feed," Sermon Central, March 1, 2002, https://www.sermoncentral.com/sermons/where-lions-feed-robert-simmons-sermon-on-endurance-43796?page=1&wc=800.

5   Elisabeth Elliot, ed., *The Journals of Jim Elliot: Missionary, Martyr, Man of God* (Grand Rapids, MI: Revell, 2021), 72.

6   C. S. Lewis, *The Screwtape Letters* (New York: Bantam Classics, 1995).

7   I. D. E. Thomas, *The Golden Treasury of Puritan Quotations*

8   R. A. Torrey and Edward D. Andrews, *Christian Living: How to Succeed in the Christian Life* (Cambridge, OH: Christian Publishing House, 2016).

U: The Unseen Providence of God

1   Derek W. H. Thomas, *What Is Providence?* (Phillipsburg, NJ: P&R Publishing, 2008).

2   J. C. Ryle, *Expository Thoughts on the Gospels* (Edinburgh: Banner of Truth Trust, 2012).

3   Sinach, "Way Maker," Integrity Music, 2016, accessed October 25, 2003, https://youtube/n4XWfwLHeLM?si=7WsPB0Kg1W7nmF3e.

4   "Abraham Lincoln," Bible.org, February 2, 2009, https://bible.org/illustration/abraham-lincoln-1.

5   Jerry Gifford, "Sermon: Virtuous Realities, Part 1 - Ruth 1, 2," Lifeway, January 1, 2014, https://www.lifeway.com/en/articles/sermon-ruth-virtue-relationships-1.

6   Jess Whitley, "The Life of Amy Carmichael," Girl Got Faith, August 11, 2017, https://girlgotfaith.com/2017/08/11/the-life-of-amy-charmichael/.

7   Elizabeth Barrett Browning, "86. From 'Aurora Leigh," Nicholson & Lee, eds., *The Oxford Book of English Mystical Verse* (1917), accessed September 23, 2022, https://www.bartleby.com/lit-hub/the-oxford-book-of-english-mystical-verse/86-from-aurora-leigh.

V: Volunteering and Serving

1   David Jeremiah, "First-Person: Mining Your Spiritual Gifts," Baptist Press, April 17, 2010, https://www.baptistpress.com/resource-library/news/first-person-mining-your-spiritual-gifts/.

2   Rev. Andrew Murray, *Money: Thoughts for God's Stewards* (Grand Rapids, MI: Revell Publishing, 1898).

3   Grace Stott, *Twenty-Six Years of Missionary Work in China*, American Tract Society, 1897.

4   Simon Sinek, "What Makes the Highest Performing Teams in the World," YouTube, 2020, https://www.youtube.com/watch?v=zP9jpxitfb4&t=21s.

5   Erwin Raphael McManus, *The Last Arrow: Save Nothing for the Next Life* (Colorado Springs, CO: WaterBrook, 2017).

6   "A Quote from Living, Loving & Learning," Goodreads, accessed November 7, 2023, https://www.goodreads.com/quotes/958314-your-talent-is-god-s-gift-to-you-what-you-do.

W: Worship

1   Gordon S. Jackson, *Quotes for the Journey, Wisdom for the Way* (Eugene, OR: Wipf and Stock, 2009).

2   George Sweeting, *Psalms of the Heart* (Wheaton, IL: Victor Books, 1988).

3   Shirley Ceasar, "This Joy I Have," Song Lyrics, accessed October 25, 2023, https://www.songlyrics.com/shirley-ceasar/this-joy-i-have-lyrics/

4   Mike Raiter, *Journey Through Colossians & Philemon: 30 Biblical Insights* (Grand Rapids, MI: Discovery House Publishing, 2002).

X: X Chromosome and Other Fallacies

1   "Fulton J. Sheen Quotes About Attitude," AZ Quotes, accessed October 26, 2023, https://www.azquotes.com/author/13447-Fulton_J_Sheen/tag/attitude.

2   "Quote by C. S. Lewis: 'When the Whole World Is Running towards a Cliff . . .'" Goodreads, accessed October 26, 2023, https://www.goodreads.com/quotes/3189180-when-the-whole-world-is-running-towards-a-cliff-he.

3   Stella Hu et al., " Linkage Between Sexual Orientation and Chromosome Xq28 in Males but Not in Females," *Nature Genetics* 11, no. 3 (November 1, 1995): 248–56, https://doi.org/10.1038/ng1195-248.

4   "ChatGPT Writes Beautiful Transgender-Affirming Bible Verse," Advocate, accessed October 26, 2023, https://www.advocate.com/technology/chatgpt-writes-inclusive-transgender-verse.

5   Rowland Croucher, "F W Boreham: A Packet of Surprises," John Mark Ministries, November 7, 2008, https://www.jmm.org.au/articles/21885.htm.

6   Chip MacGregor, *The Christian Life for the Kindred in Spirit* (Colorado Springs, CO: Multnomah Books, 1994).

7   Clarence Edward Noble Macartney, *The Greatest Words in the Bible and in Human Speech* (Grand Rapids, MI: Kregel Publications, 1995).

Y: Young and Old

1   Matthew Burden, "Heroes of the Faith: Charles Finney and D. L. Moody," The Peace and the Passion, February 25, 2021, https://thepeaceandthepassion.blogspot.com/2021/02/heroes-of-faith-charles-finney-dl-moody.html.

2   J. I. Packer, *Your Father Loves You* (Wheaton, IL: Shaw Publishing, 1986).

3   Sermon Index, accessed October 24, 2023, https://www.sermonindex.net.

4   Martin Luther, *The Familiar Discourses of Dr. Martin Luther*, trans. H. Bell (1652).

5   Tan Seow How and Cecilia Chan, *Generations Volume 1: How to Grow Your Church Younger and Stronger: The Story of the Kids Who Built a World-Class Church* (Heart of God Church, 2021).

6   Winkie Pratney, *Revival: Principles to Change the World* (Lindale, TX: Agape Force, 2010).

7   Zoe Caplan, 2020 Census: 1 in 6 People in the United States Were 65 and Over.

8   Billy Graham, *Nearing Home: Life, Faith, and Finishing Well* (Nashville, TN: Thomas Nelson, 2011).

9   "Marathon Man Akhwari Demonstrates Superhuman Spirit," Olympics.com, June 27, 2023, https:// olympics.com/en/news/marathon-man-akhwari-demonstrates-superhuman-spirit.

10 Gerald L Sittser, *Water From a Deep Well: Christian Spirituality From Early Martyrs to Modern Missionaries* (Downers Grove, IL: InterVarsity Press, 2010), 9–10

Z: Zeal

1   Charles. H Spurgeon, *The Metropolitan Tabernacle Pulpit: Sermons Preached and Revised by Charles. H. Spurgeon* (Pasadena, TX: Pilgrim Publications, 2006).

2   J. C. Ryle, *Practical Religion* (Louisville, KY: GLH Publishing, 2014).

3   Rick Reilly, "Game, Set, Career," *Sports Illustrated*, June 16, 2003, https://vault.si.com/vault/2003/06/16/game-set-career.

4   George Campbell Morgan, *The Morning Message: A Selection for Daily Meditation* (London: Hodder and Stoughton, 1906).

5   "The Fifth Gospel: The Ultimate Apologetic," Christian Research Institute, August 25, 2014, https://www.equip.org/articles/fifth-gospel-ultimate-apologetic/.

Acknowledgments

Newspaper columnist George Adams once said, "There is no such thing as a self-made man. We are made up of thousands of others. Everyone who has ever done a kind deed for us or spoken an encouraging word to us has entered into the makeup of our character as well as our successes." This project has truly had "the thousands of others" involved in its completion. This wasn't an undertaking that was done over the last twenty-seven weeks but something that has been in the making for well over four decades of ministry. Though it's impossible to acknowledge the literal "thousands of others," I must say "thank you" to a few of those voices.

Thank you, Leslie Law, for your meticulous hours of editing. Thank you, Amy Mathew, for always being there with joy to help in whatever capacity was needed. Thank you, Dr. R. T. Kendall, for sending twenty-seven emails every Sunday afternoon giving feedback and encouragement to the sermon. Thank you, Luly McCoy, for taking this from pulpit to print. Thank you, Times Square Church staff, for making it possible for us to reach the world with the gospel. Thank you, Times Square Church, for your relentless commitment to a biblical worldview in these difficult and dark times. And finally thank you to my family: Cindy, Christian, Anna, Grace, and Lauryn, for just being amazing.

Together we are believing for a billion souls to be won to Christ. And together we made it possible for them to have a biblical worldview to start their journey with Christ.

About the Author

Tim Dilena is the senior pastor of Times Square Church. With over forty years of pastoral leadership and experience, he is the third senior pastor since the founding of the church by David Wilkerson in 1987.

In 1984 Tim moved to Detroit, eventually starting Revival Tabernacle in a former 900-seat XXX movie theater. After Detroit, Tim pastored in Brooklyn, New York, and then Lafayette, Louisiana, before returning to New York City in May 2020 to pastor Times Square Church.

Tim attended Baylor University, Wayne State University, and Moody Bible Institute. He holds a Bachelor of Arts in Corporate Finance and has taken extended studies in apologetics at Oxford University in England.

He has been a speaker for the MLB, NFL, and WNBA chapels and is the author of *The 260 Journey*, a daily devotional that goes chapter by chapter through the New Testament in 260 days.

Tim and his wife, Cindy, have four children: Christian, Anna, Grace, and Lauryn.

Start reading your next book by Tim Dilena.

Why call it The 260?

The New Testament contains 260 chapters, and there are 261 week-days in every year. You'll read one chapter a day Monday through Friday to finish the entire New Testament in a year.

The 260 takes a verse or passage from that day's New Testament chapter and explains, inspires, and brings it to life. Personal stories, historical illustrations, quotes, and cross-references help make each chapter more easily understandable and applicable.

Available on Amazon.com